Strategic Valuation
of Companies

MANAGEMENT BRIEFINGS
F I N A N C E

Strategic Valuation of Companies

ALAN GREGORY

FINANCIAL TIMES
PRENTICE HALL

Pearson Education Limited
128 Long Acre, London WC2E 9AN
Tel: +44 (0)171 447 2000
Fax: +44 (0)171 240 5771
Website: www.business-minds.com

A Division of Financial Times Professional Limited

First published in Great Britain 1999

ISBN 0 273 63970 6

British Library Cataloguing in Publication Data
A CIP catalogue record for this book can be obtained from the British Library.

10 9 8 7 6 5 4 3 2 1

Typeset by Boyd Elliott Typesetting
Printed and bound in Great Britain

The Publishers' policy is to use paper manufactured from sustainable forests.

About the author

Alan Gregory is Professor of Corporate Finance at the University of Exeter, where he is head of the Department of Business and Management. He has previously been Professor in the Departments of Accounting and Finance at Glasgow University and the University of Wales, Aberystwyth. At Exeter he teaches on the Exeter MBA and MA Finance and Investment programmes.

His current research interests include takeovers and mergers, the cost of capital and stock market efficiency, and his recent published work has included a study of the long-run performance of UK acquiring firms, a CIMA-funded study of the cost of capital in the UK, the performance of initial public offerings, share price reaction to directors' trading activity and the performance measurement of 'ethical' unit trusts. His work has been published in the *Economic Journal, Accounting and Business Research*, and the *Journal of Business Finance and Accounting.*

In addition to his academic interests, he is a chartered management accountant and has acted as a consultant in the valuation of target companies in takeover bids and as a consultant to a 'big five' accounting firm in the determination of the cost of capital.

Contents

Executive summary

COVERAGE

This briefing is intended to cover valuation for the purposes of the commercial purchase or sale of a company or division and for the evaluation of strategic alternatives in general. Valuation of minority stakes and valuation for the purposes of litigation or taxation involve special considerations and are not covered in this text.

VALUATION MODELS COVERED

The three main categories of valuation model are all covered in this briefing. These are: the *earnings* based type of model, the *asset* based type of model, and the *discounted cash flow* models where the factors affecting value are the future cash flow prospects of the company and the opportunity cost of capital. Given the growing importance of the latter, the main emphasis in this briefing is on the following:

- an explanation of the basic DCF models;
- a detailed description of the 'free cash flow' (FCF) model;
- an explanation of the link between the FCF and 'shareholder value' models;
- a comparison of the different approaches to 'shareholder value' and their adavantages and disadvantages;
- a detailed discussion of the calculation of cost of capital, including the costs of complex financial instruments;
- the estimation of 'terminal' or 'horizon' values of companies.

In addition, recognition is given to the importance market practitioners attach to earnings based methods of valuation. The strengths and weaknesses of such models are discussed, and adaptations of the earnings based model are explained, including:

- the basic PE model and its link with DCF models;
- the 'earnings before interest and tax' (EBIT) multiple and when to use it;
- the application of 'cash earnings' models.

OTHER ASPECTS OF VALUATION

Besides the valuation models described above, specific aspects of valuation for takeovers and mergers are analysed. This is especially important in the light of the evidence that a majority of takeovers are not wealth-enhancing events in the long term from a shareholder value perspective.

Recent developments in finance have emphasised that managerial flexibility in choosing between strategic alternatives adds value to the company. The final chapter in the briefing describes how this flexibility gives rise to what are known as 'real options' and explains how these can be valued using option pricing techniques.

GENERAL APPROACH

The general approach in this briefing is to explain the issues involved in using any particular type of valuation model, and to illustrate the application of each one with numerical examples. Comparisons are then made between the models using further numerical illustrations of their strengths and weaknesses in particular situations. Illustrations are also given of the way in which the models can be applied to published accounting data.

Throughout the emphasis is placed upon:

■ the advantages and disadvantages of alternative approaches *in practice*;

■ how and why the models might be applied in practice;

■ the practical circumstances in which simple models may work, and when a more complex approach is needed.

Last, a major objective of this book is an explanation of the latest techniques available and how they may be applied in future.

List of abbreviations

AARR	average accounting rate of return
ACT	advance corporation tax
ADMP	active debt management policy
AE	annual equivalent
APM	arbitrage pricing model
APR	annual percentage rate
APT	arbitrage pricing theory
ASB	Accounting Standards Board
BMV	book-to-market value
BS	Black-Scholes (option pricing model)
CAPM	Capital Asset Pricing Model
CCR	continuously compounded rate
CFAT	cash flow after tax
CFPS	cash flow per share
CFR	cash flow return
CFROI	cash flow return on investment
CIMA	Chartered Institute of Management Accountants
CNBV	closing net book value
COS	cost of sales
CT	taxes paid as cash
CULS	convertible unsecured loan stock
DCF	discounted cash flow
DEP	depreciation
DPS	dividend per share
EAT	earnings after tax
EBIT	earnings before interest and tax
EBITDA	earnings before interest, tax, depreciation and amortisation
EP	economic profit
EPS	earnings per share
EV	enterprise value
EVA™	Economic Value Added
FC	fixed costs
FCF	free cash flow
FRS	Financial Reporting Standard
FT	*Financial Times*
FTASI	Financial Times All Share Index
GAAP	generally accepted accounting principles

GBV	gross book value
GDP	gross domestic product
HGSCI	Hoare-Govett Smaller Companies Index
IIMR	Institute for Investment Management and Research
INT	interest
INV	investment
IRR	internal rate of return
LIBOR	London Inter-Bank Offered Rate
MNE	multinational enterprise
MRP	market risk premium
NI	interest net of tax
NOPAT	net operating profit after taxes
NPV	net present value
OCF	operating cash flow
OGBV	opening gross book value
ONBV	opening net book value
OPAT	operating profit after tax
P&L	profit and loss account
P/CE	price/cash earning ratio
PATS	profit attributable to shareholders
PBT	profit before tax
PDMP	passive debt management policy
PE	price-earnings ratio
PV	present value
RE	retained earnings
RI	residual income
RONI	return on new investment
RPI	retail price index
SBU	strategic business unit
SEC	Securities and Exchange Commission
SSAP	Statement of Standard Accounting Practice
SVA	Shareholder Value Added
SWOT	strengths, weaknesses, opportunities and threats analysis
TR	Total Revenue (turnover)
ULS	unsecured loan stock
VBM	value based management
VC	variable costs
WACC	weighted average cost of capital
WCAP	working capital investment
XD	ex dividend

Introduction

1

1.1 COVERAGE AND PURPOSES OF VALUATION

This briefing is intended to cover valuation for the purposes of the commercial purchase or sale of a company or division and for the evaluation of strategic alternatives in general. This includes acquisitions, mergers, management buyouts, flotations and divestments, and the assessment of which areas of the business should be expanded or contracted. All businesses should be continually monitoring their performance and investigating the various strategies open to them. A key part of this process involves looking at the value contributed by existing parts of the enterprise, and the way in which value can be added by divesting or improving under-performing businesses or by buying or developing new businesses. The evaluation of such alternatives has received considerable recent attention through the marketing of such techniques as 'shareholder value analysis' or 'value based management' but all of these techniques are merely methods for operationalising discounted cash flow (DCF) valuation methods. These techniques are covered in the briefing, as are more traditional models for valuation.

Valuation of minority stakes, and valuation for the purposes of litigation or taxation involve special considerations[1] and are not covered in this text.

The issues involved in valuing companies for strategic reasons are different from those involved in valuing a company for investment analysis purposes. One school of thought is that valuation for investment purposes is unlikely to be a worthwhile activity. This is because if equity markets are price-efficient, on average shares will be fairly priced. This view is typified by Fama (1998), and the logical investment strategy if one accepts such a position is index fund investment. The alternative view is that there are 'aberrations' or 'anomalies' in market prices which may be exploitable. Examples of this view can be found in DeBondt and Thaler (1985, 1987) and Lakonishok et al. (1994).[2]

However, when a company is being valued for strategic purposes, we will be interested in a whole range of issues, such as alternative business strategies for the company if it is acquired, the realisable value of the company's assets, the saleable value of any subsidiaries and any synergistic benefits which may arise from the acquisition. A key difference is that ownership implies that we can actively change the value of the company by management action, whereas individual investors cannot. Furthermore, analysis of strategic alternatives often involves the use of information not available to the market as a whole.

There are two other aspects of valuation, which are bargaining strategy and bidder objectives. As regards the former, a key question is how much it will be necessary to pay in order to win control of a target company, or from the seller's perspective how much it will be possible to realise for a company or division. For a listed company, a bidder will have to pay some sort of premium over the current share price, but the size of that premium will depend upon a number of factors. If the target has a shareholder profile typical of that of most large companies, this will involve convincing large institutional fund managers of the case for a takeover. Key factors will be the past performance of the company and whether the acquisition is to be a cash deal or involves equity financing.

Bidder objectives are the factor that really drives the valuation process in the context of an acquisition. The value of a target to any bidder depends upon what that bidder intends to do with it. If we consider a conglomerate takeover, where the objective is simply to 'improve the running of the company', the value might be similar to a number of different bidders. However, it is quite possible that particular synergistic or strategic benefits make a target worth more to one bidder than another.[3] Bidder objectives and bargaining strategies become even richer areas when we consider the case of privately held companies or subsidiaries, since the objectives of the seller and bargaining strategies also come into play.

1.1.1 Assumed knowledge

This briefing assumes some familiarity with DCF principles although a revision of the major concepts is included in Chapter 3. A basic understanding of company accounts is also assumed. Readers who wish to brush up on their knowledge of this topic will find there are several good guides to company accounts currently in print. Particularly recommended are the *FT Guide to Using and Interpreting Company Accounts* by Wendy McKenzie, and Professor Parker's *Understanding Company Accounts* published by Penguin Paperbacks. Throughout his book, Professor Parker uses as an example the accounts of British Vita plc, and to aid readers who wish to follow his book in parallel with this briefing British Vita is used as a core example.

1.2 PARTIES POTENTIALLY INTERESTED IN VALUATION

Many of those included in the list fall into the categories of either potential buyer or potential seller. Included as buyers would be acquisitive companies, investment fund managers and management buyout teams. Fund managers might also appear as potential sellers; also in this group would be those who have a controlling stake in an enterprise and companies who want to divest themselves of subsidiaries or business areas.

In addition, there are advisers who need to perform valuations for a variety of purposes. These include valuations by investment bankers who may be concerned with activities such as the appraisal of takeover targets, valuations in takeover defences, valuations in buyouts and valuations for stock market flotations. Accountancy firms are major advisers in takeover situations and will also be involved in valuations for employee share ownership schemes, receivership and other purposes.

Lastly, company managers should be concerned with the value of their companies *on a continuous basis*. This includes not only senior management, but also the managers of subsidiaries and major business units. Unless these managers have an idea of the value of what they control, they cannot sensibly evaluate alternative business strategies. Neither can they convincingly defend themselves from hostile takeover bids, or indeed perceive whether or not they should feel potentially threatened (if managers really believe that their company is undervalued by the market, they should feel vulnerable to any bidder who realises the same). Without an idea of corporate value they lack one increasingly important method of estimating their past performance, since the objective of public companies is, at least in part, to increase the wealth of the shareholders.[4] Finally, unless managers are aware of value, they will find it hard to objectively assess whether they should be expanding through acquisitions or 'organic' growth, or whether they should be concentrating the business through closures, divestments or spin-offs.[5] As managers should be taking a long-term view of the business, they should be primarily concerned with discounted cash flow valuation models (*see* Chapters 3 to 6).

Recently, the increasing importance attached to 'shareholder value' has led to a growing awareness by managers of the need to monitor the calculated values of their businesses ('strategic business units', or SBUs). These models are used by strategists both in the evaluation of alternative business plans and in the calculation of the values of potential targets. Essentially, these techniques can be viewed as simplifications of, or attempts to operationalise, the 'free cash flow' model of valuation described in Chapter 5. One problem with this model is that it requires direct estimates of operating cash flows, cash taxes, investment in working capital and capital expenditure. As practitioners sometimes find these estimates difficult to deal with, a generic type of spreadsheet-based model has been created by consultants to ease the process. These models focus upon the link between accounting variables, cash flow and value.

Broadly, the models derive cash flows by focusing either upon accounting profits and working towards cash flows, or by directly estimating the cash return on investment. An example of the former is the residual income model of Stern-Stewart (marketed under the acronym EVA™ – shorthand for Economic Value Added), while an example of the latter is the cash flow return on investment model of Braxton Associates.

1.3 THE OPPORTUNITY COST PRINCIPLE

When valuing a company, it is important to realise that there are three values that need to be investigated. The valuation methods discussed in this and other works on valuation tend to focus on the value of the business as a going concern. Specifically, this going concern value should be the present value of the company's future free cash flows (*see* Chapter 3 for an explanation). This going concern value can be termed the 'economic value' and in current terminology is often referred to as the 'enterprise value'. This is not necessarily the actual value of the business, as there are two alternative values that arise. First, there is the possibility of breaking up the company in some way rather than have it continue in its present form. There are, of course, many ways of achieving this end, ranging from an emergency sale of the assets, through a more orderly piecemeal disposal, to the fragmentation of the business into smaller units some of which may be continuing businesses and some of which may be asset disposals. For example, a regional bus company may be able to relocate its head office and garages to the edge of a city leaving the city centre bus depot and head office to be sold off as freehold property. The relevant figure for the purposes of our valuation is the best of these alternatives, which gives us the maximised *net realisable value* of the company.

If this net realisable value exceeds the economic value, the best alternative is to break up the company. In principle, precisely this type of analysis led to some of the 'corporate raids' of the 1980s (for example, James Goldsmith's failed offer for BAT). More generally, of course, net realisable value will be less than economic value. However, there is one further consideration. Rather than buy an existing business, it is possible to replicate that business. For example, rather than buy a chain of estate agents or themed restaurants, it is possible to grow such an organisation from scratch. Thus the *full replication cost* of the business (including an allowance for the difference in timing) should also be considered. The value of the company being considered cannot logically exceed its replication cost. This is often lost sight of, but some analysis along these lines might have saved some large insurance companies which bought chains of estate agencies in the 1980s a great deal of money. Of course, quite often replication is impossible. For example, pharmaceutical companies own patents on drugs which cannot legally be replicated. Others (for example, water companies) have extensive assets which cannot feasibly be duplicated.

Despite these difficulties, at least some thought should be given to realisable values and replication cost. This the general rule can be summed up as:

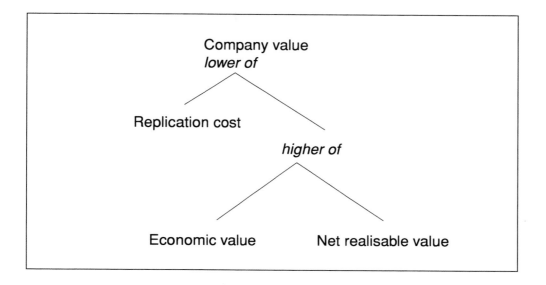

1.4 AN OVERVIEW OF THE PRINCIPAL VALUATION MODELS

1.4.1 Introduction

Essentially, there are three main categories of valuation model. There is the *earnings* based type of model, which measures value as some multiple of accounting profit, the *asset* based type of model, which is concerned with the sale or replacement value of the physical and financial assets of a company, and the *discounted cash flow* models where the factors affecting value are the future cash flow prospects of the company and the opportunity cost of capital. It is sometimes suggested that only earnings and discounted cash flow models value companies as going concerns or continuing businesses. This is not strictly the case, since asset valuations concerned with the replacement values of assets implicitly assume that the business is to continue in some form.

1.4.2 Earnings valuations

The principle behind a 'traditional' earnings valuation model is to try and estimate the so-called *maintainable profits* of the company and apply a capitalisation factor known as the *price-earnings multiple (PE)* to this profit. This suffers from two key problems. First, inflation has a confounding effect on accounting profits unless profits are stated in current cost terms. Second, most firms would expect profits to grow through time because of real increases in the levels of their activity. The traditional idea of maintainable profits ignores this feature, both in terms of the company being valued and in the selection of the PE multiple. In practice, the PE multiple is almost invariably arrived at by choosing some comparable or analogue company, group of companies or industry PE.

In current practice, most investment analysts seem to concentrate on current and forecast earnings, adjusting for any items that are not representative of the typical trading conditions faced by the company. However, recent evidence suggests that accountants still use the concept of 'maintainable earnings', although this is mainly in the valuation of unquoted companies.[6]

In general, current earnings should be multiplied by a current PE ratio, while forecast earnings must be multiplied by a *prospective* PE ratio. The aim is to find the PE multiple by searching for listed firms that have comparable growth prospects, risk factors and financial structures (*see* Chapter 2 for a detailed explanation). However, because firms with similar business risks can have different financial structures, an alternative approach is to take profits before interest charges (the earnings before interest and tax, or EBIT) and look at the ratio of the value of the whole firm to EBIT. This value of the entire firm is sometimes called the 'enterprise value' and can be defined as assets minus current liabilities and deferred taxes (equivalent to equity plus long-term debt).

A further variation has received added impetus from the growing globalisation of world markets and the inherent difficulty of making cross-border comparisons given differing accounting policies between countries.[7] A particular problem is that the tax legislation in some countries gives companies the incentive to use high rates of depreciation or accounting provision. Even within one country, companies can adopt different rates of write-off and have assets of different ages. One way round these problems is the use of multiples of what are sometimes called 'cash earnings', defined as being earnings before interest, tax, depreciation and amortisation (EBITDA). Earnings based models are described fully in Chapter 3.

1.4.3 Asset valuations

To derive the asset value of the company, we need information on both the *realisable* value of the assets (what they could be sold for, either piecemeal or as business segments) and the *replacement cost* of those assets (assuming we are interested in the business as a continuing entity). Unfortunately, in respect of fixed assets other than property, it is difficult to get such information directly from the published accounts. While for most public companies property is shown at current or recent valuation, other fixed assets are shown at historic cost less depreciation. Whether or not these will be useful guides to either realisable value or replacement cost depends upon the type of asset and the relative rates of asset price change (as contrasting examples, consider computers and aircraft). Asset based valuation models are discussed in Chapter 3.

1.4.4 Discounted cash flow valuations

The discounted cash flow (DCF) valuation model, or present value model, requires the explicit forecast of future cash flows. In theory, that forecast needs to cover the entire life of the company. This presents obvious practical difficulties, and the approach generally used to overcome this problem is to make specific forecasts for a number of years, and then to calculate a 'terminal' or 'horizon' value at the end of this specific forecast period. This value is calculated by taking a base cash flow for the year beyond the horizon period and making some form of constant growth assumption. This allows the use of simplified techniques to calculate the present value of the firm into perpetuity. An introduction to the necessary techniques is covered in Chapter 3.

An essential requirement for a DCF valuation is an estimate of investors' required rates of return. This gives rise to the cost of capital of the SBU. An essential point is that a conglomerate firm with a number of SBUs will have different costs of capital for each SBU in general, assuming they are of different risks. There are a number of alternative models that can be used for estimating cost of capital and these are described in Chapter 4.

One of the problems with DCF valuation is the difficulty of forecasting cash flows. This issue is discussed in more detail in Chapter 5. In reality, unless the industry in question has fairly stable and predictable cash flows (for example, utility industries in between regulatory price reviews), it has to be conceded that this is the hardest and most error-prone part of any valuation. Recently, several consultancy packages have been developed which make use of concepts such as 'value drivers' to forecast future cash flows. These models have been applied in the contexts of valuation for takeovers and mergers and for 'shareholder value' type exercises. While these models highlight the link between variables such as sales growth, asset growth, margins, investment and cash flows they can be misused. Although such models have a role to play, it is important to remember that projecting into the future on the basis of current accounting numbers may be a simple alternative, but there is also a danger of it being simple-minded. Recent research (Bulkley and Harris, 1997) shows that while analysts' forecasts of long-run future earnings growth are highly correlated with past earnings growth, *actual* long-run earnings growth bears almost no relationship to past growth.[8]

These models and their possible application are examined in detail in Chapter 6.

1.4.5 A basic comparison of models

Assuming that we wish to value companies as going concerns (so that asset values are not the key issue), a fundamental question is whether the DCF or PE valuation frameworks should be preferred. From a theoretical viewpoint, DCF has all the advantages in that value is calculated in the context of a rational economic framework. It also has the advantage of making all the assumptions made in the valuation process *explicit*. Furthermore, there exist theoretically developed and empirically tested models (albeit imperfect ones) from which we can derive the opportunity cost of capital. By contrast, there is no rational economic model available which can be used to derive satisfactory PE ratios, and all the forecast assumptions on risk, cost of capital and growth prospects are *implicit* in the earnings multiple chosen. Finally, the earnings multiple method makes use of the accounting profit number. This is problematic, since differing methods of accounting can give rise to different estimates of profit. Although it is the case that many of the more creative methods of accounting have been limited by successive accounting standards in the US and the UK, it still remains the case that accounting profits are more malleable than cash flows. Furthermore, in many emerging economies, local generally accepted accounting principles (GAAP) are far slacker than US GAAP.

While DCF is the preferred method, it must be remembered that a good valuation depends upon the quality of the cash flow or profit forecasts made. Typically, the most sensitive variables in any valuation are sales growth and profit or cash margins, and the usual 'garbage-in, garbage-out' caveat applies.

In general, earnings based valuation models remain widely used in both the US and UK, but the recent trend towards 'shareholder value' models has given considerable impetus to the increasing use of DCF models which was previously apparent in the UK and US. In practice, for the foreseeable future it seems likely that any valuation exercise will include the use of both DCF and earnings based techniques. This is for several reasons. At the time of any acquisition, the statistics reported at the time of a bid typically focus upon price paid to earnings, sales and sometimes book value of the target. Clearly, these multiples may be of use in any negotiations over the price paid for any target. It certainly allows comparisons to be made with deals done recently in related industries. A further useful function is that the PE multiple implied by a DCF valuation may provide a 'reality check' on the assumptions made and the final figure arrived at.

1.5 ADDITIONAL FACTORS IN TAKEOVER VALUATION

As was outlined above, in the broadest sense there is no difference in principle between the valuation of a company for, say, 'shareholder value analysis' or for a takeover or merger. Added complications occur in a takeover context though. These are discussed in detail in Chapter 7. First, we might normally expect there to be some synergistic benefits in a takeover. These could range from cost savings through to greater product market power. The obvious question that arises is how to calculate these. When valuing the benefits from synergy it is sometimes forgotten that these will often not grow in real terms, whereas many other cash flows may. An example might be head office cost savings. These apparent benefits may take some time to achieve, especially if there are major differences in cultures or systems between merger partners.

A further point to be considered is the effect of the form of financing. With cash deals, the target shareholders are bought out immediately. With equity financed deals, however, the target shareholders share the risks and benefits of the merged firm with the acquiring shareholders. This opens up additional questions over the real value of any bid and in negotiating the precise ratio of shares offered.

Lastly, it would be unwise to embark on any takeover without some warning about the possible consequences. The evidence on the long-run performance of acquiring firms is not encouraging. If one starts from the logical assumption that takeovers should be shareholder wealth-enhancing events from the viewpoint of the acquiring company shareholders, then the conclusion is that roughly two-thirds of takeovers are failures. This experience is broadly similar in both the US and UK.[9] As Warren Buffet, of Berkshire Hathaway, famously noted in a letter to shareholders in the 1992 annual report:

> In the past, I've observed that many acquisition-hungry managers were apparently mesmerized by their childhood reading of the story about the frog-kissing princess. Remembering her success, they pay dearly for the right to kiss corporate toads, expecting wondrous transfigurations ... Ultimately, even the most optimistic manager must face the reality. Standing knee-deep in unresponsive toads, he then announces an enormous 'restructuring' charge. In this equivalent of a Head Start program, the CEO receives the education but the stockholders pay the tuition.[10]

1.6 VALUING FLEXIBILITY

Recent developments in the theory of corporate finance have shown that investment under conditions of uncertainty are rather more complex than suggested by the DCF rule. This is because management often has discretion over matters such as the timing of a new project, the expansion of existing projects, and the temporary or permanent shut-down of an operation. The basic problem is that such flexibility in managerial action has an option-like property, and options cannot be valued by using DCF principles. Although a detailed analysis of this topic is beyond the scope of this briefing, an introduction to this type of problem, with some examples of how such 'real options' may arise in a takeover situation, are given in Chapter 8.

1.7 SUMMARY

This chapter has explained the purposes of valuation and the interested parties in a valuation. It has also outlined the major principles underlying any valuation for takeovers and mergers, and introduced the principal approaches to valuation currently in use. These were broadly earnings based and DCF based methods. Contemporary approaches to operationalise the forecasting of future cash flows and the DCF valuation process were also outlined. These are broadly known as 'shareholder value' approaches and come in a variety of guises such and Shareholder Value Added, EVA™ and cash flow return on investment. The importance of issues such as synergy benefits, the form of financing, the empirical evidence on the performance of the acquiring firm and the value of real options were then introduced.

Review of traditional valuation models and their contemporary operationalistion

2.1 INTRODUCTION

As was noted in Chapter 1, there are three basic approaches to the valuation of companies, which are the discounted cash flow model, the earnings multiple (or price-earnings) model and asset valuations. In this chapter, we look at the latter two models which comprise what may be thought of from a contemporary perspective as being 'traditional' approaches to valuation. As evidence of this, surveys of practice in the 1980s and early 1990s show that the most commonly used approach to valuation appeared to be that of the earnings multiple model, whether the valuation is of unlisted or listed companies, or for acquisitions or general analysts' recommendations on investing.[1]

However, practice appears to be changing, with a greater use of DCF methods. The real impetus towards DCF based valuations has been the recent phenomenon of interest in 'shareholder value' in the UK. Recent evidence shows that the professional investment community and companies are focusing on this new approach (Gregory and Rutterford, 1999). Despite this, it is clear that a significant number of companies, analysts and advisers are still concerned with earnings per share (EPS) as a measure of performance. For example, many British companies base either a part of managerial remuneration or managerial rights to exercise executive share options on targets related to EPS growth (for example, British Vita plc requires that options may not be exercised until growth in EPS of 6% over and above inflation has been achieved over a three-year period). The very fact that the *FT* and *Acquisitions Monthly* also report on matters like the earnings multiple paid and the effects of earnings dilution at the time of any bid is also evidence of a concern with these numbers in acquisition valuation.

The appeal of the earnings based approach doubtless owes much to the combination of simplicity and the ready availability of forecast earnings (at least for one year ahead), price-earnings multiples for all listed companies and industry sectors, and price-earnings multiples on completed acquisitions. Asset values are less used, although before the 1950s and 1960s they were regarded as important. One particular use of asset values was in the 'super profits' method of calculation.[2] Although asset valuations in themselves are not widely used, they are of relevance in two respects:

- Any valuation should always take account of the importance of the opportunity cost principles explained in Chapter 1.

- There is some practical interest in the asset multiple paid for any target. Recent academic evidence (Fama and French, 1992; Lakonishok et al., 1994) clearly shows some relationship between the 'book-to-market' ratio and total shareholder returns (i.e. dividends plus capital gains as a percentage of the investment made in the shares). This relationship and its possible interpretations are explored in detail in Chapter 4. Asset multiples paid on acquisition are also recorded in the Amdata database service of Acquisitions Monthly.

In general, the earnings multiple approach is associated with acquisitions and mergers and investment analysis rather than valuation for strategic purposes such as value based management (VBM). This is because of the simplifications made in a typical earnings based valuation, which make it unsuitable for long-run strategic evaluation where there is access to medium- to long-term cash flow projections.

To illustrate the calculations from published data of the multiples discussed in the chapter, the example of British Vita plc is used throughout. The accounts of British Vita plc, restated with additional information from the Notes to the Annual Report and Accounts, are given in Appendix 1 to this briefing.

2.2 LIMITATIONS OF ACCOUNTING DATA

Before investigating any accounting based models in detail, it is important to understand the limitations of current accounting practice, since in all cases earnings or asset based valuations will be reliant upon the validity of the accounting numbers themselves. We need therefore to be aware of the problems caused by 'generally accepted accounting principles' (GAAP) and their practical application and manipulation. In some cases these problems are caused by accounting conventions (the best example is probably that caused by the historic cost accounting convention in times of inflation), in some cases by different GAAP applying in different countries, and sometimes by the fact that companies report results, within the confines of GAAP, in a manner which best suits their own purposes; this whole area is sometimes termed 'creative accounting'. Until recently the latter had been something of a growth industry in the UK, but many of the worst excesses of 1980s UK accounting have been removed by the efforts of the Accounting Standards Board (ASB). In general, the US has tighter accounting standards than the UK. However, there are major international differences in GAAP, despite the work of the International Accounting Standards Commitee.

2.2.1 Problems caused by GAAP

In an ideal world, comparability would be assured not only between the results of the same company across different years (the position which largely exists in the UK because of SSAP 2 and SSAP 6) but also between companies, something which clearly does not happen at the moment in many countries. Comparison of companies in similar industries across international borders is even more difficult. For example, within the UK different policies can be pursued with respect to asset valuation, rates of asset depreciation, the capitalisation and amortisation of such intangibles as development expenditure and brand values, stock valuation (although it must be acknowledged that the UK permits less flexibilty here than is found in most other countries), the treatment of certain types of financing, deferred taxation and interest capitalisation on new asset construction. The basic problem caused by such flexibility is that, in practice, valuers tend to use *analogue* or *proxy* companies to determine either a reasonable PE multiple in the case of an earnings valuation or a price–book value ratio in the case of asset driven valuations (the latter is far less common than the earnings multiple approach); clearly, such a process is likely to be more reasonable when all companies follow the same accounting practices than when they do not.

It therefore follows that:

■ the first step in an accounting based valuation is a thorough analysis of the accounting practices used in the company being valued and in any other companies used as an analogue for earnings multiples;

■ the second step is then to restate the accounts of analogue and target companies on a common basis wherever possible.

Unfortunately, this is sometimes an extremely difficult task because of a shortage of some of the necessary information, although SSAP 2 (which requires the disclosure of accounting policies) provides some help. Some changes are easily made; for example, if the company we wish to value has capitalised development expenditure while comparable companies have not, the adjustment would consist of reducing the asset value of our company, writing off the actual expenditure in the year to the profit figure and adding back the amortisation of previous years' expenditure (both of these figures must be disclosed in the notes to the balance sheet referring to changes in assets). Similarly, if different depreciation rates are used, appropriate adjustments can be made. Note that it does not matter which accounting basis is adopted when making such changes; the aim is to ensure comparability, not to present an ideologically 'correct' version of the accounts.

However, even if all companies followed similar accounting policies, there would remain a problem with the historic cost principle of accounting. While at the time of writing international inflation rates are generally low (although there are exceptions such as Turkey), the fact remains that over the past ten years inflation rates have been higher. Given that many companies have assets not yet fully written down which can be ten years old or more, historical inflation rates can still cause distortions in inter-company comparisons.

In order to illustrate the problem, take the example of two companies in the same industry which have bought their equipment at different points in time. To simplify matters, assume that there is no change in productivity associated with older equipment, that all such equipment has a ten-year life, that inflation rates are constant and have affected all asset prices, costs and selling prices, and that the required return on all investment is also constant.[3] Further assume that the equipment is worthless at the end of its ten-year life, and that accounting depreciation is charged on a straight line basis. Imagine that there are two companies, A and B, which are identical in all respects except that A bought its assets six years ago while B bought its assets at the end of the previous year. As these firms have identical cash flows in real terms, they should have identical market values. A full explanation of how to calculate such DCF values is given in Chapter 3.

In the case of both companies, net cash flow for the current year will be identical and the market value of the companies should be identical; however, the reported accounting profits will not be. This is because Company B will end up with a depreciation charge based upon asset prices one year ago while Company A will have a depreciation charge based upon six-year-old asset prices. The effect of this difference will depend upon the historical inflation rate. For example, at an inflation rate of 5% the difference in depreciation charge for the current year will be 27.6%.[4] Since this implies a difference in reported earnings, given that the firms have identical values, it also implies that the PE multiples are not comparable.[5]

When there is a need to extend comparisons to different countries, as in the area of cross-border acquisitions and in the valuation of companies in countries which do not have developed capital markets, further difficulties are encountered because of differences in GAAP between countries. Nobes and Parker (1991) suggest that financial reporting differences can be attributed to:

- differences in legal systems
- the providers of finance
- taxation
- the accounting profession
- inflation
- theory and
- accidents of history.

Western legal systems can be classified according to whether they are based on common law (e.g. England and Wales, the USA) or codified Roman law (France, Italy and Germany), providers of finance can be classified according to whether there is a reliance on a stock market for new finance (e.g. the UK and USA) or whether there is a strong reliance on banks (e.g. Germany), and classifications based on taxation can be made according to whether the published accounts form the basis of taxation (e.g. France and Germany) or whether taxation is separately calculated (as in the UK and the USA). In the case of countries where the former is true, there will be an incentive to declare the lowest possible profit which will not occur in countries where the latter is true.

As regards the other factors affecting financial reporting, Nobes and Parker (1991) note that in high inflation countries there is a tendency to use general price adjusted accounts, while theoretical developments have led some countries to use different GAAP (e.g. the use of replacement cost accounting in the Netherlands). Finally, historical accidents explain factors like the SEC requirements in the USA, and the presence of UK-based practices in many ex-colonial countries.

2.2.2 Dealing with differences in GAAP

One way around the problems caused by inflation and different depreciation rates in general (both domestically and internationally) is the use of a *cash based* earnings multiple. Pike et al. (1993) report some use of price to cash ratios in both Germany and the UK. Unfortunately, definitions of 'cash earnings' are inconsistent. Essentially, what matters is whether the calculation is being done at the equity level (i.e. the cash earnings attributable to the shareholders) or at the level of the whole company ('enterprise level'). To avoid confusion in this briefing we use the following definitions:

- *Enterprise cash earnings.* For the business as a whole, this equals operating profit with depreciation, other amortisation expenses and non-cash adjustments added back. (Note that this differs from 'Net cash flow from operating activities' shown in the cash flow statement of UK companies because the latter adjusts for working capital changes.)

- *Equity cash earnings.* At the equity holders' level, this equals earnings after tax and interest with non-cash items (as defined above) added back. This is the definition used by Datastream and some other publications and so in these cases the cash earnings multiple (P/CE) is simply market price divided by the defined cash earnings.

- *Cash earnings per share.* Equity cash earnings divided by the number of shares in issue.

In the example used in section 2.2.1, the enterprise and equity cash earnings and hence P/CE would be identical for both companies because the only source of difference is the depreciation charge. Furthermore, the use of P/CE ratios would deal with any differences in depreciation or amortisation policies (for example, differing approaches to the write-off of intangible assets), and so it follows that they should be considered as an alternative to PE ratios in such cases or when the age structure of the assets differs between companies used in any comparative analysis.

This is especially the case when the trend is towards a globalisation of capital markets, a growth in cross-border merger and acquisition activity and the opening up of new financial markets. As observed above, Nobes and Parker (1991) note a number of causes of substantial international differences in GAAP, including the effects of tax legislation. To give an example, German companies tend to use much higher depreciation rates than UK companies because the rates are specified for tax purposes; German legislation requires that these same rates must be used in the preparation of the financial accounts. As Nobes and Parker note, these depreciation rates are unlikely to be thought of as 'fair' in the financial reporting sense. In addition, over the past few decades the UK has had a higher inflation rate than Germany, and there is a tendency for German companies to replace their assets more frequently than UK companies. It is therefore the case that German PE ratios are not comparable with UK PE ratios. To some degree, the use of cash earnings multiples avoids many of these problems of comparison. Table 2.1 gives comparative PE and P/CE multiples for major equity markets, while Table 2.2 shows comparative ratios for Datastream industry categories within the UK.

Table 2.1 International PE and P/CE ratios

Datastream index	Price/earnings ratio December 1998	Price/cash earnings ratio December 1998
UK	19.8	13.0
Germany	18.9	9.8
France	19.0	10.4
US	25.6	15.5

Source: Datastream.

Table 2.2 UK sector PE and P/CE ratios

Datastream index	Price/earnings ratio December 1998	Price/cash earnings ratio December 1998
UK-DS Resources	23.1	9.9
UK-DS Gen. industrials	12.6	7.8
UK-DS Consumer goods	26.4	17.7
UK-DS Services	21.2	13.5
UK-DS Utilities	17.4	9.0
UK-DS Financials	17.6	14.8

Source: Datastream.

Although P/CE ratios eliminate some distortions caused by differences in accounting practices, they do not eliminate all differences in GAAP; for example, consolidation rules differ between countries (e.g. US versus Japan). Furthermore, as Cooke (1991) notes in the context of Japan, not all differences in PE ratios can be explained by accounting factors; other issues such as economic confidence, savings ratios, etc., have an important impact. Allowing for this means that we should not expect cash earnings ratios to be identical across countries, although when making international comparisons P/CE ratios would appear to offer more insights than simple PE ratios. Perhaps the best solution of all in this type of situation would be the use of discounted cash flow models, since economic logic would suggest that we can reasonably expect some sort of comparability between required rates of return in different countries (*see* Chapter 4).

Having looked at the difficulties posed by GAAP in establishing comparative earnings multiples, earnings multiple approaches are explained in more detail.

2.3 EARNINGS MULTIPLE BASED APPROACHES TO VALUATION

The basic idea behind this approach is to estimate the future earnings figure for the SBU or company, and apply to this figure an estimated price-earnings multiple. This process requires two key inputs, and the questions which arise concern which earnings figure should be used:

- latest historical, historical average or forecast for one or more years into the future?
- 'bottom line' earnings, earnings before interest and tax, or cash earnings? and
- how is the multiple to be established?

First, how many year's forecasts are to be estimated has to be decided. This depends upon the nature of the business and its cyclicality, together with the maturity of the firm, its products and the industry. Generally speaking, the less the cyclicality and the greater the maturity the less far into the future we need to forecast. Typically, however, the appeal of an earnings based valuation to an adviser or analyst is that only a short-range forecast is needed. For most large UK companies, forecasts for up to two years ahead are generally available from either I/B/E/S or *The Estimates Directory*. I/B/E/S also provides a 'long-run' earnings growth forecast for five years ahead, although there is empirical evidence that this is not a relaible estimate of actual earnings growth (Bulkley and Harris, 1997). Neither is it clear how I/B/E/S treats loss-making companies.

Some cynicism might be valid when it comes to reliance on analysts' forecasts. Although analysts' forecasts typically perform better than the earnings predictions of naive time series models, both in the UK and US (e.g. *see* Brown et al., 1987; Capstaff et al., 1995), there appears to be systematic bias in their forecasting, although there is disagreement concerning the nature of this bias. Capstaff et al. (1995), in a detailed analysis of UK analysts' forecasts, show that:

- analysts' forecasts only outperform a naive time series model for forecast horizons up to 16 months;

- analysts' forecast accuracy is greater when earnings actually increase than when they decrease. This, they note, 'suggests an extreme reluctance ... to make pessimistic forecasts';

- in keeping with the findings of DeBondt and Thaler (1990) for the US, they find that UK analysts' forecasts are biased, showing excessive optimism and overestimating the change in earnings;

- analysts' forecasts can be improved upon by using additional information available in the market in the form of the market-wide PE ratio.

Recent evidence in Bulkley and Harris (1997) and Harris (1999) also shows bias in US analysts' long-run earnings growth forecasts.

2.3.1 Base earnings figure

There is considerable confusion about which base earnings number should be chosen, irrespective of whether earnings are defined as earnings after tax attributable to shareholders (EAT), earnings before interest and tax (EBIT), earnings before interest, tax, depreciation and amortisation (EBITDA) or 'cash earnings'. As noted above, care is needed in the case of the latter as the definition of cash earnings can be taken to mean the net of tax cash earnings to shareholders *or* the pre-tax cash flows to the company.

A traditional view taken by practising chartered accountants[6] was that the base earnings figure should somehow be a figure representative of long-run future earnings, a concept frequently termed 'maintainable earnings'. While we can meaningfully speak of maintainable margins, 'maintainable earnings' is an altogether more elusive concept. In a company where there is no long-run growth but simply year to year fluctuations in activity in line with economic cycles, its meaning is fairly clear. Under such circumstances, 'maintainable earnings' really means average earnings. Even here, however, we have the problem of the impact of inflation on the reported profit figures. When the business is growing, it is difficult to pin down the meaning of the term; does maintainable simply mean current year's earnings, or does it mean the earnings which can be generated from the existing asset base?

The difficulty arises with the application of an earnings multiple, since the multiples of analogue companies reflect their future expected earnings, not their maintainable earnings. Thus the real need is for two things:

- first, an earnings figure estimated using accounting policies comparable to those of the analogue companies;

- second, that analogues are selected so that the evolution of future earnings is similar to that of the company being valued.

If there are differences in financial structure (i.e. gearing/leverage differences), either an EBIT or EBITDA multiple can be used, but there is no feasible way to allow for differences in growth prospects. It also follows that extraordinary or exceptional items should not be included in any earnings figure to which a PE multiple is applied, since the effect of such items is 'one-off'. To the extent that they represent good or bad news to the company, they will have an effect on value which should be allowed for, but such an effect is not of a recurring nature and should not therefore be priced through the application of an earnings multiple. For analogue and target companies, items such as interest income or any income from financial assets should be excluded. The reason for this is that the income from such assets has a materially different risk from that of the business we are attempting to value. Furthermore, in theory the net present value of financial assets (*see* Chapters 3 and 5) is zero. It follows that the correct approach is to value the business on its earnings from operations, and then to add in the market value of any financial assets at the end.

2.3.2 Factors influencing the earnings multiple

In general, the factors which drive the price-earnings ratio are the growth in future earnings and the required rate of return. Breaking the former down, earnings growth is a function of the dividend retention rate and the return on new investment. The required rate of return is a function of the underlying risk-free interest rate plus the risk premium required on the firm's equity. In fact, if it is assumed that all of these factors are constant into perpetuity, it is possible to show that a PE ratio can be derived such that an earnings based valuation will give a result identical to a DCF valuation (*see* Chapter 3). Unfortunately, this will rarely be the case in practice. This is not necessarily a problem if one (or ideally more) analogue companies with a similar growth path in earnings can be found (*see* above). It is a major problem if no such comparable firm can be found. In such circumstances, the only safe conclusion is that the PE method is fundamentally flawed. The only alternative is a DCF valuation. In practice there will be many cases where earnings growth patterns differ between firms (for example, most pharmaceutical companies have differing product pipelines and product maturities), and this inevitably leads to the conclusion that earnings based methods are far from ideal.

The fact that the PE ratio is a function of the risk premium required also highlights the fact that the analogue needs to be of a similar risk to the target. A detailed discussion of the relationship between risk and return is given in Chapter 4, but for now we might note that risks could be expected to be similar if the analogue firm is operating in the same general business area as the target and the firms are of similar size.[7]

2.3.3 Historic or prospective earnings multiples

A historic PE multiple should only be applied to historic earnings, while prospective PE ratios should only be applied to prospective earnings. The prospective PE multiple is simply the current price divided by the forecast earnings. In Table 2.3, *The Estimates Directory* consensus forecasts for British Vita are used with the December 1997 market value to calculate prospective PE ratios for the years 1998–2000.

A common error in practice is to estimate next year's earnings, or earnings further ahead, for a target company, and then apply to this the *current* PE ratio of the industry or some analogue firm. A survey by Simon Keane (1992) found that an example of this type of mistake made by chartered accountants in valuing firms was this multiplication of a forecast earnings figure by an earnings multiple taken from the current PE ratios of comparable listed firms found in the *FT*. Unfortunately, this will generally have the effect of overvaluing the target. This is because in general earnings grow through time. Consider the following example, where an unquoted target firm ('Target Ltd', say a potential trade purchase from a divesting conglomerate) is being valued by reference to Analogue plc. Actual earnings are available for 1997, and earnings have been forecast for 1998:

	1997	1998(E)
Analogue plc:		
Earnings	£20 m	£22.2 m (E)
Current market capitalisation	200 m	
Price-earnings ratio	10	
Prospective price earnings ratio (200/22.2)	9	
Target Ltd:		
Earnings	£10 m	£11.1 m (E)

The valuation based upon the erroneous application of the *current* analogue PE to the 1998 forecast earnings yields a value of 10 × £11.1 m = £111 m. The defensible approaches to valuation involve *either* the application of the historic multiple to 1997 earnings (10 × £10 m = £100 m) *or* the application of the prospective multiple to forecast earnings (9 × £11.1 m = £100 m). In the case of this example, the two valuations are identical as the same rate of growth in earnings has been assumed for both target and analogue companies (as noted above, a similar evolution of growth rates is required to justify the use of PE ratios). The degree of error is simply a function of the rate of earnings growth in the target.

2.3.4 Defining earnings: FRS 3, FRS 10 and IIMR headline earnings

In this section, *earnings per share* (EPS) rather than total earnings is reviewed. In principle, it should make no difference whether calculations are done in total, on the bases of total earnings and market capitalisation, or on a per share basis on the bases of EPS and price per share. In practice, the number of shares in issue can vary over the year, and so the method of calculating the denominator in the EPS figure has an impact. So, historically, has the way the numerator is defined.

Until the introduction of Financial Reporting Standard (FRS) 3 in the UK, British Companies had calculated their EPS on the basis of earnings *before* 'extraordinary items'. In theory, this is desirable, as a valuer would want to exclude any major influences on earnings that were not likely to be persistent in future years. For example, the major costs incurred in shutting down a factory or division may be genuine 'one-off' costs which deflate the current year's earnings below their long-run trend. Unfortunately, giving UK finance directors carte blanche to declare certain items 'below the line' for EPS calculations led to widespread abuse. (For an entertaining description of some of the more glaring examples of such 'creative accounting', *see* Terry Smith's book, *Accounting for Growth*.) While one might naively expect the long-run mean of 'extraordinary items' to be zero, they appeared to be heavily biased towards negative values.

This led the Accounting Standards Board (ASB) to radically reform the position so that it is, in practice, virtually impossible for any item to be classified as an extraordinary item. This has generally had the effect of making EPS more volatile, something that the ASB had hoped would sway analysts away from focusing on just one number as the summary of corporate performance. One practical reponse has been that in the UK, the Institute for Investment Management and Research (IIMR) has defined an alternative 'headline earnings' number, which differs from the ASB (and therefore published annual report and accounts) version of earnings per share. The principal difference is in the treatment of gains or losses on capital items, which are included in the ASB definition but excluded under the IIMR definition. A summary of the IIMR 'headline earnings' exclusions compared to FRS 3 earnings is as follows:[8]

■ gain/loss on disposal of fixed assets;

■ asset write-downs;

■ provisions for losses on disposal of operations to be discontinued;

■ losses or gains on disposal of operations to be discontinued;

■ amortisation of goodwill.

It is important to note that the *FT* (but not necessarily other newspapers') definition of the PE ratio uses the IIMR definition of EPS.

In the case of British Vita there is a modest difference between the IIMR calculation and that required by FRS 3 in 1997, but because of the sale of some discontinued operations the 1996 figures differ. Details of the calculations are shown in Table 2.3. All line number references are to the British Vita accounts in Appendix 1. Earnings multiple calculations are shown for both methods in the bottom section of the table. Thus the PE multiple in mid-December quoted in the *FT* was the 10.41 as calculated.

Finally, FRS 14 was brought into effect from December 1998. This specifies the calculation of the weighted average number of shares in issue when this figure alters during the year for a number of reasons. It also requires the publication of a basic and diluted EPS figure. Diluted EPS arises when, for example, company share options or convertible bonds are outstanding.

2.3.5 Cash earnings, EBITDA and EBIT multiples

As discussed above, the case for a 'cash earnings' or EBITDA multiple is driven by possible differences in depreciation, and amortisation rates (and other provisions in the case of 'pure' cash earnings). If 'cash earnings' are calculated at enterprise level, the focus in all three cases is on cash flows pre-interest, and it is not particularly helpful to relate these flows to the value of the equity alone. In general, cash earnings to the enterprise, EBITDA and EBIT multiples are not quoted in the market and need to be 'backed out' from the accounting data and market prices. This is easily achieved and is illustrated in Table 2.3 with the British Vita data.[9] The general principle is to add back the necessary adjustments (for example, EBITDA requires the adding back of depreciation and amortisation to the EBIT figure) and divide this into the *enterprise value*. Enterprise value (EV) is defined as being the equity market capitalisation plus the value of long-term debt financing. In theory, the value of this debt should be current market values, but in Europe only large companies generally have quoted bond issues, and bank financing and lease financing are heavily used. Because of this, in practice the book value of debt is generally used instead of market values.

Thus a summary of the definitions used for these multiples is:

EBIT multiple	=	EV/EBIT
EBITDA multiple	=	EV/EBITDA
Enterprise cash earnings multiple	=	EV/Enterprise cash earnings
P/CE multiple	=	Equity/Equity cash earnings

Table 2.3 Case example: British Vita plc

Item ref.	Item	Calculation basis (refers to items in Appendix 1)	1996	1997	1998E	1999E	2000E
a	Year-end shares in issue	From accs	220.90	221.70	221.70	221.70	221.70
b	Weighted average shares	From accs	220.20	221.20	221.70	221.70	221.70
c	EPS FRS 3	From accs/ests	16.80	19.80	21.60	23.40	25.20
d	EPS co. stated	From accs	17.20	19.80			
e	EPS IIMR	17 (continuing) + 74	17.53	20.03	21.60	23.70	25.20
f	DPS	From accs/ests	8.25	8.75	9.30	9.90	10.53
g	CFPS	47/76 (direct for est.)	26.93	31.74	32.50	34.00	39.60
h	EAT	17 (implied for est.)	36.90	43.80	47.89	51.88	55.87
i	EAT (headline)	17 (continuing) − 44	37.90	44.30	47.89	52.54	55.87
j	EBIT	11 − 7	48.90	55.50	n.a.	n.a.	n.a.
k	EBITDA	11 − 7 + 42	80.00	82.80	n.a.	n.a.	n.a.
l	Enterprise cash earnings	47	70.40	81.40	n.a.	n.a.	n.a.
m	Cash earnings	17 + 42 + 46 (implied)	59.30	70.20	72.05	75.38	87.79
n	Net assets	36	299.00	287.20			
o	Market price, mid-Dec. 98 (p)	Financial Times		208.50			
p	Market capitalisation, mid-Dec. 98	Financial Times		462.24			
q	Book value long-term debt	34		34.40			
r	'Enterprise Value' (EV)	p + q		496.64			
	Multiples						
	PER (shares in issue)	p/a		10.55			
	PER (FRS 3)	o/c		10.53			
	PER (IIMR)	o/e		10.41			
	Prospective PER (FRS 3)	o/c			9.65	8.91	8.27
	Prospective PER (IIMR)	o/e			9.65	8.80	8.27
	EV/EBIT	r/j		8.95			
	EV/EBITDA	r/k		6.00			
	EV/Enterprise cash earnings	r/l		7.07			
	P/CE	o/m		6.58			
	Prospective P/CE	o/m			6.89	6.59	5.66
	Market-to-book	p/n		1.61			

These multiples, which can be calculated for analogue companies or can be calculated at industry level, are useful in situations where there are major differences in depreciation rates and/or gearing between companies. They are also used in international comparisons. For example, at the time of the Deutsche Telekom privatisation, a particular problem facing analysts was that although large telecommunications companies can, in principle, be compared internationally, there were two particular problems in making such comparisons. The first was the problem of the conservative nature of German accounting in general (*see* above). The second was that the gearing level of Deutsche Telekom was much higher than that of comparable operators such as British Telecom. While these problems are easily accommodated by a DCF analysis (*see* Chapters 4–6), the only practicable solution for analysts wishing to make the comparison on an earnings basis was to use EBITDA multiples.

2.3.6 Valuing synergies using the earnings multiple approach

As noted, the chosen earnings multiple (whether EAT, EBIT or EBITDA) is usually based on observations of other companies' PE ratios. Typically, the process involves finding companies in a similar line of business to the target and of a similar size.

When the valuation is being prepared for a possible acquisition, a rational approach is to value the company in both its 'as is' state and in its post-acquisition state, including the value of any synergystic benefits. Unfortunately, this latter value is not a simple thing to calculate when using the PE approach since the PE ratio must alter as growth prospects change, so that if the improvement results in progressive changes over a number of years, it is by no means obvious what the PE ratio should be. By contrast, no such problems arise when using a discounted cash flow approach, since the discount rate only alters when economic risk changes; efficiency changes merely alter both short- and long-run projected cash flows (the latter via the assumed growth rate). The basic cause of this problem is that synergistic benefits are unlikely to grow at the same rate as revenues and direct operating costs. Given that such benefits often include overhead cost savings, and that these are often of a fixed cost nature, these savings might only grow in line with inflation. Multiplying these savings by an earnings multiple that reflects some *real* growth prospects is likely to overvalue the target.

2.3.7 Conclusions on earnings multiple approaches

At first sight, the application of a market derived earnings multiple to estimated future earnings seems reasonable, but on closer investigation it is obvious that they must be used with some caution, for the following reasons:

- First, there are problems relating to the comparative calculation of the earnings numbers themselves, which are:
  - partly attributable to differing accounting practices; and
  - partly attributable to the problems caused by the historic cost accounting convention – as was noted, the use of cash earnings multiples can help to overcome this;

- Second, there are real difficulties encountered in attempting to derive a suitable earnings multiple because:
  - differing earnings growth patterns and risks make finding a suitable analogue company difficult;
  - this is not to say that the approach cannot reasonably be used – it can be, provided these problems are recognised and overcome;
  - however, this is by no means a trivial task and it is hard to see why the use of the earnings multiple approach should be positively recommended compared to the DCF alternative, which has the advantage of making the assumptions concerning future growth explicit rather than implicit.[10]

They have a role to play in takeover valuation, simply because they are one of the standard items discussed in any deal. This is not to say they are 'correct', merely that one would typically look at the issue of implied multiples. They have no real validity in the context of strategic valuation however, where long-run cash flow budgets would be available within the firm. In such cases, a DCF valuation would always be preferred.

Before leaving the topic of earnings multiple based valuations, we should note there are special cases where market practitioners regard PE multiples as irrelevant in determining values, because other factors (usually asset based) drive market value. Examples include oil exploration companies, investment trusts, insurance companies and property companies. Earnings based approaches also fail in the case where firms are in a loss-making position, or in start-up situations (for example, EuroDisney at flotation).

2.4 ASSET BASED VALUATIONS

Asset valuations are generally calculated as 'secondary' information, either for the opportunity cost model described in Chapter 1, or to compare strategic alternatives (such as a break-up), or as a 'reality check' where the asset value is compared to the value from a DCF or earnings model. Under certain circumstances (essentially, when the company is not viable as a going concern), the lower bound to opportunity value is the net realisable value of the assets; on other occasions, the upper bound to value will be the relacement cost of the assets, although as we noted in Chapter 1, care is needed in the definition of replacement cost, since this must reflect the replacement of assets with the same service potential and must also reflect the value of all the assets, including those which are not normally valued in financial terms, such as personnel, market share, geographical location and so on. In short, what is being calculated is really the *replication cost* of the business. Note that such a cost would also need to reflect any timing disadvantage which resulted from replicating the firm; given the time involved in setting up an enterprise from scratch, such costs may be substantial.

The need for a look at asset values, then, is partly to check that the business cannot be replicated more cheaply than it can be bought; while this is of most relevance in a takeover situation, it might also serve as an indicator of a possible overvaluation in other cases, since the implication of market value exceeding replication cost may be that there is some scope for competing firms to enter the market. Realistically, however, such a value will be very difficult to arrive at, and will probably include a great deal of subjectivity. It is probably of most relevance to the valuation of small, unlisted companies where replication might be relatively straightforward, although such a figure can be reasonably calculated for quite large businesses, such as retailers and hotel chains; the key issues are the ease and speed with which a replication can be put together. There is also a need for such calculations to check on whether a higher value can be achieved by the business in a form other than its present one; this involves looking at selling off individual SBUs as separate entities (*break-up value*), or selling off the assets piecemeal (*liquidation value*). Finally, there is a need to check on the value of the underlying assets of the business because this has implications for the security underpinning the business itself, and also the potential financing needs of the company.

In practical terms, the general approach to calculating either replacement or realisable values is:

- start with balance sheet values;

- adjust for changes in general price levels;

- adjust for other known differences in asset values (e.g. under/over provision of pension costs).

2.4.1 Break-up values

In looking at the idea of break-up values, we are simply recognising the principles behind valuation which we apply elsewhere in this briefing. Essentially, the value of any business is dictated by its future cash generating potential. A company will be worth more as a series of separate businesses rather than as a whole either if cash flow can be gained by cutting out some central overheads or if those individual businesses can be made to generate additional cash flows by being run in a different manner. Such an eventuality may come about because of greater incentives, freedom from centralised decision making, increased co-operation between management and workforce, greater use of initiative, freedom of access to external capital rather than reliance on rationed internal funds, or simply by synergystic gain from combination with some different company. Obviously, business units can themselves be parcelled together in a way which maximises value; if, for example, we are investigating the possible break-up of a conglomerate group which among its businesses has a consumer electrical appliances division and a gas fire manufacturing division, we may well find that the optimal value is created by combining these two operations into a consumer products company which is sold off. The general rules are simple (even if their application is not):

- First, find the value of each SBU as a 'stand-alone' unit. This can be compared with the realisable value of the unit's assets to see whether there is a prima facie case for discontinuing the activity.

- Second, search out any alternative combinations of business units as it may be the case that a business which appeared to be worth abandoning is actually worth keeping in conjunction with some other activity.

There are several points to watch when appraising this break-up valuation:

- the overhead costs which would be borne by the independent SBU and the remaining business – note that we might rationally expect some synergy in overheads;

- inter-SBU transfers of goods and services – however these are priced for management accounting purposes,[11] when considering the value of a SBU as an independent entity any such goods and services must be priced at an 'arm's length' market price (recognising such factors as selling costs and quantity discounts) since if the entity is sold off, any trading which continues with the rest of the group will be conducted on such a basis.

2.4.2 Liquidation values

In general, liquidation values can only be arrived at with any accuracy by direct inspection. It is obviously possible for outside valuers to arrive at crude 'guesstimates' in cases where the company has a reasonably simple structure (for example, this may be practicable in the case of high street retailers), but the dangers of the approach can be illustrated by several unfortunate examples. One spectacular case from the recent past was that of Polly Peck where just prior to the suspension of the company analysts were estimating that a substantial asset value per share would be realised on any break-up of the company.

If we consider the assets in balance sheet order, property values are normally stated at a recent valuation rather than historic cost. Since the date of such valuation is disclosed, it is possible to arrive at an approximate current value by the application of property price indices; transaction costs on buying or selling would need to be allowed for in arriving at replacement or realisable values. However, it is important to realise that professional property valuations are prepared on the assumption that an open market exists with willing buyers and sellers. It is perfectly possible that it might take some considerable time to find such a buyer. If, say, the break-up and piecemeal sale of the property portfolio of a major high street retailer was being contemplated, attempting to sell such a large amount of property at once might have a significantly depressing effect on values, particularly if there was some geographical concentration of the assets. There is also the question of special-purpose properties, such as industrial plants and ports. Attempting to define a realisable value for such cases is fraught with difficulty because of the need to consider the possibilities of alternative use and any attendant land clearance and alteration costs involved; special surveys would be the only way of accurately arriving at such values.

Other fixed assets, such as plant and equipment, vehicles and fittings are normally carried in the balance sheet at historic cost less depreciation. However, certain assets (for example, the British Airways aircraft fleet) are sometimes shown at valuation, although companies are often reluctant to use such an approach because of the accompanying need for higher depreciation charges.

Unless a recent valuation of assets is available, balance sheet values of these assets are often a very poor guide to either liquidation or replacement value. The answers to the questions which need to be asked about these assets can rarely be found from the annual report. We really need to know the production technology employed, and how this relates to that employed by competitors (if the technology is outdated, the balance sheet value might considerably overstate the realisable value), the state of repair of the assets, the degree to which these assets are movable and the degree to which the assets have a specialist use. Perhaps the best illustration of the last two points is the sale of, say, a complex chemical plant; unless there is a buyer for the operation as a going concern, the liquidation value of the assets is likely to be just the scrap value of the equipment, and if there was any toxicity problem the entire fixed asset value could be negative.

Any investments shown on the balance sheet are simply valued at market prices if the investments are easily saleable. Note that the market value of such investments at the accounting year end is a mandatory disclosure, but any revision to current market values requires a detailed breakdown of the investments held; this information will only be available from the accounts if the investment held is a substantial one (more than 2% if the investment is in a listed UK company). However, if such a substantial stake in a listed company is owned, we would need to consider the likely impact of any sale (or purchase, in the case of replacement cost) on market prices; furthermore, it must be borne in mind that some stakes in quoted smaller companies can be virtually unsaleable in any quantity unless there is a matching purchaser for the shares. In the case of investments in unlisted companies, valuations would need to be prepared on a 'willing buyer' basis, and on a forced sale basis if liquidation values were being considered.

With the exception of stocks, the book, liquidation and replacement values of most of the current assets are likely to be fairly close to one another, unless inflation rates are high. Besides the obvious issue of bad debts, another issue which needs to be considered is the definition of cash and liquid assets. In general, the netting off of cash balances is not permitted by accounting regulations, but positive balances are combined in the consolidated balance sheet of the company. The problem here is identifying just where the cash is located. It is perfectly possible that a large percentage of an apparently large cash balance is locked into a country with tight exchange control regulations; this issue can be addressed in a valuation with access to internal records but not otherwise.

Stock values can either be very objective and close to both realisable and replacement values (as in the case of the large supermarket chains), or extremely subjective (contract work in progress valuation being the best example). In between these extremes, we have the cost of manufactured stock. The general accounting rule is that stocks should be valued at the lower of cost or realisable value; unfortunately, in the case of manufactured goods, 'cost' is highly subjective, since SSAP 9 requires cost to include manufacturing overheads. Since overhead allocation is a very arbitrary process it follows that the resultant stock values are also arbitrary. A point which needs to be considered here is that the realisable values of the stocks of regularly produced branded products are fairly easy to estimate; on the other hand, the realisable values of specialist products may not be.

These stock valuation problems are relatively trivial compared to the problem of estimating values of long-term contracts. According to SSAP 9, the balance sheet value should be cost (which will include overheads and can even include capitalised interest charges), less amounts taken to the profit and loss acount,[12] less any provisions for foreseeable losses. Any payments due on these contracts should be separately disclosed under debtors. Key issues which need to be thought about include the degree of completion and the likelihood of any problems, including both construction difficulties and possible claims against the company.

2.4.3 Replacement values

It should be evident from the above that, although in most cases we can start from accounting values and derive sensible estimates of realisable (liquidation) values, the same can only be done for the replacement costs of physical assets. This is because the full costs of replication of the service capacity of the business in question will include such items as the value of key personnel, brands, goodwill and so on.

One measure that is used by financial analysts is the q-ratio; this is simply the ratio of the market value of the company to the estimated replacement cost of the *physical* assets. One problem with this is the definition and calculation of replacement costs; nonetheless, this is a measure which is used by US analysts. In Chapter 6 (pp 157–9), we show how the current replacement value (and hence a q-ratio) for British Vita's assets can be roughly estimated. In principle, the accumulated depreciation figure from the balance sheet is used to estimate the average age of the assets. The assumption then made is that all asset prices move in line with general inflation, although specific price indices can be used where available. This is obviously imperfect, but better than ignoring the impact of inflation altogether.

Finally, before leaving our discussion on asset valuations, we should note that some types of business are normally valued by reference to their asset bases and not by their earnings; the most obvious examples include property companies, oil companies and investment trusts. Note that discounted cash flow approaches can be used in such cases, but they are not always helpful. They are likely to be very useful in the case of oil and property companies, but will generally not be so in the case of investment trusts, where in the case of quoted investments the asset values will already reflect consensus market valuations. On average, both investment trusts and property companies trade at a discount to net asset values; with oil companies, both extraction costs and the period of extraction need to be estimated using DCF principles.

2.5 SUMMARY

The chapter described the main traditional approaches to valuation, which were:

- the earnings multiple approach

- asset valuations.

The general process in the former is to find a quoted analogue company for the firm being valued. Value can then be estimated using either:

- current earnings $\times$ a current earnings multiple; or

- forecast earnings $\times$ a prospective earnings multiple.

It was noted that because of problems of differences in accounting policies and international differences in GAAP, some form of cash based earnings multiple might be preferred to the more normally quoted PE multiple. Cash earnings can be estimated at either enterprise or equity levels, the latter giving rise to the 'cash earnings per share' number.

Gearing differences between analogue and target can be allowed for by focusing on enterprise value to EBIT multiples, but growth pattern differences between target and analogue cannot be satisfactorily allowed for.

In general, because of the shortcomings of earnings based valuation models, DCF is a preferred alternative.

Asset values should always be estimated both to take account of the opportunity cost principles explained in Chapter 1 and to serve as a 'reality check' on the calculations performed. Relevant asset values are replacement costs and realisable values. In general, these are estimated by starting with the balance sheet figures and adjusting for price level and other changes.

Fundamental DCF models

3.1 INTRODUCTION

This chapter starts with a short revision of basic discounted cash flow (DCF) principles. The use of the following are then covered:

- constant growth models
- dealing with inflation
- estimating the inflation rate
- specific period forecasts
- dividends and free cash flow
- comparison of price-earnings and DCF models
- dealing with uneven cash flows.

Readers familiar with all these concepts should pass on to the more detailed analyses in Chapters 4 and 5.

3.1.1 An introduction to DCF principles

We start with some simplifying assumptions which can be relaxed later:

- there is no inflation;
- future cash flows can be predicted with certainty;
- interest rates remain constant and known.

Given these assumptions, it is easy to develop a rational method of assessing the value of future cash flows. Suppose that you are owed £1000 which is payable exactly one year from now and that you are a wealthy individual with ample funds invested at the current rate of interest of 10%. You are offered an amount to be decided upon to settle the loan today. What should this amount be in order to make you indifferent between collecting the cash now and waiting for one year?

- You would accept something less than £1000 because if you had the cash now, you could invest it yourself and earn interest.

- In fact, you would want an amount which, when invested at 10% p.a., gives you £1000 in a year's time.

- Since at 10% you receive at the end of the year cash equivalent to 110% of your investment, the answer is found by dividing £1000 by 1.1, which gives an amount of £909.09.

- If the debt was settled by giving you this amount today, you would invest it at 10%, obtain interest of £90.91 and have £1000 at the end of the year.

- Thus we can say that £909.09 is the *present value* of £1000 in one year's time at 10%.

What if you were owed the £1000 in three years' time rather than one year from now? The principle is the same, except that you gain interest on the interest which is added to your account each year. If you start with £100 today, and interest rates are 10% p.a., you end up with the following balances at the end of each year:

End of year	Interest for year at 10%	Principal plus interest
1	£10	£110
2	£11	£121
3	£12.10	£133.10

This can be generalised as stating that the *future value* (principal plus interest) is found from the present value by:

$$\text{Future value} = \text{Present value} \times (1 + r)^n$$

where r is the interest rate per period expressed as a decimal (e.g. 5% gives an r of 0.05) and n is the number of compounding periods. Thus for our example with £100 invested at 10% p.a. for three years we get:

$$\text{Future value} = £100 \times (1.1)^3 = £133.10$$

We can also see that since future values can be calculated from present values, the reverse must be true, and simple rearrangement of our equation gives:

$$\text{Present value} = \text{Future value} \div (1 + r)^n$$

Thus we can solve our problem of how much you must receive today to settle a debt of £1000 in three years' time; the solution is:

$$\text{Present value} = £1000 \div (1.1)^3 = £751.31$$

- We can thus convert any future cash flow into a present value equivalent in a manner which takes account of the *opportunity cost of capital* (interest costs here).[1]

- Furthermore, these present values are *additive*, which means we can handle problems where there are cash flows arising at different points in time.

- Therefore if you are owed £1000 in one year and a further £1000 in three years, the present value of the whole is simply £751.31 + £909.09 = £1660.40.

Performing the present value calculation (known as *discounting*) can be simplified by using tables of *discount factors*. These are calculated as $1 / (1 + r)^n$ and are shown in Appendix B at the end of the briefing. As discount factors are the reciprocal of $(1 + r)$, the future value is *multiplied* by the discount factor in order to obtain the present value; for example, applying this to our example of £1000 receivable in three years' time yields:

> Present value = £1000 × 0.7513 = £751.30

Once this basic principle is understood, it is easy to see how this can be applied to valuing any investment project or business. Take the following example:

EXAMPLE

XYZ operates in a declining industry and the following estimates of annual profits are available:

Year ended	Sales less direct cost of sales	Other costs	Profit
31/12/99	£100 000	£50 000	£50 000
31/12/00	£110 000	£70 000	£40 000
31/12/01	£130 000	£70 000	£60 000
31/12/02	£120 000	£80 000	£40 000
31/12/03	£100 000	£90 000	£10 000

- At the end of this period, you believe that the age of the assets and falling demand will mean that it is no longer worth continuing in business.
- At this point, assets could be sold for a scrap value of £2000.
- Other costs include a figure of £12 000 p.a. for asset depreciation.

So far, we have ignored the question of risk, but suppose that investments of similar risk normally earn 20% p.a. (Chapter 4 deals with the question of risk and the discount rate).

Three simple steps are needed to value the business:

- Establish the cash flows (not profits) each year.
- Discount these at 20%.
- Sum them to calculate the gross present value of the future business cash flows as at 1/1/99.

The first step is important since opportunity costs of capital relate to cash; in the case of this example we therefore need to add back depreciation, with the fall in asset values being reflected in the final cash sale figure of £2000 in 2003. Assume that all cash flows arise on the last day of the year:

XYZ plc
Present value (or DCF) calculation:

Year end	Accounting profit	Depreciation added back	Cash flow	Discount factor at 20%	Present value
31/12/99	50 000	12 000	62 000	0.8333	51 667
31/12/00	40 000	12 000	52 000	0.6944	36 111
31/12/01	60 000	12 000	72 000	0.5787	41 667
31/12/02	40 000	12 000	52 000	0.4823	25 077
31/12/03	10 000	12 000	22 000	0.4019	8 841
31/12/03		Sale of assets	2 000	0.4019	804
Total present value					164 167

This 'Total present value' (or DCF value) of £164 167 is the economic value of the business. It is also the rational maximum price that any investor would be prepared to pay for XYZ plc.

In the case of this example, it was assumed that the business had a five-year life. More realistically, businesses have very long lives and this leads to the problem of how to deal with *continuing* or *horizon* values at the end of the forecast period. This matter is explored in depth in Chapter 5.

3.1.2 An introduction to annuities

In the valuation process, a situation frequently encountered is where the cash flows are constant for a number of years. As a simple example, suppose we wish to value a business with stable cash flows of £20m p.a. for the next five years and 12% p.a. is the opportunity cost of capital.

One solution is to multiply each year's flow by its discount factor but a quicker approach is to use the sum of the discount factors (known as an *annuity factor*) and multiply this by the constant cash flow. (Tables of annuity factors[2] are given in Appendix B.) Applying the five-year 12% annuity factor to the cash flows in the example gives:

Present value = £20 m × 3.6048 = £72.096 m

A slightly more difficult case is where constant cash flows are expected to arise for a number of years in the future, but not immediately. For example, what would happen if management felt they could improve the cash flows of the above business? Suppose the revised forecast is:

- £22m in year 1;

- £25m in year 2;

- then £27m p.a. for years 3 to 5 inclusive.

This can be valued in the following manner:

- Calculate the present value of the year 1 and year 2 cash flows in the normal manner.

- The cash flows from years 3 to 5 inclusive represent a three-year annuity of £27m p.a.

- The present value of such an annuity (using a three-year 12% annuity factor) is £27m × 2.4018, or £64.849m.

- This is the value of the annuity assuming the first year of cash flow is year 1; in this case the first year is year 3. Therefore this must be discounted using a *year 2* discount factor, since the unadjusted calculation gives us the present value at the beginning of year 3 (or the end of year 2).

The business therefore has a DCF value:

Year	Item	£m	Discount factor	Present value
1	Cash flow	22	0.8929	19.643
2	Cash flow	25	0.7972	19.930
2	Yr 2 PV of annuity	64.849	0.7972	51.698
Total PV (£m)				91.271

This type of calculation can be particularly useful when calculating the economic value of property, a case where the annuity values can be calculated for successive rent reviews and discounted back to give present values.

3.1.3 Perpetuities

A perpetuity is simply a cash flow that continues for ever. The formula for calculating the present value of a perpetuity is simply:

$$\text{Present value} = \text{Cash flow} \div r$$

As an example, take the case of a shop let on a perpetual basis for a rental of £25 000 p.a. If the opportunity cost of capital is expected to be 12.5% for the foreseeable future, the economic value of the shop is £25 000/0.125 = £200 000.[3]

Perpetuities are useful tools in the valuation process because we frequently want to know the value of the business once it has reached a 'steady state'. This is the simplest example of a continuing or horizon value calculation. Take the following example of Alpha plc:

EXAMPLE

Alpha plc:

- Latest cash flow (year 0) £100 000 p.a.

- Growth will be 10% p.a. for the next five years.

- After this, the cash flow will remain constant at £161 000 p.a.

- Cost of capital: 15% p.a.

Steps:

- Calculate the present value of the first five years' cash flows (£438 460).

- Calculate the value of the perpetual £161 000 p.a. *at the end of year 5* = £161 000/0.15 or £1 073 330.

- Discount this back to the present giving a value of £1 073 330 × 0.4972 = £533 630.

- Add this to the present value of the cash flows in years 1–5 giving a total business value of £972 090.

While perpetuities in nominal or money terms might be uncommon (a major exception being perpetual bonds), perpetuities in real terms (i.e. a cash flow that increases in line with inflation) might be of more relevance. The impact of inflation is explained below.

3.1.4 Non-year end cash flows

The above DCF calculations have assumed that all cash flows occur at the end of the forecast year. Given the approximations involved in the forecasting process, this is probably adequate except in special cases. Such cases might include large-scale, short-life ventures, or cases where particularly high inflation rates or high levels of risk are expected. Adjusting the DCF calculation to take account of cash flows which occur at periods other than the year end is not difficult, and merely involves an adjustment to the discount rate. In general, the relationship is:

(1 + Period rate) = *n*th root of (1 + Annual rate)

As an example, take an annual rate of 36%. What is the quarterly compounding rate? In this case, we need the fourth root of 1.36 which gives us a figure of 1.0799 for (1 + Period rate), in other words a discount rate of 7.99% per quarter.

The discounting stage of the valuation simply proceeds with a normal DCF analysis, using n periods per annum. Some firms use the approach in investment appraisal to calculate discount factors assuming all cash flows arise on a *mid*-year basis.

Some knowledge of capital market conventions is necessary when using yield to redemption data on bonds. In both the US and UK government bond markets, yields are actually calculated on a half-yearly basis since US treasury bonds and UK gilts bear half-yearly coupons. This means that a *quoted* yield of 10% is *actually* 5% per half year; using the reverse of the above formula, we can calculate that 5% per half year represents an annual percentage rate of 10.25%. By contrast, some eurobonds and most other European government bonds, such as the French *obligations du trésor*, have only one coupon payment per annum, so that their quoted yields are annual percentage rates. This does have implications for the calculation of expected inflation rates (*see* below) and the estimation of risk-adjusted discount rates (*see* Chapter 4).

3.2 DCF WITH CONSTANT GROWTH INTO PERPETUITY

In the above example of Alpha plc, zero growth was assumed. In practice, companies in a 'steady state' perhaps might be expected to grow at approximately the rate of increase in gross domestic product. It is useful to be able to derive a formula for calculating the present value of a constant-growth business.

In such a case, the cash flows are increasing at a constant rate (1 + Assumed growth rate) as is the discount rate (1/(1 + Cost of capital). The value of such a cash flow stream is easily found by the application of the standard formula for the sum of a geometric progression (for a detailed explanation, see the notes at the end of this chapter). The present value of the cash flows is given by:

$$\text{Present value} = \frac{\text{Cash}_0(1 + \text{Growth})}{(r - \text{Growth})}$$

Since $\text{cash}_0(1 \times \text{Growth})$ is simply the anticipated cash flow in the first year this yields:

$$\text{Present value} = \frac{\text{Cash yr 1}}{(r - \text{Growth})}$$

In practice, this is a very useful formula for calculating horizon values. Suppose that in the example of Alpha plc the assumptions are changed as follows

---

EXAMPLE

Alpha plc

Changed assumptions regarding growth beyond year 5: the £161 000 in year 5 is now expected to grow at 2% per annum.

This gives the following horizon value *at the end of year 5*:

$$\text{Value at end year 5} = \frac{161\,000 \times (1.02)}{0.15 - 0.02} = £1\,263\,231$$

Of course, this horizon value would (as before) need to be discounted back to year 0 and added to the present value of the year 1–5 cash flows to give the value of the business.

3.3 INFLATION AND VALUATION

There are two basic ways of tackling the problem of inflation in the valuation process. The first is to simply take account of the relevant rate of inflation when estimating the cash flows and express all those at the price levels expected on the date of the cash flow occurring; this is known as estimating cash flows in *money terms* or *nominal terms*. These cash flows must then be discounted at a money rate cost of capital, in other words one which takes account of the effect of anticipated inflation on investors' required rates of return. The alternative approach is to estimate all cash flows on the basis of today's general price levels, in other words *real terms*. These figures are then discounted using a *real* discount rate, that is a cost of capital which excludes the implicit inflation expectations of investors. Properly applied, the two approaches give identical present values.

Thus the general rule is:

■ estimate *real* cash flows and discount at a *real* cost of capital; or

■ estimate *nominal* cash flows and discount at a *nominal* cost of capital.

Note that it is impossible to avoid forecasting inflation for the entire time horizon of the valuation; in the first approach, it is necessary to estimate the effect of inflation upon the different cost and revenue flows of the firm, whereas in the second case, given that we generally observe costs of capital from the markets,[4] we need to strip out the impounded inflation rate. This is because any view of opportunity cost of capital obtained from the financial markets is a compounding of the required real rate of return and the consensus anticipated inflation rate for the time horizon of the investment.

The following example of Exe Properties plc is used to illustrate the two approaches to dealing with inflation:

EXAMPLE

Exe Properties plc has a property portfolio on which rents are fixed for the next five years at £500 000 per annum. The company has the following costs:

- staff costs of £50 000 p.a. which are expected to increase at the rate of general inflation (as measured by the retail price index (RPI)) plus 1%;
- other costs of £30 000 p.a. which will increase in line with the RPI.

Other information:

- RPI is expected to increase at 5% p.a., and the appropriate cost of capital for property firms is 15.5% p.a.
- The property portfolio will be sold off for around £5 million at current property price levels; property prices will increase by 2% p.a. in real terms.

To show that the two approaches are equal, the company is valued in both real and money terms and the practical issues are then explained.

First, it is helpful to calculate the various price indices:

Exe Properties plc: calculation of price indices

Year	RPI calculation			Labour rate index			Property prices index		
0			100			100			100
1			105			106			107
2	105	× 1.05	= 110.2	106	× 1.06	= 112.4	107	× 1.07	= 114.5
3	110.2	× 1.05	= 115.8	112.4	× 1.06	= 119.1	114.5	× 1.07	= 122.5
4	115.8	× 1.05	= 121.6	119.1	× 1.06	= 126.2	122.5	× 1.07	= 131.1
5	127.6	× 1.05	= 127.6	126.2	× 1.06	= 133.8	131.1	× 1.07	= 140.3

The first calculation made is the present value in nominal or money terms:

Exe Properties plc: present value in nominal terms

All figures in £000s

Year	Rental	Staff costs	Other costs	Property sale	Cash flow	PV @ 15.5%
1	500	53	31.5		415.5	359.7
2	500	56.2	33.1		410.7	307.9
3	500	59.6	34.7		405.7	263.3
4	500	63.1	36.5		400.4	225.0
5	500	66.9	38.3	7015	7409.8	3604.9
						4760.8

Obtaining a solution in real terms involves the following steps:

- deflating the cash flows using the general rate of inflation (i.e. the RPI rate) using the relationship:

> Real cost = Nominal cost ÷ (1 + General inflation rate)

- discounting at a real cost of capital. The relationship between real and money rates is:

> (1 + Real rate) = (1 + Money rate) ÷ (1 + General inflation rate)

In the case of the latter, inflation has a compounding effect, and it is not possible to simply deduct the 5% inflation rate from the 15.5%.

This is now applied to the example of Exe Properties plc:

EXAMPLE

Exe Properties plc: present value in real terms

Step 1: Calculation of real discount rate:

$$(1 + \text{Real rate}) = 1.155 \div 1.05 = 1.10, \text{ i.e. a real rate of}$$
$$0.1 \text{ or } 10\% \text{ p.a.}$$

Step 2: The present value calculation in real terms:

Year	Cash flows calculated in real terms			PV @ 10%
1	415.5 × 100/105	=	395.7	359.7
2	410.7 × 100/110.2	=	372.7	307.9
3	405.7 × 100/115.8	=	350.3	263.3
4	400.4 × 100/121.6	=	329.3	225.0
5	7409.8 × 100/127.6	=	5805.8	3,604.9
				4,760.8

Although the calculations yield an identical result on paper, in practice it is generally safer and easier to perform the analysis in nominal terms. This is because there will often be differential rates of price change applying to different types of cost and revenue (obvious examples include labour costs, which historically have risen in real terms, and computers which historically have experienced substantial real reductions); since these have to be estimated anyway, there is little advantage in translating all the money cash flows back into real terms. Perhaps more importantly, taxation is levied on monetary cash flows, and working capital has to be funded in these terms. Attempting to assess taxation (particularly when related to capital allowances) and working capital flows in real terms can be somewhat difficult and is certainly prone to error; as there is no advantage to be gained from this, the recommendation must be to use cash flows in money terms discounted by a cost of capital stated in money terms.

3.4 ESTIMATING THE FUTURE INFLATION RATE

The analysis in section 3.3 above demonstrates that it is not possible to avoid estimating the future inflation rate. There are three main methods of obtaining such estimates:

- economists' or brokers' estimates;
- estimates derived from index-linked government bonds;
- estimates derived from successive iterations based on nominal government bond rates.

The problem with the first source is that almost all available estimates suffer from the weakness of being short term in outlook, typically using a forecast horizon of between one and three years. There is also the problem of disagreement between estimates; this can be overcome by simply using an average of the various forecasts, which can be shown to be more accurate than using individual forecasts in the long run. Unfortunately, the former problem renders such forecasts virtually useless for the planning horizons we typically need in company valuations.

Thus the latter two approaches are preferred. In principle, such methods are applicable to any country with a liquid bond market. However, using inflation-linked loan stocks requires a ready and liquid market in these securities. To some degree, the UK has this, but this feature is not found in many other countries.

The problem which both approaches address is the determination of both the long-run real rate of interest and the long-run inflation rate. The simplest method (in the UK) is to look at the long-run yield to redemption on index-linked gilts. In December 1998 this was just over 2%. There are some problems with this figure as an estimate of investors' required real rate of return, however. First, the market is much 'thinner' than that for other gilts. Second, these returns may understate anticipated real rates of interest if they reflect the fact that the holder is partly protected from inflation and may therefore accept a lower return for lower inflation risk. Thirdly, these gilts are only *partly* hedged against inflation risk because the RPI for eight months previous to the due date is used in calculating the index-adjusted coupon and redemption values; this is why the *Financial Times* uses two different assumed inflation rates when presenting real yields to redemption. Nonetheless, despite these problems it is one easily accessible view of anticipated real interest rates. Simple application of the relationship between nominal rates (as found from the 'straight' gilt rate) and the index-linked gilt rate leads to an estimate of the average inflation rate over the life of the two gilts. (It follows that the life of the gilts should be comparable.) Thus the steps are:

- For a given life of gilt, find the index-linked gilt and ordinary gilt rate
- Using the relationship (1 + General inflation rate) = (1 + Money rate) ÷ (1 + Real rate), find the implied inflation rate.

For example, suppose we seek an estimate of the long-run rate of inflation in December 1998, we can use the relationship to find the approximate ten-year inflation rate by using the following gilt information from the *FT*:

EXAMPLE

Using index-linked and UK gilt yields to find the long-run inflation rate:

Gilt:	Yield to redemption:
Index-linked 2.5% 2009	(1) 1.88% (2) 2.00%
Treasury 8% 2009	4.31%

Assuming inflation of (1) 5% and (2) 3%.

Taking the 3% yield as more representative of current inflation rates, the calculation of ten-year inflation expectations yields:

$$1 + \text{Inflation} = 1.0431 \div 1.02 = 1.0226 \text{ or an average}$$
$$\text{inflation rate of } 2.26\%$$

The above is probably the simplest approach for the UK, but it is not applicable in the majority of countries where there are no index-linked government bonds available. In such cases, the alternative approach is to use the term structure of interest rates to 'back out' the implied future inflation rate. Implicitly, this method requires a direct estimate of the long-run risk-free rate of interest which is assumed to be constant. One approach to this estimation problem is to look at historical rates of return, which raises the problem of which historical period to look at. For example, using UK data obtained from the Barclays Capital *Equity-Gilt Study* (1998), we can observe the following real rates of return on gilts (geometric averages):

Period	*Real return*
	(on a gross income reinvested basis)
1918–1997	2.13%
1945–1997	0.26%
1954–1974	− 4.46%
1977–1997	5.69%

It seems unlikely that investors would rationally accept negative real returns, and their historical existence is almost certainly due to a failure to foresee experienced rates of inflation in the 1960s and 1970s. Equally, expectations formed during this period may explain the high real returns experienced since 1977. Thus taking the very long-run historical average may give the most representative figure for long-run real interest rate expectations. From a current perspective, it is interesting to note that this return is close to the current yield on long-dated index-linked gilts (which in December 1998 were between 1.96% and 2.12%, depending on the rate of future inflation assumed in the yield calculation).

Having established an estimate of the long-run real rate of return, it is possible to use gilt market data to derive anticipated inflation rates. If we assume that the underlying real return which investors require remains constant, we can approximate the market's anticipated inflation[5] by realising that the yield on any gilt is a compound sum of the anticipated inflation rate in each year and the required real rate of return. Thus if, at the end of 1998, we wish to calculate the implied anticipated inflation rates through to 2001, we need to solve:

$$(1 + \text{Yield}_3)^3 = (1 + \text{Inflation}_1)(1 + \text{Inflation}_2)(1 + \text{Inflation}_3)(1 + \text{Real})^3$$

The way we find the inflation figures for each year is as follows:

- Solve the expression for a one-year gilt, finding the implied inflation rate.
- Use this number to solve for the inflation rate in year 2.
- For example, the two-year inflation rate (Inflation_2) is found by:

$$(1 + \text{Inflation}_2) = (1 + \text{Money rate}_2)^2 \div [(1 + \text{Real rate}) \times (1 + \text{Inflation}_1)]$$

- Repeat for the appropriate number of years.

As an example, the following gilt yields were found in December 1998 (note that if available, gilts trading at par should be selected for this purpose to avoid any distortions caused by differing tax treatments on high and low coupon gilts):

EXAMPLE

This example demonstrates the above approach using information from the *FT*, assuming it is early 1999.

Calculation of implied inflation expectations from nominal gilt yields:

Gilt:	Yield to redemption
Treasury 8% 2000	4.93%
Treasury 7% 2001	4.75%
Treasury 7% 2002	4.62%

Continued overleaf

Using the very long-run estimate of the real gilt rate from Barclays Capital (1998) of 2.13% as representative of future real interest rates, we obtain the following estimates for inflation:

1999–2000:

$$1 + \text{Inflation}_1 = 1.0493 \div 1.0213 = 1.0274, \text{ or } 2.74\%$$

Feeding this into the next calculation:

2000–2001:

$$1 + \text{Inflation}_2 = 1.0475^2 \div (1.0274 \times 1.0213^2) = 1.0239, \text{ or } 2.39\%$$

2000–2001:

$$1 + \text{Inflation}_3 = 1.0462^3 \div (1.0274 \times 1.0239 \times 1.0213^3)$$
$$= 1.0218, \text{ or } 2.18\%$$

It must be emphasised that this is an approximation, since we have not allowed for coupon and redemption dates. If we have a forecast horizon of, say, ten years we can either continue with the procedure outlined above or we can use a long-run average rate calculated by using the usual real/money relationship. In December 1998, the yield on ten-year gilts was approximately 4.46%. If 2.13% is the long-run real rate we have an expected ten-year average inflation rate of:

$$(1 + \text{Real}) = 1.044 \div 1.0213 = 1.022, \text{ or } 2.28\%$$

This is almost identical to the ten-year rate found from the calculation made using index-linked gilts. In general, unless we expect major changes in the rate of inflation, a pragmatic approach would be to estimate specific rates for two to three years (perhaps cross-checking with those supplied by various forecasting agencies) and to use a long-run average rate for the remainder of the valuation period.

3.5 INTERNATIONAL INFLATION RATES

The above approach can be applied to any developed government bond market. However, an alternative approach is to rely on what is known as the *International Fisher Effect*, which hypothesises that in markets where there is free movement of capital, real risk-free rates of interest should be identical between countries. In December 1998, US ten-year treasury bond yields were 4.79%. The fact that these are higher than the UK yield of 4.46% implies, according to the International Fisher Effect, that expected US inflation is fractionally higher than UK inflation.[6]

3.6 DIVIDEND GROWTH AND FREE CASH FLOW MODELS

Taking a single-period perspective of valuation, it is possible to express the value of the company today (exdividend) as a function of next year's dividend (assumed to be payable at the end of the year), the year end value and the required rate of return, r:

$$\text{Value} = \frac{\text{Year end value} + \text{Year end dividend}}{(1 + r)}$$

In turn, the year end value will depend upon the year 2 dividend and year 2 estimated closing price, which is itself a function of year 3 dividend and closing value, and so on. Interpreting 'dividends' in the broadest sense as any flow of cash to the shareholders (thus, for example, including share repurchases), we have:

$$\text{Value}_0 = \sum_{t=1}^{t=n} \frac{\text{Dividend}_t}{(1 + r)^t} + \frac{\text{Value}_n}{(1 + r)^n}$$

In words, the formula states that value is the discounted sum of the future dividends plus the terminal value of the shares. (The Greek letter sigma (Σ) means the 'sum of' and the sub- and superscripts tell us to sum the discounted dividends from year 1 through to year n, the final year of dividend receipt.) Note that the model is based on dividends (again in the broadest sense) *not* earnings. If earnings were used, we would be double counting because the benefits of future investment would be included without taking into account the funds that need to be committed (reinvestment of retained earnings) to achieve those benefits.

So far, the above model assumes that the valuation is being done for a specific holding period. The question that always arises is how Value$_n$ is arrived at. The answer, of course, is by continuous iteration of the model. Now imagine that n becomes very large, say 100 years. What happens to the last term of our expression? Value in year n is likely to be a big number, but after discounting the last term becomes insignificant compared to the present value of the dividends. Thus the further we go into the future, the less important the terminal value of the firm becomes. The precise relationship is dependent upon the cost of capital and growth rates, but unless required returns are low and growth rates high, continuing value as a percentage of today's value is unlikely to be significant after such a time period, as illustrated in the following example:

EXAMPLE

Continuing value as a percentage of today's value with various different growth and required return (cost of capital) assumptions. The dividend for the current year is assumed to be 10p; it is also assumed that the share has just gone *ex dividend*.

Required return	Growth	Dividend year 0	Value year 0	Continuing value % of value in year 0 after:				
				5 years	10 years	25 years	50 years	100 years
10%	5%	0.10	2.10	79%	63%	31%	10%	1%
10%	2%	0.10	1.28	69%	47%	15%	2%	0%
5%	2%	0.10	3.40	87%	75%	48%	23%	6%
5%	4%	0.10	10.40	95%	91%	79%	62%	38%

To make this discounted dividend formula usable in practice requires some simplifying assumptions. The simplest solution is to assume that dividends grow at a constant rate. Such a model was described in section 3.2 above (for 'cash year 1' read dividend in year 1). This is a standard model for share valuation, sometimes known as *Gordon's Growth Model*. Its application is illustrated by the following example:

EXAMPLE

Suppose a company has 50 million shares in issue, and that dividends of 26.1 pence per share have just been paid in January 1999. Assume that the historical *real* growth rate of dividends is a good predictor of future growth, and that in January 1987 dividends were 13.4 pence per share. In January 1987 the RPI stood at 100; in January 1999 the RPI stands at 164.5.

The steps involved are as follows:

■ Calculate the real dividends by deflating figures using the RPI.

■ Calculate the average historical real growth.

■ Calculate the real cost of capital (for now assume this is 7%; *see* Chapter 4 for calculation of cost of capital).

■ Estimate future real dividend growth (here assumed to be the historical real growth).

■ Estimate value using the growth formula.

Real dividends:

Taking 1999 as the base year, the real dividend from 1987 in 1999 price levels is $13.4 \times (164.5/100) = 15.87$.

Continued overleaf

Historical growth rate:

There are 102 years of growth, so (1 + Growth) can be found by solving for the twelfth root of 15.87 pence divided by 13.4 pence:

$$(1 + \text{Growth}) = \sqrt[1/12]{\frac{26.1}{22.04}} = 1.0142$$

As 1.0142 = (1 + Growth), this gives us a real growth factor of 1.142%.

Estimate future value:

Remember that the relevant dividend figure is the year 1 real value, which by assumption here is 26.1 pence × 1.0142 or 26.47 pence per share. This gives price per share of:

$$\text{Price} = \frac{26.47}{(0.07 - 0.0142)} = 474.37\text{p}$$

Multiplying by the 50 million shares in issue gives:
50 m × £4.7437 = £237.2 million

Obviously, the assumption of constant growth will be unrealistic in the majority of cases, particularly where historical growth has been unusually high or low. Analysts who use this type of approach usually make specific dividend forecasts for a number of years and then resort to general growth patterns. An example of a US adaptation has the investment analyst making a specific forecast for years 1 to 5, an industry average forecast for years 6 to 10 and a general growth forecast for year 11 onwards. Some alternative models (*see* Chapter 6) also assume that abnormally high or low growth patterns or returns revert to a 'normal' level over time.

Several problems arise in applying the dividend discount model in reality:

- What happens to firms that do not pay dividends?
- What is the relationship between dividend retention and growth?
- What effect does the tax treatment of dividends have on the value of the firm?
- What is the effect of different mixes of equity and debt, or holding cash deposits from one year to the next?

Some firms take the view that there is little point in paying out dividends if the money can be invested internally in positive NPV projects. If they are correct in this view, the effect of increased retention should be to increase the future growth rate in dividends; at *some* point in the future higher dividends will be paid, presumably when the marginal return on new investment projects starts to decline. This must happen eventually, since no firm manages to keep a profitable market entirely to itself forever. The arguments concerning dividend policy are complex and beyond the scope of this briefing.[7] The issues involved include the theoretical argument of 'dividend irrelevance' which should apply in perfect capital markets, through to arguments based upon taxation treatments of dividends and capital gains, transactions costs arguments, agency theoretic arguments and 'signalling' effects.

One way of side-stepping some of these issues is to focus on the cash flows to the firm as a whole, rather than to the equity holders *per se*. In practice, this type of model is much more widely used and forms the basis of all the proprietary 'shareholder value' models available at present. This alternative to the dividend growth model is known as the 'free cash flow model' and is described below.

3.7 THE FREE CASH FLOW MODEL

Although similar to the dividend discount model, it can be intuitively more appealing in a variety of situations and can also help in situations where cash is being generated but not paid out as dividends. In order to develop the free cash flow model, which is the one that will be concentrated on for the remainder of the briefing, the company's profit and loss account and cash flow statements are broken down into their principal components:

Profit and cash flow components		
	Cash flow	*Profit & loss*
Sales turnover	TR	TR
Cash operating expenses		
– variable	VC	VC
– fixed	FC	FC
Operating cash flow	OCF	OCF
Depreciation	–	DEP
Operating cash flow/profit before tax	OCF	PBT
Cash taxes	CT	CT
Changes in deferred & other tax provisions	–	DT
Operating cash flow/profit after tax	CFAT	OPAT
Working capital investment	WCAP	–
Investment in fixed assets	INV	–
Free cash flow	**FCF**	
Interest income net of tax	INT	INT
Interest net of tax	NI	NI
Cash flow/profit attributable to shareholders	CFS	PATS

Note that cash flow attributable to shareholders is *net* of investment, and is therefore equal to dividends plus the change in cash deposits. It is also possible to look at the free cash flow (FCF) figure in terms of its financing (the above looks at its operational creation):

Financing flows and FCF		
Interest income net of tax	INT	(+ve)
Interest payments net of tax	NI	(−ve)
Dividends paid	DIV	(−ve)
Change in cash deposits and investments	DCDI	(+ve/−ve)
New borrowings	D+	(+ve)
Loan repayments	D−	(−ve)
New share issues	E	(+ve)
Free cash flow	**FCF**	

This illustrates the comparability of the FCF model with the dividend discount model; if there are no borrowings or cash deposits, DIV = FCF and the two models are equivalent. However, when cash deposits are involved (which in reality they will be, given the lumpy nature of investment), the two models can give different results.

It happens that the FCF model is simpler to use, as the following basic example illustrates:

EXAMPLE: FCF and dividend discount models compared

Suppose that Constant plc is financed entirely by equity and has a constant net cash flow of £100 p.a. with no growth opportunities; all this is paid out as dividends each year. Constant plc's cost of capital is 10% p.a.

Exceptionally, there is now available an investment opportunity which will require an investment of £315.25 at the end of year 3 and produce cash flows of £35 p.a. in perpetuity with effect from year 4.

This a positive NPV project (the NPV in year 3 is +£34.75). Constant's finance director intends to finance the investment by witholding the dividends for the next 3 years and placing the money in risk-free investments which earn the fair risk-free rate of 5% p.a.; this will yield a terminal value exactly equal to the necessary £315.25.

The aim is to compare the two models. Before doing so, it is helpful to think of the value of the business from the logical perspective of the value of the 'continuing' business, plus the value of the new investment opportunity:

- First, the value of the continuing business is not altered in any way, since initially we are using the cash and investing it in a zero NPV investment.

- It therefore follows that no change in shareholder wealth results from this so we have a present value of 100/0.1 = £1000.

- To this we add the NPV of the new investment, £34.75 in year 3, discounted back to present value terms which is £26.11.

- This gives a total value of the firm of £1000 + £26.11 = £1026.11.

Following the outline given above, this is exactly the result we get from the FCF model:

Item	Yr 1	Yr 2	Yr 3	Horizon value (Yr 3)
CFAT	100	100	100	135 ÷ 0.1 = 1350
INV	0	0	315.25	
FCF	100	100	−215.25	1350
Discounted Value @ 10%	90.91	82.64	−161.72	1014.28

Adding up the discounted cash flows yields £1026.11 which agrees with the 'logical' answer.

Unfortunately, the dividend discount model does not. As no dividends are payable until year 3, the discounted value of the future dividends is simply £1350 in year 3, discounted back to year 0 (today) which gives us the £1014.28 shown as the PV of the horizon value above. However, the dividend model takes no account of the cash flow movements in years 1–3 because they do not represent dividend payments. This is why the value differs from that found from the FCF model. Essentially, the dividend discount model has taken the view that the cash deposits were invested in a negative NPV project as they were earning 5% and not 10%. This is not the case, since the company *could* have paid out those dividends and gone for a rights issue in year 3;[8] clearly, if the shareholders had put that money into risk-free investments themselves, they would be in the position suggested by our 'logical' calculation and FCF formula.

The only way of rescuing the dividend model is to recognise that the risk of the business is changing constantly between year 1 and year 3, and the appropriate discount rate therefore changes (essentially, in year 1 it is 1/11 risk-free and 10/11 'risky', in year 2 it is 2.05/12.05 risk-free, and so on). Clearly, this is a rather unsatisfactory approach, and hence the FCF valuation is preferred.

There are also other reasons why in practical terms using the free cash flow formula is simpler:

- the exact sources of cash flow creation/consumption are broken down in a form comparable with the familiar profit and loss account;

- once debt financing is allowed for, problems can arise with using the dividend discount model if we do not allow for the impact of changing payout ratios on the gearing levels of the firm.[9]

In general, the FCF model uses the following steps to value the firm:

- Discount the FCF at the weighted average cost of capital (WACC), which gives the value of the entire firm.
- Then:
  - deduct the value of the debt claims;
  - add the value of any financial assets.
- This yields the value of the equity.

3.8 PRICE-EARNINGS MODELS AND THEIR RELATIONSHIP WITH FCF AND DIVIDEND DISCOUNT MODELS

It might seem that FCF valuation is a reasonably complex methodology. As such, it is important to consider when such an approach is necessary, and when the 'traditional' approach of a PE valuation based upon next year's earnings might perform well. Knowing when the PE method is likely to work and why is useful since it is avoids some computational complexity and is clearly used extensively in practice. The PE multiple, which was discussed in Chapter 2, is a complex function of future growth rates, risk, payout ratios, inflation rates and opportunity cost of capital. In the FCF method, risk and cost of capital are reflected in the discount rate, with growth rates and payout ratios appearing in the cash flow forecasts. The FCF method explicitly models the complex relationships involved between these variables. When these relationships can be simplified, as in the case of constant growth models, the PE approach may be appropriate; however, when this is not the case, calculating a reasonable PE is not likely to be possible.

The example below explains the relationship which exists between the PE ratio and FCF methods.

EXAMPLE

Dart plc, has a policy of steady expansion and has predictable and constant growth rates. Dart is all equity financed and has a cost of capital of 15% p.a.; the year 0 asset base consists of £4000 fixed assets and £1000 working capital. Forecast cash flows and profits are as follows:

		Year 1	Year 2	Year 3	Relationship
Operating cash flow	OCF	1900	2090	2299	38% opening total assets
Depreciation	DEP	400	440	484	10% fixed assets
Taxes (paid as cash)	CT	600	660	726	*
Investment in:					
Working capital	WCAP	100	110	121	Increases in line with expansion
Fixed assets	INV	800	880	968	**
Cash flow (= OCF − CT − WCAP − INV)	FCF***	400	440	484	
Profit	PATS	900	990	1089	

*   For simplicity, depreciation is assumed to be tax allowable and a 40% tax rate is assumed.

**   Investment is a replacement of existing assets (note implicit assumption of no inflation) and expansion of existing base by 10%.

***   All FCF is paid out as dividends.

It can be shown that, with the assumption of constant relationships made above, the two valuation approaches are equivalent. This is because the PE ratio is related to the required rate of return and the future growth. First, notice that the growth rate in both FCF and profit is 10% p.a. As these cash flows are increasing at a constant rate, the constant growth formula from section 3.2 above can be applied. In this case, 'year 1 cash' is the FCF and r is the required return of 15% p.a., so we have a value of:

$$V = \frac{400}{(0.15 - 0.10)} = £8000$$

If the PE approach is to give the same result, the prospective PE ratio must be £8000 ÷ 900 = 8.89. This prospective PE ratio remains constant each year. In year 2, with a PE of 8.89 the firm is worth 990 × 8.89 = £8800. If this is the case, shareholders would have just received a dividend of £400 and a capital gain of £800 since year 1, which gives the required return of 15%. Thus in principle, given constant growth, payout ratios and return on new investment (RONI), the PE ratio and FCF models can be compatible. The general relationship is given by:

$$PE = \frac{1 - (\text{Growth}/\text{RONI})}{(r - \text{Growth})}$$

The derivation is given in the notes to this chapter. To apply this to the above example:

- The return on new investment is £900/5000 = 0.18 or 18.

- Using the formula for the PE ratio gives:

$$PE = \frac{1 - 0.10/0.18}{(0.15 - 0.10)} = 8.89$$

- Checking the valuation on a PE basis yields 8.89 × £900 = £8000.

While this works with constant rates of investment and growth, it does not work with lumpy investment patterns. Look back at the example of Constant plc above. The initial prospective PE ratio is 10.92; this begins to rise in years 1 and 2 in anticipation of increased profitability, but by year 3 the *prospective* PE has fallen back to 10 as there are no further growth prospects in the offing. In theory, it is possible to derive a formula for the PE under all types of scenario, but in practice it is easier to use the FCF formula whenever investment patterns are lumpier and growth is eratic.

However, the above shows that the two approaches are equivalent in the type of situation frequently assumed when calculating the continuing or horizon value of a company. It can be valid to use PE ratios to calculate these horizon values, provided the PE is calculated using assumptions about cost of capital, growth and returns on new investment which are compatible with those used in the rest of the forecast.

3.9 THE FCF MODEL AND 'LUMPY' INVESTMENT FLOWS

So far, we have analysed situations where future investment takes place on a continuous basis. However, in reality investment in fixed assets tends to follow a 'lumpy' or discontinuous pattern. The FCF model is capable of dealing with this by simply taking the free cash flows described as before and discounting these at an appropriate rate. One problem is that a consequence of this type of cash flow pattern is that we cannot use the growth based models we described above since they assume a constant rate of cash flow growth.

Fortunately, there is a way around this problem by using a method based on the concept of 'annual equivalent cash flows'. In principle, any net present value can be turned into an annual equivalent cash flow; the cash flow is found by dividing the NPV by an annuity factor for the required life of the cash flow.

Take the simple example of a single project company below:

Example

Newco plc has just been established: £1 million has been invested in the company, which has been used to purchase the necessary capital equipment with a life of ten years.

Assume:

- there is no inflation;
- the equipment will have a scrap value of zero at the end of its life;
- the annual net cash inflows (after tax) will be £0.17 million for the next ten years;
- the required rate of return on this type of investment is 10% p.a.

Calculating the NPV gives a positive value of £44 576.

In terms of annual equivalence, having this much positive NPV today (year 0) in exchange for a £1 million outlay is the same as receiving, for the next ten years, an amount of £44 576 ÷ (a ten-year annuity factor @ 10% p.a. [6.145]) or £7254.5 per annum with no investment in year 0. This is because the NPV of these two cash flow streams (the outlay of £1 million and ten years inflow of £0.17 million, compared with £7254.5 p.a. for ten years) are identical. This turns out to be a very useful concept in valuing companies where projects are repeated on a cyclical basis.

In the case of Newco plc, in year 10 it will reinvest in the necessary equipment and repeat the whole cycle all over again. This gives the following FCF pattern:

Newco plc – free cash flow cycle:

				£000					
	yr 1	yr 2	....	yr 10	yr 11	....	yr 20	yr 21	......
Cash inflows	170	170		170	170		170	170	
Investment				1000			1000		
Free cash flow	170	170		−830	170		−830	170	

One valuation approach is to continue estimating these cash flows over a very long period and discounting them. A faster method is to recognise that the annual equivalent cash flow can be viewed as occuring every year of the ten-year cycle; since this cycle is continuously repeated, we have the equivalent of a perpetual cash flow of £7254.5 p.a. At a discount rate of 10%, this gives an NPV of £72545 (£7254.5 ÷ 0.1). In rational markets, the value of Newco would therefore be £1.0725 million (NPV plus the initial capital investment).

This approach is also very useful when it comes to calculating the value of a company part way through the life of one of its investments. Suppose we wish to value Newco plc at the end of year 6. Before we can do this, we need to make an assumption about the dividend payout policy followed by the company; broadly, we can either assume that this is to pay out all surplus cash flows as dividends, and then make a rights issue for the necessary proceeds, or we can assume that the company has retained enough cash (and invested it at a fair rate of return) to finance the equipment replacement when it falls due. We shall assume the latter, and further assume that the cash retained has been invested in financial assets yielding a return of 10% p.a. The necessary retention must be sufficient to produce £1 million at the end of ten years; in other words, £1 million is the *future* value of an annuity of an unknown amount at 10% p.a. Using tables for the future value of such an annuity indicates an annual retention of £62 745; the balance of each year's cash flow is assumed to be distributed by way of dividends.

This offers a useful insight into the valuation of steady-state companies with lumpy investment patterns, but in order to make it practically applicable the basic analysis needs to be adapted to cope with inflation. This is not difficult because the annual equivalent cash flow can be expressed in real terms and indexed up each year as appropriate.

APPENDIX 3.1 DERIVATION OF THE CONSTANT GROWTH FORMULA

The generalised form of the present value calculation used above can be written as:

$$\text{Present value} = \frac{\text{Cash yr 1}}{(1 + r)^1} + \frac{\text{Cash yr 2}}{(1 + r)^2} + \frac{\text{Cash yr 3}}{(1 + r)^3} + \dots \frac{\text{Cash yr } n}{(1 + r)^n}$$

When cash flow simply increases at some constant rate (expressed as a decimal) over a base year cash flow (Cash_0), the above can be rewritten as:

$$\text{Present value} = \frac{\text{Cash}_0(1 + \text{Growth})}{(1 + r)^1} + \frac{\text{Cash}_0(1 + \text{Growth})^2}{(1 + r)^2} + \dots \frac{\text{Cash}_0(1 + \text{Growth})^n}{(1 + r)^n}$$

This carries on into perpetuity and so n becomes very large. Note that the terms on the right-hand side are growing at a constant rate: $(1 + \text{Growth})/(1 + r)$. This is is a geometric progression to infinity. There exists a formula for the sum of such a progression, which is:

$$\text{Sum} = \text{First term} \div (1 - \text{Common ratio})$$

The common ratio is $(1 + \text{Growth})/(1 + r)$, and the first term refers to the right-hand side of the present value equation, which gives $\text{Cash}_0(1 + \text{growth})/(1 + r)$. Substituting this into the expression and rearranging gives:

$$\text{Present value} = \frac{\text{Cash}_0(1 + \text{Growth})}{(r - \text{Growth})}$$

APPENDIX 3.2 PROOF OF THE EQUIVALENCE OF DIVIDEND DISCOUNT, FCF AND PE MODELS UNDER CONSTANT GROWTH ASSUMPTIONS

Given a simplifying assumption of constant growth and payout ratios, and all-equity financing, dividends are simply FCF. Taking the dividend model as the case example:

From the dividend discount model we have:

$$\text{Value}_0 = \frac{\text{Dividend}_1}{(r - \text{Growth})}$$

Dividends are simply earnings (Engs) multiplied by one minus the proportion retained (RE), i.e.:

$$\text{Dividends} = \text{Engs}(1 - \text{RE})$$

Given the assumptions about constant returns, growth comes from reinvesting future earnings, so that growth is a function of the proportion of earnings reinvested multiplied by the return on new investment (RONI), or growth = RONI $\times$ RE, and therefore by rearranging that:

$$\text{RE} = \text{Growth} / \text{RONI}$$

It therefore follows that:

$$\text{Value}_0 = \frac{\text{Engs}_1(1 - [\text{Growth} / \text{RONI}])}{r - \text{Growth}}$$

Dividing both sides by Engs gives:

$$\frac{\text{Value}_0}{\text{Engs}_1} = \frac{(1 - [\text{Growth} / \text{RONI}])}{r - \text{Growth}}$$

$\text{Value}_0/\text{Engs}_1$ is the *prospective* PE ratio.

The cost of capital in DCF models

4.1 INTRODUCTION

The DCF models discussed in this briefing all require as an input some cost of capital. Depending on whether the model focuses on valuing the equity directly (as in the case of the dividend discount model) or indirectly (as in the case of the FCF model), we need either an equity cost of capital or a weighted average cost of capital (WACC) to form the discount rate. The equity cost of capital is, of course, a component of the WACC.

The last thirty years or so have seen a great deal of innovation in capital markets. Complex financing arrangements are now common and include convertible loan stocks, swaps, caps and collars. The problem is how to:

- value such financing packages (necessary to discover the value of the equity[1]);
- work out the cost of capital of such forms of financing.

Two general observations are in order. First, unless there are some external value adding factors associated with financing (generally these will be debt tax shields, liquidation costs and any government subsidised loan arrangements – *see* below), the *total* value of the business is unaffected by how it is financed. In effect, with the exception of these external factors, financing arrangements affect how the cash flows of the business are divided but not how such cash flows are created. Second, with more complex forms of financing we need to understand the principles of discounted cash flow analysis *and* the basic principles of option pricing. With these, it is possible to value any type of financing package on offer. Options are an important part of contemporary financing. Any form of finance which gives one or other party the right to do something (but not an obligation) involves an option. Examples include convertible loan stocks (a simple convertible allows the holder to exchange debt for equity) and caps (which allows the holder to have the interest rate set at a maximum level).

Options are explained later in the chapter. The following topics are covered:

- estimating the cost of equity;
- estimating the cost of debt and preference share capital;
- estimating the cost of complex financial instruments;
- estimating WACC;
- using WACC.

Broadly, the approaches to estimating the equity cost of capital are as follows:

- use of long-run historical averages for the company;
- use of long-run historical averages for the market;
- forward projection for the company;

- forward projection for the market;

- a single-factor risk pricing model – the Capital Asset Pricing Model (CAPM);

- a multi-factor risk pricing model.

The last two require as inputs a 'risk premium' or 'price' for each risk factor; as in the case of the first four approaches, the premia can be estimated from historical premia or by forward projection. The use of historical averages is self-explanatory. Forward projection is normally undertaken by using the dividend discount, or Gordon's Growth Model, described in Chapter 3.

Essentially, the second and fourth models assume that the cost of capital for all large firms is similar (this is found in the Boston Consulting Group's model of shareholder value, for example). Some consultancy practices (e.g. Holt Value Associates) use this assumption but allow the cost of capital to vary with firm size.

4.1.1 An introduction to risk, required returns and portfolios of investments

Current approaches to risk pricing have their foundation in the analysis of portfolio risk undertaken by Harry Markowitz in the 1950s. This work leads to several important implications:

- Rational investors will hold well diversified portfolios.

- Given that this is so, on individual investments they will be concerned not with the *total* risk of such investments, but with the *additional* risk which they impose upon the portfolio.

- Increasing the number of investments in a portfolio decreases the risk to a point, but it is impossible to diversify away all risk.

- Certain types of risk are easily disposed of simply by holding large numbers of different investments. These can be viewed as company-specific risks, and examples include the technical failure of a newly developed product, legal actions, etc.

- By contrast, the sorts of risk which cannot be diversified away are mainly those of an economic nature.

To a greater or lesser extent all firms are affected by bad economic news but some are affected more than others. The central message of portfolio theory is that it is the additional contribution to portfolio risk which matters; company-specific risks tend to cancel each other out in a large portfolio, but *all* the investments in the portfolio will be moved in the same direction to some extent by these common economic factors. In a well diversified portfolio it is this exposure which is the important component of additional risk.

In principle, the approaches to cost of capital outlined above approach the problem of associating this risk with required return in a different way.

The single- and multi-factor risk pricing models take the view that some companies suffer from this type of economic exposure more than others; for example, those firms where product demand is discretionary, such as tour operators, hi-fi manufacturers and fashion retailers, are much more vulnerable to economic downturns than those where product demand tends to be non-discretionary, such as food manufacturers, food retailers and utility companies. These models share the view that when describing a firm as 'risky' there is a need to distinguish between *diversifiable risk* (sometimes called *specific* or *non-systematic risk*) and *non-diversifiable risk* (also called *systematic* or *non-specific risk*). Since investors can diversify away the former type of risk for the expense of some transaction costs but cannot get rid of the latter type of risk, it is *only* this latter, non-diversifiable, risk which they should expect to be compensated for. However, the models differ in their approach to pricing this risk. The single-factor CAPM model assumes that one index (*beta*) can be applied to one catch-all risk factor known as *market* risk. The multi-factor (arbitrage pricing theory or APT) model assumes a number of different risk factors (for example, interest rate and inflation rate risks) will be priced.

The company-specific approach simply assumes investors' required returns are implicit either in the historical returns achieved or in the future required returns derived from a dividend discount model. Those who advocate the use of a market-wide figure simply assume that risks are broadly similar across all large firms. Some (such as Holt) assume that smaller firms and more highly geared firms are riskier and need to earn larger returns (that is, they have a higher opportunity cost of capital).

4.2 THE HISTORICAL PERSPECTIVE

A long run of historical data is available for both the US and UK markets. For the US, Ibbotson Associates has published data going back to 1922, while for the UK, Barclays Capital publish the *Equity-Gilt Study* each year at the end of January. Barclays Capital give the estimates of the total real returns on UK equities as shown in Table 4.1.

Table 4.1 Historical total real returns (i.e. capital gains plus dividends) for the UK, 1918–97

Period	Real geometric mean return %	Real arithmetic mean return %
1918–97	8.01	10.53
1945–97	7.00	9.69
1977–97	11.21	11.84

Source: Barclays Capital, Equity-Gilt Study (1998).

The first issue to be addressed is whether, when using historical data, cost of capital figures should be based upon geometric or arithmetic averages. This turns out to depend upon two major issues:

- whether successive years' stock market returns can be viewed as independent drawings from a stationary independent probability distribution;
- the investment holding period assumed.

These are critical issues because there is a difference of more than 2.5% p.a. between the estimates based upon the 1918–97 experience. Those who argue for the use of arithmetic premia assume that annual returns can be viewed as the independent drawings described above, and implicitly assume that investors' holding periods are one year. In the first place, there is evidence of negative autocorrelation in long-term returns, which calls into question the first assumption. Second, whereas geometric averages are not dependent upon the holding period assumed (the geometric average would be identical whether one-month, one-year or ten-year return intervals were used), the arithmetic average obtained increases as the holding period assumed is reduced.

As an illustration, if the figures for ten-year annualised holding period returns given in the Barclays Capital study (1998) are used, for successive ten-year non-overlapping periods ending in December 1997 (with the exception that the first period is the nine years to December 1927), the arithmetic average return obtained is 8.28%, much closer to the 8.01% obtained from the geometric average. Given that the choice of holding period interval can have a marked effect on the arithmetic average, and further given that in valuation the emphasis is upon long-term returns, on balance the arguments would seem to favour the use of a geometric return. Similar arguments arise in the calculation of the equity risk premium required for the CAPM (*see* below).

4.3 FORWARD PROJECTION OR EXPECTED RETURNS

The calculation of implied future returns is fairly straightforward, although inevitably requires assumptions to be made concerning future growth. The basic approach, whether being carried out at market or individual firm level, involves using the dividend growth model described in Chapter 3 to estimate the required rate of return implied by the current share price. Thus the steps involved are:

■ take the current gross dividend (or dividend yield);

■ estimate the future growth in dividends;

■ using today's share price (or 100 if using the dividend yield), solve the dividend growth model for r, the required return on the share or market.

The following example calculates the required return on the UK market in December 1998 in real terms, under the assumption that real dividends will grow at 2% p.a.

EXAMPLE: UK market data as of December 1998

Dividend yield on FTSE 100 index (gross): 2.75%[2]

Applying the dividend growth model;

$$100 = \frac{2.75(1 + 0.02)}{r - 0.02}$$

Multiplying and rearranging gives:

$r = (2.81 + 2) / 100$, so $r = 0.0481$ or 4.81%

Finally, note that if growth is assumed to be 2.25%, r becomes 5.06%.

The above example assumes that average dividends will grow in line with GDP. Historically, this has been the case. Barclays Capital shows that between 1919 and 1997, real dividends grew by 2.19% while GDP grew by 2.16%. However, Barclays Capital (1998) point out that dividend payout ratios can change, as can profitability rates (compared to GDP) and the ratio of foreign to domestic profits. While it is true that these can cause dividend growth to differ from GDP growth, it must be borne in mind that recent larger increases in dividends may not be sustainable in the face of global competitive pressures, labour market pressures and the need for reinvestment.

4.4 A SINGLE-INDEX RISK PRICING MODEL: THE CAPM

The Capital Asset Pricing Model (CAPM) is derived by finding the equilibrium rate investors would require as compensation for a given quantity of risk. The model is derived by making some critical assumptions after which it is possible to derive a risk pricing model which prices the required return by using a single index of risk called *beta*. The CAPM has three components:

- the general market-wide price of risk, known as the *market risk premium* (MRP);

- an investment-specific index of risk exposure, *beta* (β);

- a risk-free rate of return (r_f).

The CAPM states that the required return (r) on any risky investment, *i*, is given by:

$$r_i = r_f + (\beta_i \times MRP)$$

In the above expression, r_f is the expected 'risk-free' rate of return, which in a single-period context can be approximated by the return on treasury bills but from a long-term valuation perspective is better approximated by the yield to maturity on government bonds. The market risk premium (MRP) is the return expected from holding a portfolio which represents the entire market of risky investments (the *market portfolio*), less the expected risk-free rate of return (put more formally, MRP = $r_{\text{Market portfolio}} - r_f$). Strictly, the CAPM requires that *all* assets are marketable and divisible, but in practical terms 'the market portfolio' is normally taken to be the stock market, and the return on this portfolio is approximated by the return on an arithmetic value weighted price index with dividends reinvested. In the UK, the index which is normally used is the FT All Share Index (FTASI) and in the USA, the Standard & Poor 500 Share Index.

While the assumptions underlying the CAPM may be regarded as anywhere between simplifying and preposterous, the critical factors are whether the assumptions lead to a model which is a good predictor of share returns and whether we have a model which is practically useful. The assumptions are:

- no transactions costs;

- all assets are infinitely divisible and marketable;

- short sales are allowed;

- no personal taxes;

- all individual investors are price takers and cannot influence the price of any risky asset by their actions;

- investors are concerned only with risk and expected returns;

- unlimited borrowing and lending can take place at the risk-free rate;
- all investors have homogeneous expectations concerning risk and return;
- investors have the same single-period investment horizon.

It should be noted that many of these assumptions can be independently relaxed without violating the basic conclusions of the model. For example, it is possible to develop a version of the model which takes account of personal taxation; under certain circumstances the model remains unchanged (Litzenberger and Ramaswamy, 1979). Given certain further assumptions, it is possible to extend the model to a multi-period setting.

The potential appeal of the CAPM is its simplicity. If it works, we have the prospect of being able to calculate the required rate of return on any risky investment by reference to just three factors. All that is required are estimates of the risk-free rate, the market risk premium and the beta of the individual investment. Risk-free rates of return are readily observable, the market risk premium can be estimated either historically or by reference to expected returns (*see* below) and it is also possible to obtain betas from published sources for any company quoted on most of the world's larger stock markets.

However, the evidence on the CAPM and whether it adequately describes returns is ambiguous at present.

4.4.1 Tests of the CAPM

Unfortunately, the strict answer to the question of whether or not the CAPM is 'true' is that it is doubtful that we can ever know. The problem is that we simply do not know the composition of the *true* market portfolio – all we have are proxies for this. The issues here are complex and beyond the cope of this briefing but the well-known Roll (1977) critique argues that the CAPM is untestable. Potentially, therefore, all the tests which follow can be described as flawed in some respect. However, there are a large number of tests which can be viewed as investigating whether the CAPM gives us a useful estimator of equity returns. Most of the available evidence relates to the New York Stock Exchange.

The early evidence seemed to show that there was no reward for bearing non-diversifiable risk (as predicted by the CAPM), and that return is a linear function of systematic risk (again as predicted by the CAPM), although it was the case that the return line was flatter and had a higher intercept than the basic form of CAPM predicted.[3]

More recently, the empirical investigations of the CAPM have been the subject of some controversy. Fama and French (1992) concluded that once 'size effects'[4] are allowed for, beta has little role in explaining the cross-section of share returns. Fama and French also show that the 'book-to-market value' (BMV) ratio is important in explaining returns. This led to the *Wall Street Journal* running an article which proclaimed that beta was 'dead'. In the UK, Strong and Xu (1997) have demonstrated that this 'book-to-market' effect is also significant in explaining the cross-section of UK returns. One theory[5] is that this effect is due to high BMV firms being financially distressed, and that high ratios are observed essentially because the share price is depressed.

However, there is considerable dispute about whether the Fama and French conclusion on the CAPM is valid. Recent research calls into question their findings, at least to some degree:

- Kothari, Shanken and Sloan (1995) show that the Fama and French result is critically dependent upon the return interval used to measure beta. Using annual returns shows that beta risk is priced, although firm size also has a role in explaining returns.

- Kim (1995) shows that a critical problem is caused because firm betas are statistically estimated (and hence invariably subject to measurement error), while firm size is known precisely. If allowance is not made for this the importance of beta in explaining returns will be underestimated in statistical tests. Correcting for this, Kim shows that beta is important in explaining the cross-section of US stock returns. Firm size has an important, though diminished, role once this correction is made.

- Jaganathan and Wang (1996) show that if beta is allowed to be conditional on an economic risk factor, and the 'market' portfolio includes the value of human capital, the 'conditional' CAPM holds.

- Roll and Ross (1994) and Ashton and Tippett (1998) show that estimates of beta are extremely sensitive to mis-specification of the market portfolio. In particular, the latter show that such mis-specification can result in researchers reaching the incorrect conclusion that factors such as book-to-market ratios are significant in explaining returns.

The above studies might seem to argue the case for rescuing beta, but there remain problems for the CAPM:

- None of the studies show that the *simple* version of the CAPM holds – either 'size effects' are important or we need to estimate a conditional CAPM using a complex market portfolio. Alternatively, the problem of beta being highly sensitive to mis-specification of the true market portfolio may be impossible to address.

- The CAPM should predict all returns – it seems clear that at the very least firm size is an additional important factor in practice

4.5 APPLYING THE CAPM

Assuming the CAPM is viewed as being a useful practical tool for estimating the cost of equity (at least for larger firms), estimates are needed for the risk-free rate, the market risk premium and the beta for the investment being considered. Note this is not generally the same as the beta of the company making the investment or purchase. The reason for this is that investors expect compensation for the degree of investment risk being taken on in any new investment.

This can be illustrated by a simple example. Suppose a brewing company decides to take over a hotel chain. Brewing companies generally have low betas (less than 1.0) while hotel companies tend to have higher betas. If purchasing brewers used their own betas in calculating return, they would underestimate the rate of return required by investors for taking this degree of risk. The correct approach is for the brewing firm to use a beta representative of the hotel industry, adjusting if necessary for differences in financing structure (*see* below). Assuming the purchase goes ahead, investors will regard the combined firm as a portfolio of hotel and brewing operations, and adjust their required returns accordingly.

4.5.1 The risk-free rate

There are several alternative candidates for the estimate of the risk-free rate of return. The UK has a wider range of alternatives than many countries because of the availablity of index-linked gilts:

- treasury bill rate
- short-dated gilts (less than five years)
- medium-dated gilts (5–15 years)
- long-dated gilts (more than 15 years)
- undated gilts
- index-linked gilts.

Ideally, the risk-free instrument chosen should have a similar *duration* to the firm being valued. Duration is the weighted average time it takes to receive a bond's cash flows, and is useful as a measure of a bond's price volatility for any given change in yield.[6] The duration of a bond can be estimated easily, as the future cash flows (coupon plus redemption) are known with certainty. The *FT* now publishes gilt durations for each of its price indices. For example, the durations listed in Table 4.2 applied in December 1998.

Table 4.2 Gilt durations, December 1998

UK gilts	Duration (years)
Up to 5 years	2.43
5–10 years	5.96
10–15 years	8.73
Over 15 years	11.88
Irredeemables	23.24
Index-linked, 5–15 years*	9.88
Index-linked, over 15 years*	16.74

* Assuming inflation of 0% (assuming inflation of 5% makes little difference to the duration).
Source: Financial Times.

The real problem is how to calculate the duration of an equity or a company. The first difficulty is that cash flows are perpetual. However, this is not insurmountable and is a problem for calculating the duration of an irredeemable in any event. The solution is simply to project far enough into the future for the present value of any payment to become insignificant. More pressing is the problem of estimating future dividend patterns. As with any duration calculation, low initial cash flows and long maturities lead to increasing duration. With current dividend yields of 2.75% (December 1998), and the low implied required returns of investors, equity 'durations' will inevitably be long. Taking the average long-run dividend yields, equity returns and dividend growth patterns found historically (1919–97) from the Barclays Capital *Equity-Gilt Study* (1998) yields an estimated duration of about 18 years for the UK.

Given that, more generally, the coupon payment pattern on index-linked gilts is similar to that on equities (i.e. rising through time), and the duration on long-dated gilts is broadly similar, the recommendation is that the *real* risk-free rate is estimated using the index-linked 5–15 years figure for the UK. For other countries, the choice of rate will depend on matching duration but in general it is likely to be the case that longer-dated gilts are the best measure of the risk-free rate of interest provided market prices reflect a thickly traded bond market.

4.5.2 The market risk premium

The estimation of this parameter is contentious, and as the impact of the estimate on any valuation is large, it is important to understand the arguments. The methods which can be used to estimate this premium are:

- estimating the long-run risk premium as the mean historical difference between the return on the stock market and the treasury bill rate;

- estimating the long-run risk premium as the mean historical difference between the return on the stock market and the gilt rate;

- estimating the long-run mean return on equities and comparing this to the long-run real return on gilts;

- estimating the long-run return on equities and comparing this to the current risk-free rate;

- estimating the implied forward return on the market and comparing this to the current risk-free rate.

To further complicate the issue, the first four methods can use either the arithmetic or geometric means. For the reasons given in section 4.2 above, in general the use of the geometric mean is preferred in this briefing. However, taking a geometric mean *premium* is a flawed approach.

To illustrate the differences between these approaches, the data in Table 4.3 are taken from the Barclays Capital *Equity-Gilt Study*.

The estimates of the risk premium based upon 1918–97 data can therefore range between a minimum of 8.01% − 2.13%, or 5.88% and a maximum of 8.76% if the geometric mean premium is utilised. Even more extreme is the premium obtained if the aritmetic risk premium over treasury bills of 9.16% is used.

Table 4.3 Geometric mean returns and premia for the UK

Period	Total real return on equities	Total real return on gilts	Mean risk premium over gilts	Mean risk premium over treasury bills
1918–97	8.01	2.13	7.37	8.76
1945–97	7.00	0.26	n.a.	n.a.
1977–97	11.21	5.69	n.a.	n.a.
Comparable yield periods*	6.1	2.3	n.a.	n.a.

* Intervals of at least 25 years where the opening and closing dividend (equities) and redemption (gilts) yields were the same (Barclays Capital, *Equity-Gilt Study*, 1998, p. 19).
Source: Barclays Capital *Equity-Gilt Study*.

These figures are problematic from several points of view:

- At the time of writing they imply either a large degree of overvaluation in the stock market or a dividend growth rate in real terms much higher than that seen historically.

- They ignore the fact that *today's* market prices are the best estimate of the *current* opportunity cost of capital – these are the prices that today's investors are prepared to invest at.

■ In the context of the CAPM, it is conceptually incorrect to estimate the risk premium using historical risk-free rates and add this to a *current* risk-free rate – to do so uses two different measures of the risk-free rate in the CAPM formula.

The first of these points has become much more of a problem with the valuations seen in recent years. One way of explaining these valuations is that investors are prepared to live with a lower risk premium in the future than they were in the past. Related to this, Barclays Capital argue that using long-run historical periods with similar opening and closing dividend yields (and gilt yields) might capture any valuation changes. This gives the lower risk premium of 6.1% – 2.3%, or 3.8%.

Taking account of the third point would mean taking the historical estimate of 8.01% as the long-run expectation of future real equity returns. Comparing this to the current rate on index-linked gilts of around 2% still results in a risk premium of around 6% and hence still leaves the problem of implied overvaluation in the market. In section 4.3 above we argued that current market levels implied a future real return on equity of around 5%. If 8.01% were to be the correct estimate of investors' future returns the implications for the FTSE 100 with a current yield of 2.75% are either:

■ that the market is overvalued by close to 100% (assuming real dividend growth of 2.25%); or

■ that future real dividend growth will need to be 5.1% – more than twice the best forecast of GDP growth, and around 2.3 times greater than historical growth.

The latter seems completely implausible. One way that it is possible to justify the current level of the stock market is to assume that investors' risk preferences have caused valuation patterns to change. If this is the case, then a better estimate of the true risk premium on equities is found by comparing the projected future return on equities with the current long-run real gilt rate. It is also worth noting that there is theoretical support for believing in a lower estimate of the market risk premium. A puzzle for academics has been precisely why the equity risk premium has been so high historically.[7] Taking the 5% projected return from section 4.3 above and comparing this to the current long index-linked gilt return of around 2% (*see* section 3.4) suggests a risk premium of 3% for the future. Furthermore, an advantage of the projected premium approach is that it allows premia to be estimated for markets without long historical series of returns.

4.5.3 Estimating beta

Although betas can be estimated from fundamental data, the most common approach is to estimate them by statistical analysis of share returns. The method involves running a regression of the 'excess' returns on the share (the return on the share over and above the risk-free rate) on the 'excess' returns on the market portfolio.[8] Adjustments can be made for both 'thin trading' problems in individual shares and for the tendency of betas to revert to the mean value of 1.0 over time. Few analysts bother with such an approach as there are readily available sources of individual equity betas for most major markets. For example, Standard & Poor is a source of US betas, the London Business School is a source of UK betas and BARRA International publish betas for a number of major markets. Bloomberg's also provide estimates of beta. Thus betas can be readily obtained, but note that what these services provide is an estimate of *equity* betas. As discussed below, on occasions (such as in the example given above of a brewing company acquiring a hotel company), what is required is an estimate of an *asset* beta. The most practically applicable approach to finding this is to:

- find analogue or proxy companies for the target company (or division) being valued;[9]

- adjust for the effect of differing financial structures.

The latter raises some complex issues which are explained below.

As an example of the published information available for UK companies, the following is an extract from the London Business School Risk Measurement Service, which is published quarterly:[10]

	Market cap. (£m)	Beta	Variability	Specific risk	Std error	R-squared
British Vita	474	1.13	30	26	0.20	23

First, we can work out the cost of British Vita's equity provided we know the return required on long-dated gilts (this is obtainable on a daily basis from the *Financial Times*; issues relating to the choice of an appropriate gilt rate are discussed above) and the market risk premium. Assume that the current real risk-free rate is 2% and that the market risk premium is 3%. Given these data inputs, we can calculate the real cost of British Vita's equity as:

$$R_{British\ Vita}(\%) = 2 + (1.13 \times 3) = 5.4\%$$

This cost of equity could be used directly in a weighted average cost of capital calculation if British Vita's project cash flows were being appraised in real terms.

If they were being appraised in nominal terms, we would need to uplift the cost of capital to allow for forecast inflation.

The other data given by the service are *variability*, which is the standard deviation of the returns on British Vita shares, *specific risk* which is the standard deviation of returns attributable to the diversifiable part of the risk, and R-squared, which is a statistical term that describes what percentage of the variability is explained by market risk factors. In this case, 23% of British Vita's total risk is explained by general market risk factors.[11] The 'standard error' referred to is that of the beta. Applying the normal rules of statistical inference allows us to conclude with 95% confidence that the true beta of British Vita lies between the mean and plus or minus two standard errors. While this may make the observed beta appear unreliable, it should be noted that we are more normally interested in the betas of portfolios of companies. A statistical property of these betas is that portfolio betas are far more accurate than the betas of individual companies.

4.6 ALTERNATIVES TO THE CAPM

There is a general class of these alternatives called *multi-index models*, which contrast with the single-index CAPM. The theoretical basis of these models is the *arbitrage pricing theory* (APT), which is derived in a perfect markets framework where the arbitrage transactions of informed investors result in the fair pricing of fundamental risk factors. By a risk factor being 'priced' we mean that investors require some return for taking on that type of risk. Unfortunately, APT does not give us a theoretical framework for the determination of these factors, although it does exclude some factors by definition (for example, returns in previous periods cannot be 'factors', since if they were, this would imply market inefficiency – something incompatible with the theory itself). We are therefore forced to try and find these factors by trial and error. As an example, Chen, Roll and Ross (1986) examined the relationship between macroeconomic variables and returns and suggested that industrial production, unanticipated inflation, the term structure of interest rates and bond default risk premia were important factors.

More recently, Burmeister and McElroy (1987, 1988) have conducted further tests of the APT, and found that the model explains stock returns better than the CAPM. Specific factors found by them to be relevant were:

- the default risk on bonds;
- the term structure of interest rates;
- unanticipated inflation;
- the change in expected sales;
- the return on the 'market portfolio' not captured by the first four factors.

While this list looks similar to that of Chen, Roll and Ross (1986), the factors are measured in a slightly different manner. At present, it appears to be the case that inflation, term and default risk structure of interest rates, and industrial output all have some role as risk factors in the US.

In the UK, Clare and Thomas (1994) find that the results obtained depend upon the method used to form portfolios of stocks for estimation purposes. If the CAPM beta is used the following are priced:

- oil prices
- a measure of corporate default risk
- the consol/dividend yield (the 'comfort index')
- inflation risk
- private sector bank lending
- the current account balance and
- the redemption yield on UK corporate debentures and loans.

However, if portfolios are formed on firm size, only the following turn out to be priced:

- inflation risk
- the 'comfort index'
- the excess return on the market.

The issue of interest here is whether we have a model that can be used to calculate costs of capital. The CAPM gives us the relationship between return and a single risk factor. That risk factor was systematic risk, and the unit price of that risk is the market risk premium (MRP). The unit (or index) of risk exposure for individual investments is given by beta. In an arbitrage pricing model (APM), there are a number of factors (estimates vary, but most investment houses using the model use between five and seven), each of which has a price (MRP_j, for each factor, j), with each security having its own set of factor betas. If we take a simple example, with two risk factors, say a GDP growth risk premium (MRP_1) and an inflation risk premium (MRP_2), an empirically derived model might be:

$$r_i = r_f + \beta_{i1}MRP_1 + \beta_{i2}MRP_2$$

More generally, where there are J risk factors, the risk return relationship can be written as:

$$r_i = r_f + \sum_{j=1}^{J} \beta_{ij}MRP_j$$

A practical problem with the application of this model is that if there are, say, five factors to consider, we would need, for each target firm being valued, five beta factors, and we would need to establish the market risk premia associated with each of the factors. By contrast, the CAPM needs one risk premium and beta factors are readily available from published data sources. There are as yet no published UK sources for either factor prices (MRPs) or multi-factor betas.

4.6.1 The Fama and French 'three-factor' model

Recently, a well known model that has been applied is the 'three-factor' model of Fama and French.[12] They believe that both 'book-to-market' (BMV) and size effects capture macroeconomic risk factors that are important in determining stock returns, and based upon their empirical analysis propose the following model, basically an extended CAPM:

$$r_i = r_f + \beta_i(r_m - r_f) + \gamma_i(\text{SMB}) + \delta_i(\text{HML})$$

where:

SMB = the value − weighted return on small firms minus the value − weighted return on large firms;

HML = the value − weighted return on high BMV firms minus the value − weighted return on low BMV firms.

However, as noted above, there is considerable dispute about whether the Fama and French (1992) conclusion on the CAPM is valid or whether the above model has any theoretical underpinnings. As Ashton and Tippett (1998) observe, their findings 'ought to be a warning to those who would place undue reliance on results like those reported in the Fama and French ... papers.'

All this leaves the practitioner with something of a dilemma. Clearly, the CAPM has serious weaknesses. However, in the UK and continental Europe, the data is not generally available to apply the alternative APT model. One approach to this dilemma is to attempt to extend the CAPM to allow for the fact that the most common empirical finding in tests is that 'the smaller firms effect' also appears to influence return.

4.6.2 Adjusting cost of capital for firm size

At the outset, it must be acknowledged that there is no *theoretical* basis for extending a CAPM to take account of the effects of firm size. The CAPM should correctly price all returns. The empirical evidence is that it does not.

One way round this problem is to use a small-firms premium added to the CAPM-derived cost of capital. One approach that has been used in testing the performance of unit trusts is to estimate a two-factor model where the exposure to 'size effects' is captured by the difference between an index of smaller company performance (either the Hoare-Govett Smaller Companies Index (HGSCI) or the FT250) and the return on the FT All Share Index (FTASI). For example, we might make estimates assuming the following model of returns:

$$r_i = r_f + \beta_i(r_m - r_f) + \gamma_i(r_{hg} - r_m)$$

where:

$$r_m = \text{the return on the FTASI;}$$
$$r_{hg} = \text{the return on the HGSCI.}$$

The first coefficient is then a 'normal' CAPM beta coefficient. The second coeficient (gamma) captures the exposure to size effects, and the second bracketed term on the right-hand side is the 'price' of small company risk – in this case the difference between the HGSCI and the FTASI. How large this premium is depends upon the time period chosen. The HGSCI has been backdated to 1954, while the FTASI was formed in 1962. Taking the more recent period since the FTASI was formed, the additional return on smaller companies is around the order of 1.5%. Taking a longer period can produce figures of up to 3%. In general, smaller companies have underperformed in recent years but showed substantial outperformance up to the mid-1980s.

To show how the degree of exposure to size effects varies across companies, at the University of Exeter we sorted all firms into decile groupings each year from 1979 to 1997 and then calculated unweighted average returns for each. We then ran the above regression and obtained the result in Table 4.4.[13]

Table 4.4 Average exposures to the 'small firms' effect as measured by the HGSCI

Decile	Beta	Gamma
1 (largest)	1.074	0.216
2	1.105	0.715
3	1.057	0.932
4	0.996	1.118
5	0.960	1.087
6	0.922	1.126
7	0.873	1.093
8	0.856	1.137
9	0.886	1.301
10 (smallest)	0.684	1.313

Thus if these gamma coefficients are representative of the 'typical' firm in, for example, decile 4, we might adopt the following approach to calculating its equity cost of capital:

■ Calculate CAPM cost as before (risk-free rate plus beta times MRP).

■ Add on the 'gamma factor' multiplied by the price of small firms risk.

■ Taking 1.5% as the estimate of this, we have an *additional* cost of: 1.5% × 1.118, approximately 1.7%.

■ This is added to the CAPM cost.

4.7 THE EFFECT OF CHANGING GEARING LEVELS ON THE EQUITY COST OF CAPITAL

In order to be able to understand the relationships between changing debt levels and the cost of equity capital, we need some form of theoretical framework that predicts how weighted average cost of capital (WACC) and the cost of equity should be influenced by the gearing level. The obvious starting point is the well known Modigliani and Miller framework discussed in most finance texts. Essentially, their analysis shows that interest payments themselves are merely a transfer of wealth from one class of security holder (equity) to another (debt); slicing up cash flow in this way contributes nothing to corporate value. However, when debt interest is tax allowable there *is* a real gain in corporate value, since the tax relief effectively represents a subsidy on debt from the government.

Modigliani and Miller show that the effect of increasing gearing is to increase the cost of equity capital.

- When debt interest is not tax allowable, this exactly offsets the benefit obtained from cheaper debt financing, so WACC remains constant at all levels of gearing.

- When debt interest *is* tax allowable, the benefits from increasing the level of debt more than offset the increasing cost of equity, and so WACC declines as gearing increases.

Of course, this result depends upon a number of assumptions, the most critical of which are:

- the absence of liquidation costs;

- that individuals, as well as firms, can borrow and lend at the risk free-rate (this is necessary to allow arbitrage between debt and equity which is central to Modigliani and Miller's analysis);

- an additional assumption (discussed in more detail below) that debt income and equity income are taxed at the same rate. It is on this issue of personal taxation that many of the difficulties in estimating the effect of gearing on cost of capital are encountered.

The most obvious problem is that in reality lenders will require higher levels of return to compensate for increased risk as debt levels increase; indeed, this is exactly what we should expect to happen according to the CAPM. Rubeinstein (1973) and Buckley (1981) have shown what will happen to the cost of capital when the presence of risky debt is allowed for, with the result being that although the cost of borrowing will rise at high levels of gearing, the optimal structure is still 100% debt and WACC still declines linearly with increases in gearing. This relationship is expressed by:

$$\text{WACC} = r_{eu}\left(1 - T_c \cdot \frac{D}{D + E}\right)$$

where r_{eu} is the cost of equity for an ungeared firm, E is the market value of equity and D is the *market* value of debt.

While this may be valid for reasonable levels of gearing, it is worth pointing out some real-world problems which may help to explain why the result might be invalid at high gearing levels:

- When companies increase their gearing levels, they increase the probability of making losses in any one year, and this means a delay in obtaining the tax relief on debt interest.

- Should the company go bankrupt it will never obtain these benefits; the effect is that the expected present value of the tax relief on debt does not increase linearly with gearing.

- If liquidation is a costly process we should expect the value of the geared company to decrease by the present value of the expected liquidation costs.

- Lenders to highly geared companies often impose restrictive covenants which limit managerial actions, particularly in terms of dividend payments; this might be viewed as a cost of higher gearing which again serves to reduce the value of companies with high levels of debt.

4.7.1 The Modigliani and Miller analysis and the CAPM

The Modigliani and Miller analysis is compatible with the application of the CAPM to the estimation of the cost of equity capital. The beta of a portfolio of investments is a weighted average of its constituent betas. Modigliani and Miller prove that the relationship between the value of geared and ungeared companies is that a geared firm is worth the value of an ungeared firm *plus* the present value of the debt tax shields

We can view a geared company as consisting of a portfolio of debt and equity. Expressing the relationships between the cost of ungeared equity cost of capital and the geared cost as gearing levels change in terms of beta gives us the following:[14]

$$\beta_{eu} = \frac{\beta_{eg} \cdot E + \beta_d \cdot D(1 - T)}{E + (1 - T)D}$$

The beta subscripts, *eu*, *eg* and *d* refer to the beta of equity of an ungeared and geared company, and the beta of debt respectively. In the absence of personal tax T is the rate of corporation tax. The weighting given to the geared equity and debt betas given in the denominator is equivalent to the value of an ungeared firm.

The importance of this formula is that by modelling the relationship between geared and ungeared betas, it enables us to use analogue proxy companies with levels of gearing different from that of the company or division we wish to calculate a cost of capital for,[15] and also lets us examine the effect of different financing alternatives upon value.

4.7.2 Extensions to the Modigliani and Miller analysis

At least two problems remain with the above analysis. First, the implicit assumption in the Modigliani and Miller analysis is that management do not alter the capital structure in the light of changes in the firm's circumstances. This is sometimes referred to as the assumption of a *passive* debt management policy (PDMP), and contrasts with the alternative assumption of an *active* debt management policy (ADMP).[16] Second, the analysis assumes that the personal tax rates on dividends, capital gains and debt are equal. Although the recent reforms in UK tax legislation which were incorporated in Gordon Brown's first budget represent moves towards the equal treatment of these types of income, there remain clear differences in their tax treatment for at least some classes of investor.

Active debt management

The assumption of an ADMP changes the conclusions from the basic PDMP case in an important respect. If management actively manage debt so as to maintain gearing constant at market values the effect is that the tax shields on debt have a lower value. This is because it is only the next period's tax shield which is known with certainty and can therefore be discounted at r_d (Modigliani and Miller assume all future debt tax shields can be so discounted). Beyond that, since the amount of debt covaries with the market value of equity, the appropriate discount rate is the equity cost of capital. The net result is that the relationship between geared and ungeared equity betas now becomes:

$$\beta_{eu} = \frac{\beta_{eg} \cdot E + \beta_d \cdot D.Z}{E + ZD}$$

whereas in the case of a PDMP, Z takes the value $(1 - T_c)$; under an ADMP, Z becomes:

$$Z = \left(1 - \frac{r_d}{(1 + r_d)} \cdot T_c\right)$$

Differing personal tax rates on equity and debt income

The second problem we noted above is that personal tax rates on capital gains, dividends and debt interest are not equal. Strong and Appleyard (1992) analyse this problem in detail, and they note that the critical tax rates for equity and debt are those of the marginal investor. Note that the marginal investor in debt is not the same as the marginal investor in equity. A further problem that Strong and Appleyard discuss is that of three possible assumptions concerning the nature of the capital structure equilibrium. If the tax rates on equity and debt are assumed to be equal for the marginal investor (since the post-election budget tax reforms, this is the position if a UK pension fund is the marginal investor in both), then the basic PDMP and ADMP results above hold.

An alternative is to assume that the Miller (1977) equilibrium position holds. This assumes that the marginal investor has a tax rate of zero on equities but pays tax on debt income. This would be the case if, say, UK investors held equities through a PEP scheme but held corporate bonds as individual investments. In such a case, the tax shield value of debt is reduced to zero because the cost of debt rises as higher rate tax payers have to be induced to hold debt despite the tax disadvantage. The net result is that in equilibrium, the tax advantage at the corporate level is exactly offset by the tax disadvantage at the personal level. The Miller equilibrium also follows from an assumption of higher personal tax rates on debt income than on equity income and an increasing marginal tax rate on debt income. In effect, then, T in the above formulae become zero. Furthermore, in the CAPM the term R_f has to be multiplied by $(1 - T_c)$. However, given changes in recent UK budgets, it seems implausible to argue that the Miller equilibrium is likely to hold in the UK. It seems far more likely that the Modigliani and Miller (1963) equilibrium would hold rather than the Miller (1977) equilibrium.

Strong and Appleyard also analyse an intermediate position where there is a relative tax disadvantage to debt income at the personal level, but no increasing marginal tax rate on debt income as in the Miller equilibrium. In such circumstances, the risk-free term in the CAPM is revised to r_f^* and needs to be adjusted for the differential tax rates by:

$$r_f^* = r_f \frac{(1 - T_{pd})}{(1 - T_{pe})}$$

and T in the above formulae for beta is given by:

$$T = \frac{(1 - T_c)(1 - T_{pe})}{(1 - T_{pd})}$$

where the subscripts c, pe and pd on T refer to the rate of corporation tax, personal tax on equity, and personal tax on debt income respectively for the *marginal* investor.

Given the difficulties of determining the tax position of the 'marginal investor' it is perhaps not surprising that a recent survey of the practices used by large UK firms in setting their cost of capital found that none attempted to incorporate personal tax rates into their analysis.[17] For the remainder of this briefing the assumption will be made that the tax rates on equity and debt income for the marginal investor in each are equal, and that the Modigliani and Miller equilibrium therefore holds. The consequence is that the relevant tax rate, T, is simply the corporation tax rate.

4.8 COST OF OTHER CLASSES OF CAPITAL

In order to calculate the WACC, it is necessary to know the cost of the other forms of financing commonly found in practice. Broadly, these are:

- short-term debt
- long-term debt
- preference shares
- warrants
- convertible loan stocks.

The general principle underlying the estimation of the costs of these forms of financing is the same as that used in estimating the equity cost of capital. That is, we need to estimate the *current opportunity cost* using *market* rates and values, not historic or book rates and values. In the case of variable interest rate debt where there is no significant default risk, market value will be approximately equal to book value. However, this will not be the case for fixed interest instruments or forms of financing which have option-like properties, such as warrants and convertibles.

4.8.1 Cost of debt

Short-term debt

When calculating the WACC, the objective is to use the long-run gearing ratio of the firm. Short-term debt should therefore be included only if it is part of the long-run core financing of the business. In general, for debt maturing within one year, market values will be close to book values, in the absence of any significant default risk. The appropriate cost of capital is the current interest rate on this risk class of debt, less corporation tax.

Long-term debt

As noted above, for variable interest debt, it is sufficient in the absence of significant default risks to assume market value equals book value, and that the opportunity cost of capital is the current yield on equivalent risk variable interest debt (or the rate implied by the premium over LIBOR, if known). Again, allowance needs to be made for corporation tax relief on the debt.

In the case of fixed interest debt, the cost of capital (pre-tax) is given by the yield to redemption on the debt, if traded. Yield to redemption is simply the internal rate of return (IRR) on the bond and is calculated by solving the following expression for r:

$$D_0 = \sum_{t=1}^{t=n} \frac{Coupon_t}{(1 + r)^t} + \frac{Redemption\ value}{(1 + r)^n}$$

where:

$$D_0 = \text{current market price;}$$
$$n = \text{life of the bond.}$$

EXAMPLE

Edwards plc has £50 m nominal of 10% debt in issue, with a redemption date ten years from now. Debt interest is tax allowable at 31%, and coupons are paid semi-annually. The debt is redeemable at par. The current price of the debt is £129.75.

The equivalent gilt yield (i.e. on a semi-annual coupon basis) is found by solving:

$$129.75 = \sum_{t=1}^{t=20} \frac{5}{(1 + r)^t} + \frac{100}{(1 + r)^{20}}$$

for r, which gives $r = 0.03$ or 3%. Thus the equivalent gilt yield is $2r$, or 6%, but the APR is $(1.03)^2 - 1 = 0.0609$ or 6.1%. Thus the current after-tax cost of debt is 6.1% $\times$ $(1 - 0.31) = 4.2\%$.

For irredeemable debt, the yield to redemption is identical to the 'running yield', and as the current market price is simply the present value of a perpetuity, r is found from:

$$r = \frac{Coupon}{D_0}$$

If debt is not traded, the implied market value can be calculated by using the market yield to maturity on equivalent grade debt in the above expression. The opportunity cost of capital to the firm is given by $r \times (1 - T)$.

4.8.2 Cost of preference shares

For preference shares, the opportunity cost of capital is again found by solving for the implied rate of return on the share given today's price and dividend. That is, the cost of preference shares is the IRR on the share, found in exactly the same way as r was calculated in the case of quoted debt.

The only difference is that whereas the debt interest payments were tax allowable, dividends to preference shareholders are not, so that the final step of multiplying r by $(1 - T)$ is not carried out.

4.8.3 Cost of capital on complex financial instruments

For companies which have only ordinary shares and simple or 'plain vanilla' debt, there is no real need to know how to deal with options.[18] When more complex forms of financing are involved, it helps to understand the basic principles of options and their pricing. Any financial instrument that involves a contingent claim on some other asset essentially has option-like properties. The two most common examples found in corporate financing are convertibles (loan stocks or preference shares) and warrants. Swaps can also involve options; in fact, any swap can be decomposed into a series of forward and, if applicable, option contracts. Because of the potential complexity of swaps, they are not covered in detail in this briefing, but a brief explanation of their treatment for cost of capital purposes is given below.

The basic option pricing models

An option can be defined as the right to buy (a *call option*) or the right to sell (a *put option*) an asset at a set price on some specified future date. The theoretically correct method of appraising such options is to value them using option pricing techniques. Two widely used models are the binomial model and the Black-Scholes model.

The simplest option pricing model is the binomial model. A basic example is that of a single period, where the end price can take on one of two values. Although this may not be a realistic scenario in many cases, if we take a sufficiently short interval of time, it may be a reasonable approximation of reality to think of share prices having either an up-tick or down-tick of given size. The binomial model can easily be extended to cope with any number of change intervals, and is useful for pricing an option on dividend-paying stocks which can be exercised early (a so-called 'American' option).

The easiest way to understand this model is through a single-period two-state example. Suppose the current share price of JPR plc is £3 per share. JPR is a specialist company in the biotechnology industry, and its future depends upon the success of a new process which is currently undergoing final trials, the result of which will be known in one year's time. If the outcome of these trials is successful, the share price will jump to £4 per share (+33.3%); if the process fails the share value will fall to £2.50 (-16.67%). Option pricing rests upon the 'no arbitrage' principle which underpins finance theory. This implies that two asset portfolios with identical state payoffs must sell for identical prices, otherwise risk-free profits can be earned in excess of the risk-free rate of interest. Given a market in traded options, it is possible to combine a position in options with a position in the underlying shares such that the combination is risk free. The 'no arbitrage' principle requires that the options are fairly priced so that this particular combination yields the risk-free rate of return.

To see this, suppose that we hold 1000 shares in JPR; there is a ready market in call options on JPR shares, including those which have an exercise price equal to the current share price (such options would be said to be *at the money*) and an exercise date exactly one year from now. If the share price rises to £4, a call option with an exercise price of £3 will be worth £1 at expiry. Conversely, the same option is worthless if the share price falls to £2.50. The proportionate change in the values of the option and share are:

$$\frac{\text{Option price range}}{\text{Share price range}} = \frac{£1 - £0}{£4 - £2.5} = 0.667$$

This number is the *option delta*; the inverse of this tells us how many options need to be written per share held in order to establish a risk-free position. Selling 1/0.667 options (i.e. 1.5) for every share held in JPR yields the following possible outcomes:

	Share price £4	*Share price £2.50*
Value of shareholding	£4000	£2500
Loss on exercise of option	(1500)	0
Net position	2500	2500

This is an identical payoff whichever state occurs; the position is a risk-free one. The fair return on such a position is the risk-free rate of return. Suppose that this rate is 10% p.a. The net investment made is 1000 shares at £3 each, less the receipts from selling 1500 call options at £c each. Thus the value of the call option must be the amount which equates the value of this net investment to the end of period return:

$$2500 = (3000 - 1500c) \times (1.10)$$

Multiplying out and solving for c gives us the value of each call option, which is £0.485.

There is an alternative method of getting the same answer, sometimes called the *risk-neutral* or *risk-adjusted probability method*. Essentially, the method internalises any risk premium into a 'synthetic' probability which would apply *if* investors were risk-neutral (indifferent to risk).[19]

Given this assumed risk neutrality, the 'synthetic' expected return on a JPR share must be equal to the risk-free rate of return. Suppose the 'synthetic' probability of a share price increase is p; the probability of a decrease must then be $(1 - p)$. The first step is to find the value of p that equates the expected return on the share to the risk-free rate. Suppose the upside percentage movement is u, and the downside movement is d. We then have:

$$r_f = pu + (1 - p)d$$

Rearranging gives the 'synthetic' probability of a rise in the share price as a function of the price movements and the risk-free rate:

$$p = \frac{r_f - d}{u - d}$$

Applying this to the JPR example results in a synthetic probability of:

$$p = \frac{0.10 - (-0.1667)}{0.3333 - (-0.1667)} = 0.5334$$

If the shares are worth £4 each, the option has a value of £1; if the shares are worth £2.50, the option has a value of zero. The expected value of the option *at expiry* if investors are risk-neutral is therefore:

$$(p \times \text{Value if price rises}) + ([1 - p] \times \text{Value if price falls}) =$$
$$0.5334 \times £1 = £0.5334$$

The current value is the present value of this amount at the risk-free rate:

$$£0.5334/1.1 = £0.485, \text{ as before.}$$

In principle, this calculation can be carried out where there are successive jumps in the share price. The steps are straightforward:

- Start with the final period.
- Calculate the option values at the start of the final period using the *risk-neutral* method.

- Using the synthetic probability p and the risk-free rate, calculate the expected value of the option at the start of the previous period.

- Repeat until the value at the start of the first period is found.

Thus for two periods there are two iterations necessary, and so on. The binomial method can be used for smaller and smaller time periods if appropriate.

However, if we extend the binomial model into continuous time, it is possible to derive the Black-Scholes Option Pricing Model.[20] This model is widely used in practice. The Black-Scholes model calculates the value of a call option C as:

$$C = S.N(d_1) - X.e^{-Rf.t}N(d_2)$$

S is the current share price, X is the exercise price and $e^{-Rf.t}$ is a continuously compounded discount factor for t years at the risk-free rate, where t is the number of years to expiry of the option. $N(d_1)$ and $N(d_2)$ are cumulative probabilities, the values of which can be found from normal area tables. $N(d_1)$ is known as the hedge ratio[21] and $N(d_2)$ can be interpreted as the probability that the option will finish 'in the money' (Copeland and Weston, 1988, p. 276). The values of d_1 and d_2 are given by:

$$d_1 = \frac{\ln(S / X) + R_f.t}{\sigma.\sqrt{t}} + (0.5.\sigma.\sqrt{t})$$

and:

$$d_2 = d_1 - \sigma.\sqrt{t}$$

These calculations can either be carried out manually, in which case normal area tables are required, or is simple to calculate using a spreadsheet package such as Excel and the 'NORMDIST' function (see Appendix 4.1).

Financing instruments involving options

Even apparently simple debt financing can have options built into it. Many debenture and loan stock issues, particularly in the US, have what are known as 'call provisions', which allow the company to buy back the loan stock at a set price (designed to protect the firm against interest rate falls in the case of fixed interest securities), which essentially amount to the debt holder having 'sold' the company a series of call options. Similarly, many loan agreements stipulate a 'cap' to interest rates which is also an option-like arrangement. In so far as both of these are priced through an interest rate premium on the bond or loan, their incorporation into the WACC is simple, and we do not really need option pricing formulae to do so. However, there exist two important sources of finance where there does not exist such a simple solution; these are warrants and convertible unsecured loan stocks (CULS).

A warrant is a pure option in that it allows the holder to buy shares in the issuing company at a specified price on a certain date(s). Warrants are normally associated with bond issues (from which they can be detachable and separately tradeable), new equity issues or dividend distribution (e.g. BTR). Executive stock options are similar to warrants in that they are written by the company and are claims on new issues of equity (*see* below). CULS are similar to a combination of a warrant and a loan stock, where the warrant is not detachable and separately tradeable. The coupon rate on the loan stock will be less than the current rate on comparable corporate loan stocks, reflecting the value of the attached warrant. In order to be able to perform company valuations, we need to know the cost of capital of these forms of financing and their fair market value, since the value of the equity is the value of the firm less the value of any claims on that firm.

Using the Black-Scholes model to value warrants

There is an important difference between options and warrants in that the former are written by outsiders on existing shares, whereas the latter are written (issued) by the company and involve the issue of *new* shares; thus warrants have a dilution effect which options do not. This can be allowed for, and subject to certain assumptions[22] the relationship can be shown to be:[23]

$$W = \frac{N_s}{N_s + N_w} \, .C$$

where N_s and N_w are the number of shares and warrants in existence at present.

> **EXAMPLE**
>
> Suppose that Rush plc has a current share price of £3.50, has 100 million shares in issue and issues 10 million warrants (1 warrant carries an entitlement to 1 share) with an exercise price of £5 and an exercise date five years from now. Assume that the risk-free rate on five-year gilts is 5% and the standard deviation of the share price is 25% per annum.[24] The beta of the shares is 1.0 and the market risk premium is 3%.

To value the warrants, we need to note that the gilt yield quoted is *not* a continuously compounded rate. As UK and US government loan stocks pay semi-annual coupons, the quoted gilt yield equates to an annual percentage rate (APR) of:

$$APR = (1 + (0.05/2))^2 - 1 = 0.0506 \text{ or } 5.06\% \text{ p.a.}$$

To convert an APR to a continuously compounded rate (CCR), take the natural logarithm of one plus the APR:

$$CCR = LN(1.0506) = 0.0494 \text{ or } 4.94\%$$

Using this CCR of 4.94%, it is possible to: (a) value the warrants; and (b) calculate the implied cost of capital on the warrants.

Using the spreadsheet formulae in the appendix to this chapter gives values for $N(d_1)$ of 0.7054, $N(d_2)$ of 0.492 and a value for the call option of £0.6274.

The fair value of the warrant is therefore:

$$W = 0.6274 \times \frac{100}{100 + 10} = £0.5704$$

The implied cost of capital on these warrants can be found by calculating the beta and applying the CAPM. The beta of warrants (β_w) can be shown to be related to the beta of equity by the following (see Copeland and Weston for a full explanation):

$$\beta_w = \beta_e.N(d_1).S/C.$$

Applying this to the Rush plc example gives the result:

$$\beta_w = 1.0 \times 0.5331 \times 350/62.74 = 2.97$$

This indicates that the warrant is much riskier than the underlying equity because of the fact it is considerably 'out of the money'. In general, the closer the exercise price is to the current price and the longer the time to expiry, the nearer the beta of the warrant will be to that of the equity.

The final step is to calculate the cost of capital on the warrant (r_w), by applying the CAPM:

$$r_w = 5\% + (2.97 \times 3\%) = 13.9\%$$

Clearly, in the majority of cases, given the length of time between issue and exercise of many warrants, we would expect dividend payments to be made. One way of approximating a solution to this problem is to value the call option component by reducing the initial term S in the Black-Scholes model by the present value of the expected dividend. In such a case, as the dividend assumed to be known with certainty, the appropriate discount rate is the risk-free rate.

However, the correct approach to valuing a call option on a dividend-paying stock (assuming early exercise is possible – that is, the option is an *American* style call) is to use the binomial option pricing model. This directly allows for the fact that if the dividend payment is sufficiently large, it may be worth exercising the option early in order to buy the share before it goes *ex dividend*. As this binomial approach to valuing American options is useful in valuing the 'real' option to delay investment in a project (*see* Chapter 8), an example of this approach is given below. Note, however, that this method is not without difficulty – again, dividends are assumed to be known with certainty, and in the example below share prices are assumed to move only at year ends.

Using the binomial model to value warrants

To value warrants on dividend-paying stock when early exercise is possible, the binomial model has to be used. The dividend payment that will be made at all future points in time needs to be known – these can be conditional on whether an up or down movement occurs in share prices. The model employed is the 'risk-neutral' approach explained above.

EXAMPLE

Suppose that Giggs plc issues a warrant which can be exercised at any time in the next two years. The company will pay a dividend at the end of year 1. The following information applies:

Inputs	Values
Current or spot price	500p
Upside change	25.00%
Downside change	20.00%
RF (APR)	5.00%
Dividend, end of year	30p
Exercise price	400p

For simplicity, assume that the share price will only move at the end of the year.

The first step is to calculate the synthetic probability:

$$p = \frac{0.05 - (-0.2)}{0.25 - (-0.2)} = 0.5556$$

The second step is to calculate the value of the call option (which the warrant represents) at the end of the first year. For this, we need to calculate the share prices implied at the end of the first and second years, and the payoff on the option at expiry. Two assumptions are made: first, that the share price falls by the amount of the dividend when the share goes *ex dividend* (XD); second, that exercise of the warrant takes place immediately before the shares goes XD in year 2. There are four final positions, depending on whether the share has moved up (U) or down (D) in successive years:

Year 1		Year 2		
State:	Share (XD)	State:	Share (CD)	Option
U	595	UU	744	344
L	370	UL	476	76
		LU	462.5	62.5
		LL	296	0

Applying the synthetic probabilities to the period 2 option values gives the values at the end of year 1 if not exercised. Two values are possible, depending on whether prices went up or down in year 1. For example, if prices went up (U), the expected value of the option at the end of year 1 is:

$$\frac{(0.5556 \times 344) + ([1-0.5556] \times 76)}{1.05} = 214$$

A similar calculation shows that if prices went down in year 1, the expected value at the end of year 1 is 33p. However, the presence of a dividend now means there is an alternative. Instead of passively waiting until the end of year 2 to exercise the warrant, holders can exercise immediately before the share goes XD in year 1 and obtain the dividend payment. In such a case, the XD price plus the dividend is obtained in exchange for the exercise price paid. This results in the following alternative payoffs, depending on the year 1 share price movements and whether or not the option is exercised before the share goes XD:

Option values:			
	No exercise	Exercise & obtain dividend	Maximum payoff
U	214	225	225
L	33	0	33

Thus the optimal strategy is to keep the option 'alive' if the share price has gone down in year 1, but to exercise early and take the dividend if prices have gone up (the payoff having been calculated as 595p + 30p dividend − 400p exercise price). Having calculated this, the last step is to use the synthetic probability and risk-free rate on the maximum payoffs to calculate the value of the option at the beginning of year 1:

$$\frac{(0.5556 \times 225) + ([1-0.5556] \times 33)}{1.05} = 133$$

The warrant beta can be calculated as before, substituting the option delta (the change in the option price ÷ the change in the share price) for $N(d_1)$.

Using option pricing models to value convertibles

Once the procedure for valuing warrants is understood, it is possible to approximate the cost of capital of a CULS, which is roughly equivalent to a warrant plus an ordinary unsecured loan stock. Unfortunately, the accurate valuation of a CULS is a very complex task because of several factors. In the first place, the exercise price on a straight option is clear cut; unfortunately, on a CULS what is being surrendered on exercise is the value of the underlying loan stock. If the redemption and exercise dates are the same and redemption is at par, no particular problem exists, but when this is not the case, the underlying value of the CULS at each possible exercise date needs to be estimated. In reality, there will also be problems connected with dividend payments and optimal timing of option exercise. Given that the requirement here is to approximate the value of convertibles in order (a) to estimate cost of capital and (b) to estimate the residual value of the equity, it is probably sufficient to use the approximation of valuing a convertible as a warrant (with due allowance for dividend payout) plus an equivalent unsecured loan stock.[25] The steps are straightforward:

■ Value the loan stock element, using the yield to maturity on an equivalent straight loan stock.

■ From this, calculate the after-tax cost of debt.

■ Value the warrant element, as described above, using the binomial model if necessary.

■ Calculate the warrant element beta and cost of capital as described.

■ Weight the debt and warrant costs by the values of the loan and warrant components.

EXAMPLE

Hughes plc currently has 40 million shares in issue with a market price of £2 each. In order to finance an expansion, it has just issued £10 million worth of 4% CULS. Per £100 nominal, the loan stock is convertible into 40 ordinary shares at the option of the loan stock holder in three years' time (this means that the effective exercise price is £2.50). Alternatively, if the loan stock is not converted, it is redeemable by the company at par in three years. The current yield on equivalent ULS issues is 6.5%, the gilt yield is 4.5% (which equates to a continuously compounded risk-free rate of 4.45%) and the market risk premium is 3%.

Following the CULS issue, the company's shares have a beta of 1.2, a standard deviation of 30% p.a., and given the expansion plans the company is not expected to pay a dividend for the next three years. For simplicity (*see* above) tax relief on interest is assumed to be 31%. Finally, to avoid complications concerning the value of the firm, assume that the gearing level remains constant[26] and that there is no other debt in issue at present.

First, the fair value of an equivalent ULS is found by discounting the three-year 4% coupons at 6.5% (using a 6.5% annuity factor), and adding to this the present value of the £100 redemption value in five years at 6.5%:

$$(4 \times 2.6485) + (100 \times 0.8278) = £93.38$$

The warrant element is now valued in a manner similar to that used above. S, the current share price, is £2, and X, the exercise price, is £2.50.

Using the spreadsheet given in the appendix to this chapter gives $N(d_1) = 0.5348$ and $N(d_2) = 0.3328$ and C = 0.3416.

For each £100 of loan stock, there will be 40 shares if the warrants are exercised, which would create 100 000 × 40 or 4 million shares. Thus the value of each warrant is:

$$W = \frac{40}{40 + 4} \times 0.3416 = £0.3106$$

Since 40 of these attach to each £100 worth of CULS, the warrant value is £0.3106 × 40 = £12.42, thus giving us a total CULS value of £12.42 + £93.38 = £105.80 per £100 nominal.

Having calculated fair values, it is possible to calculate the cost of capital. On the ULS element, this is simply the equivalent yield less the assumed tax shield, which gives $6.5\% \times (1 - 0.31) = 4.5\%$. On the warrant, using the formula for beta given above gives:

$$\beta_w = 2/0.3416 \times 0.5348 \times 1.2 = 3.76$$

This implies an expected return of:

$$r_w = 4.5 + (3.76 \times 3) = 15.8\% \text{ p.a.}$$

The expected equity return is:

$$r_e = 4.5 + (1.2 \times 3) = 8.1\% \text{ p.a.}$$

Finally, we are in a position to work out the company's WACC:

Finance	Market value (£m)	Annual cost	Cost × Market value
Equity	80.000	8.1%	6.480
CULS:			
Warrant element	1.242	15.8%	0.196
ULS element	9.338	4.5%	0.420
Total	90.580	7.8%*	7.096
* 7.096/90.580			

Note that the weighted cost of the convertible is $(0.196 + 0.420)/(1.242 + 9.338) = 5.82\%$.

Finally, note that a common feature of such instruments is the 'forced conversion' clause, which allows the company to redeem the bonds for equity if the shares have stood above the effective exercise price for a number of days (usually between 30 and 60). In effect, this gives the company a call option on the CULS, which in principle can be valued using option pricing models. However, this is an extremely complex process since the exercise date is unknown. For the purposes of cost of capital calculations this effect can probably be ignored, but in practical terms it does mean that the warrant element is less valuable than it would be without such a feature.

Swaps

Another prevalent feature of modern financing is the swap. Reduced to basics, the swap is merely the exchange of one set of cash flows for another. The swap can be a currency swap or an interest rate swap. In the former, typically a company borrows in one currency and 'swaps' the liability for one denominated in a different currency; both principal and interest rate differences are exchanged.

Although it is possible to value such simple swap arrangements, in efficient and frictionless markets its NPV should be zero; however, imperfections and regulatory and tax arbitrage opportunities sometimes allow borrowing to be arranged more cheaply in some countries than in others. From a valuation and cost of capital perspective, one reasonable treatment is to value swapped loans using the currency rates of interest into which the swap has been made (this gives us a 'quasi-market value'), less the tax shields received on such borrowing, weighted by the quasi-market value of this debt.

The interest rate swap involves no exchange of principal, just the exchange of interest-rate obligations. For example, BlueChip plc can borrow £100 million fixed at 6% p.a. for five years, or alternatively can borrow at LIBOR plus 0.25%. Because of its size, Lesser plc cannot borrow on fixed-rate terms so advantageously, paying 8% for a loan of this size and duration, but can borrow at LIBOR + 0.75%. Because of their differing cash flow patterns and economic exposure, BlueChip would really like to borrow at variable rates while Lesser wants to borrow at fixed rates. A swap might be arranged so that BlueChip borrows fixed-rate money, Lesser borrows at floating rates and the terms of the swap are that Lesser pays BlueChip 7% fixed, while BlueChip pays Lesser LIBOR plus 0.5%. Compared to their alternative borrowing strategies, both gain; BlueChip pays 6% − 7% − LIBOR + 0.5% = LIBOR − 0.5% (compared to the LIBOR + 0.25% it would have had to pay), while Lesser pays 7% − (LIBOR + 0.75%) + (LIBOR + 0.5%) = 7.25% (compared to the 8% it would have had to pay).

Although this may seem to be exploiting some comparative advantage, in an efficient markets context BlueChip has taken on some of the default risk of Lesser. While such effects can be valued, as can differential interest rate expectations, the simplest approach for cost of capital purposes is to treat such swaps as zero NPV investments and value the debt of BlueChip as though it were floating rate (which is effectively what has been created), and that of Lesser as though it were fixed rate. Tax shield values should be based upon the expected tax savings, which for floating rate debt requires an estimate of future interest rates. In general, the best way of estimating these is to look at the yield curve on government debt (corporate debt can be used if the market is large enough, as in the case of the US) and work out the implied future interest rates in a manner similar to that used in Chapter 2 to estimate the future inflation rate. For example, to work out the implied interest rate (the spot rate) for year 2, from the one-year rate together with the yield on two-year debt:

$$(1 + \text{Yield on 2-year debt})^2 = (1 + \text{1-year spot rate}) \times (1 + \text{2-year spot rate})$$

If government debt is used to estimate such rates, an appropriate risk premium would need to be added.

Leasing

In a world of rational lenders, leasing simply displaces borrowing capacity. It is now generally recognised that the correct way to evaluate financial lease contracts is to calculate the difference in cash flow resulting from leasing versus direct acquisition, and to discount these differences at the marginal after-tax cost of borrowing (e.g. Brealey and Myers, 1996, chapter 26). This is because the opportunity cost of capital on the lease agreement is the same as the company's cost of other (straight) debt capital. In general, leases only have a positive net present value to the lessee when there is some tax advantage involved, and this can only occur when the lessor is in a less favourable tax-paying position than the lessee; the most usual reason for this is temporary tax exhaustion (normally because of unused capital allowances) on the part of the lessee.

In terms of the treatment of leases in the WACC calculation, the theoretically correct approach is to weight this after-tax opportunity cost of borrowing by the value of the lease contract. However, from a practical perspective it will normally be difficult to establish the necessary numbers and an acceptable short cut under most circumstances will be to weight the after-tax cost of the company's debt capital by the book value of the lease.

4.9 WEIGHTED AVERAGE COST OF CAPITAL

Although personal tax rates have an impact, through the capital structure equilibrium which holds, upon the relationship between risk and required return, and between geared and ungeared equity betas, the returns observed in the capital market on equity and debt are before personal taxes. Furthermore, in the case of debt the yield is before corporate tax. It therefore follows that the correct estimate of WACC will always be:

$$\text{WACC} = r_e \frac{E}{V} + r_d(1 - T_c)\frac{D}{V} + r_p\frac{P}{V} + r_w\frac{W}{V} + r_{uls}(1 - T_c)\frac{ULS}{V}$$

where E, D, P, W and ULS are the total market capitalisations of equity, secured debt, preference shares, warrants (including the warrant portion of any CULS issue) and unsecured loan stock (including the ULS portion of any CULS issue) respectively, and V is the sum of these market capitalisations. Such a WACC can be applied to the post corporation tax free cash flows of the company to value the whole entity.[27]

Note that for project or divisional valuation, the WACC should be representative of the cost of capital for that project/division as a stand-alone entity in its own right. The general principle is to calculate the cost of equity, debt, etc. for that division given its systematic risk and the debt financing it would support in its own right.

This may be the same as the corporate WACC but in general will involve the following steps:

- finding an analogue company or companies with similar business risks to the division;

- estimating a gearing level that the division would have as a 'stand-alone' enterprise;

- calculating the implied 'ungeared' equity beta;

- calculating the implied equity beta at the revised level of gearing;

- estimating the post corporation tax costs of other classes of capital;

- calculating the WACC using these revised costs and the 'quasi-market' weighting implied by the revised gearing levels.

4.10 CASE EXAMPLE OF WACC ESTIMATION

In this section, a brief example of calculating the WACC for a large UK company is given. The company chosen here is not British Vita plc, which has a straightforward capital structure (but *see* Chapter 6 for a discussion of this company's WACC and an application to shareholder value models), but Tesco plc, which has several different types of corporate bond traded in the market.

EXAMPLE: WACC for Tesco plc

The 1998 financial statements reveal that Tesco has the following long-term debt:

4% unsecured deep discount loan stock	£83m nominal, redeemable at a par value of £125m in 2006
Finance leases	£25m
$10\frac{3}{8}$% bonds	£200m, redeemable at par in 2002
$8\frac{3}{4}$% bonds	£200m, redeemable at par in 2003
$7\frac{1}{2}$% bonds	£250m, redeemable at par in 2007
Other loans	£34m

Continued overleaf

The mid-market prices (from Bloomberg) for these bonds in early 1999 are:

4% unsecured deep discount loan stock   £92.50

$10\frac{3}{8}$% bonds   £113.187

$8\frac{3}{4}$% bonds   £111.625

$7\frac{1}{2}$% bonds   £114.437

The long gilt yield was approximately 4.6% at this time, and a market risk premium of 3% is assumed.

Tesco's share data from the 1998 accounts has not been given because of a subsequent capital change, but its beginning of year market capitalisation was approximately £11 400m. The London Business School Risk Measurement Service gives a beta for Tesco of 0.8 in December 1998.

Solution

The first step in the calculation of Tesco's WACC is the estimation of a cost of equity. Given the size of Tesco's market capitalisation relative to its debt, this will dominate the WACC calculation.

Applying the CAPM gives an equity cost of capital of:

$$4.6\% + (0.8 \times 3\%) = 7\% \text{ (nominal)}$$

The second step is the calculation of the implied IRR on each of the bond issues. Since all bonds are priced in multiples of £100 nominal, and from the accounting data we know that each is redeemable at par, we have, using the example of the 2002 $10\frac{3}{8}$% bond, the following:

$$113.187 = \frac{10.375}{(1 + r_d)^1} + \frac{10.375}{(1 + r_d)^2} + \frac{10.375}{(1 + r_d)^3} + \frac{10.375}{(1 + r_d)^4}$$

Solving for r_d, the IRR on the bond, yields 6.52%. Note that for simplicity the bonds have been valued assuming annual coupon payments and an assumption of a valuation at the beginning of 1999 with year-end redemption and coupon payments.

Calculating IRRs (yields to redemption) on the other bonds give yields of:

4% bonds	5.17%
$8\frac{3}{4}$% bonds	5.99%
$7\frac{1}{2}$% bonds	5.43%

The final step is now to weight the after-tax cost of all these components (see Table 4.3). For simplicity, it has been assumed that the lease financing and other loans carry an interest charge of 6% and that the relevant rate of corporation tax is 31%.

Table 4.3 Weighted after-tax cost

Capital class	Pre-tax cost	Post-tax cost	Market capitalisation (£m)	Weight	Weighted cost
Ordinary shares	7%	7%	11 400	11 400/12 309	6.48%
4% unsecured deep discount loan stock	5.17%	3.57%	125 × 92.5/100 = 115	115/12 309	0.03%
Finance leases	6%	4.14%	25	25/12 309	0.00%
10⅜% bonds	6.52%	4.50%	200 × 113.187/100 = 226	226/12 309	0.08%
8¾% bonds	5.99%	4.13%	200 × 111.625/100 = 223	223/12 309	0.08%
7½% bonds	5.43%	3.75%	250 × 114.437/100 = 286	286/12 309	0.09%
Other loans	6%	4.14%	34	34/12 309	0.01%
Total			12 309		6.77%

Thus the nominal WACC for Tesco plc is 6.77% p.a. Assuming an inflation rate of approximately 2.5% p.a., this translates into a real rate of:

$$(1.0677/1.025) - 1 = 0.0417 \text{ or } 4.17\%$$

4.11 HURDLE RATES AND COST OF CAPITAL

Until recently, the prescription of modern finance theory was that hurdle rates should be set at project level (although in practical terms this was typically suggested as meaning divisional level), and that the hurdle rate should reflect the beta of the project or division. If the project beta was the same as the corporate beta, the project discount rate would therefore be the firm's WACC. There is still virtually unanimous agreement in the literature that in the case of unconstrained capital investment projects of a non-dynamic nature (those that do not have the possibility of being actively managed (Strong and Appleyard, 1992) in the sense that they do not have the flexibility conferred by abandonment, temporary shutdown or expansion), the theoretically correct approach to valuation is to calculate the net present value (NPV) of the project's future cash flows at the firm's WACC. However, it is now recognised that in many cases there are dynamics in the project management process that can be compared to call and put options on shares. These dynamics give rise to what are sometimes called *real* options.

The correct way to analyse these is to value the options using the appropriate option pricing techniques (*see* Chapter 8 for an introduction). Some authors (e.g. Stark, 1990) have argued that in practice firms may approximate the value of some of these options by making adjustments to the hurdle rates used. This approach is not recommended here, but this argument has been used to explain why, in practice, UK hurdle rates may be considerably in excess of observed costs of capital. Recent research published by CIMA finds no evidence in the articulated practices of senior managers of leading UK companies to support such a claim.[28]

4.12 SUMMARY

In this chapter, various approaches to estimating the equity cost of capital have been investigated. Different methods of calculating the equity risk premium were also explained. In general, the recommendations were:

- use a risk premium based upon forward projection;
- estimate the equity cost of capital using either the CAPM or a multi-index model if available.

An explanation was then given of how to adjust equity costs of capital or equity betas for changes in capital structure. This is useful when:

- changes in gearing levels are planned (e.g. in management buyouts);
- the 'analogue' company approach to estimating beta is being used.

Estimation of the cost of debt and preference share capital was then explained. Broadly the approach can be summarised as:

- estimate yield to redemption on fixed-interest debt, less tax relief at the current rate of corporation tax;
- take current rates for variable-interest debt, less tax relief at the current rate of corporation tax;
- estimate the yield to redemption on preference shares.

The cost of capital on complex financial instruments usually involves the calculation of option values. In general, such instruments can always be broken down into the following components:

- options (e.g. warrants);
- forwards (e.g. swaps);
- bonds or quasi-bonds (e.g. ULS components of CULS, preference elements of convertible preference shares).

The final step is the estimation of the WACC. This simply involves weighting the post corporation tax cost of each component (only debt interest being tax-allowable) by the *market* values of each component.

While this can be used to value the whole company, it may not be appropriate for the valuation of divisions as risk and gearing may differ. In such cases the analogue company approach can be used to calculate a divisional cost of capital.

APPENDIX 4.1 EXCEL SPREADSHEET FORMULAE FOR THE BLACK-SCHOLES OPTION PRICING MODEL

	Column:			
Row:	A	B	C	D
1	A BASIC BLACK-SCHOLES MODEL			
2				
3				
4	Inputs			Value
5	Current or spot price			48
6	Days to expiry			78
7	Std Deviation			0.31
8	CC Risk-free rate			0.1
9	Exercise price			43
10				
11	Outputs			
12				
13	d1			=(LN(D5/D9)+((D8+(0.5*D7^2)) *D6/365))/(D7*(SQRT(D6/365)))
14	N(d1)			=NORMDIST(D13,0,1,TRUE)
15	d2			=D13−(D7*(SQRT(D6/365)))
16	N(d2)			=NORMDIST(D15,0,1,TRUE)
17				
18	Value			=(D5*D14)−(D9*(1/EXP (D8*D6/365))*D16
19	Hedge ratio, write			=1/D16

5

Forecasting free cash flows and calculating horizon values

In this chapter, the key forecast variables are first explained, along with value drivers and the relationship between them. The issues involved in forecasting these variables and value drivers are then examined.

The analysis is then extended to forecasting free cash flows. In particular, attention is paid to the calculation of FCF for the specific forecast period and how long this period should be. (Shareholder value based models for operationalising these forecasts are covered in the next chapter.) Finally, methods of calculating the terminal or horizon value of the company are explored.

5.1 RELATIONSHIPS BETWEEN VARIABLES

A key factor in performing successful valuations is an understanding of the relationships between the forecast variables, which allows an appreciation of which variables are likely to have the greatest impact on business value. As a general principle, all forecasts should be analysed to show the effect of a change in each of the variables, a process known as *sensitivity analysis*. It is also a good idea to set up the forecast on a spreadsheet model in such a way as to allow several variables to be changed simultaneously, a process sometimes termed *scenario modelling*. In terms of valuation sensitivity, the most critical variable in the forecast is usually the sales revenue. In general, as the ratio of fixed costs to variable costs increases, any given change in the sales revenue has a greater impact. This phenomenon is sometimes known as *operational gearing* or *leverage*.

A recent consequence of the developments in 'shareholder value' models is the labelling of these key variables as so-called *value drivers*.

5.1.1 Value drivers

In general, a value driver is any variable that has an influence on the market value of the enterprise. These can be either key variables for the company as a whole (e.g. sales growth or margin) or key variables for an individual subdivision (e.g. reducing delivery costs per customer for a distribution division). The basic principle of what has become known as *value-based management* is to identify the key value drivers for each unit of the organisation, and then focus attention on improving the value contributed by each of these drivers. In part this is achieved in some organisations by linking compensation to value drivers at the appropriate level.

Given the focus in this briefing on company valuation, the emphasis will be placed upon top-level value drivers rather than individual business or operating unit value drivers. Rappaport (1998) classifies value drivers according to whether they are related to operational, investment (financial management) or financing activities as follows:

Value drivers:

- Operating:
  - sales growth
  - operating profit margin
  - tax rate
- Investment:
  - working capital investment
  - fixed capital investment
- Financing:
  - cost of capital.

The other key factor is the time period over which these value drivers apply, termed the 'value growth duration' by Rappaport. A general principle of economics is that abnormally high profits are competed away over the longer term. In general, this leads to an expectation that advantages conferred by particularly favourable value drivers are likely to disappear eventually; in other words, the 'value growth duration' has a limited life.

5.2 GENERAL PRINCIPLES OF FORECASTING

For any valuation, background information on the economy, the industry and the company itself needs to be obtained. A crucial factor here is the type of valuation. In many cases, such as management's own valuation in the case of shareholder value analysis, the acquisition of a privately held company, consultants' valuations and so on, access to internal information is possible. This will cover areas such as:

- strategic plans
- contract details
- cost structure
- management's own forecasts.

In other cases, such as independent investment analysis and hostile takeover attempts, this information is not available and the valuation is based mainly upon information available in the public domain, plus that which can be gained through personal contacts and other sources (for example, it may be possible to get an approximate idea of the value of a company's property by inspecting land registry documents and externally viewing buildings). From a predator's perspective, it can be possible to gain more information by actually bidding for the company (the extent of the information gained will depend upon whether any details have been disclosed to a third party; the City Code requires information symmetry between rival bidders).

5.2.1 Economic indicators

A vital input to the valuation process is the forecast of economic indicators. Inflation forecasts were explained earlier in the briefing; other macroeconomic variables which will need to be estimated include:

- interest rates
- exchange rates
- growth in gross domestic product (GDP)
- unemployment rates
- taxation rates.

GDP growth, unemployment and interest rates are all indicators of the general health of the economy, and therefore have an important influence on sales and cost forecasts. In particular, interest rates have had a substantial effect on most companies since recent governments have used interest rates as a central plank of economic policy. Given this importance in policies for controlling inflation and growth, interest rates can have a double impact on companies because they can influence both demand for products and financing costs. In the case of exchange rates, it may be obvious why we need a forecast for those companies which export, buy imported raw materials or have overseas subsidiaries, but perhaps not so obvious a forecast is needed for companies which do not indulge in any of these activities. The first point which needs to be considered here is the influence of exchange rates on demand in remote, but nonetheless important ways; these are discussed below. The second point is that exchange rates interact with both interest rates and inflation rates.

In theory, interest, inflation and exchange rates should all be interrelated, at least in the long run, so that it is possible to check for consistency in the long-run forecasts for each of these variables. In the absence of exchange controls and other restrictions, international financial market equilibria should ensure the following:

- the required risk-free rate of return should be equal in all countries;
- thus the difference in interest rates should be explained by differences in the expected inflation rates;
- this difference in interest rates will drive the difference between spot and forward rates of exchange;[1]

- the difference between forward and spot rates should equal the expected change in the spot rate;[2]

- the difference between forward and spot rates should equal the difference in expected inflation rates.

It must be emphasised that these equilibria do not necessarily hold in the short run.

Turning to the issue of obtaining forecasts for all the required economic variables, obvious sources are stockbrokers and the various economic forecasting agencies, but as with the inflation predictions discussed earlier, an average of these forecasts tends to give better results than any individual forecast. Again, there is the problem that forecasts are often available for a period shorter than we would wish. Depending on the country the information is needed for, it may be possible to obtain forecasts for up to five years ahead, but often this is not possible. In such cases, for the longer term one alternative may be to use long-run averages, so that for example we might forecast the long-run rate of growth in GDP for the UK to be around 2% per annum.

5.2.2 Industry factors

For each SBU, general industry factors need to be considered. First, there are questions concerning the market itself. These might include:

- fashion changes and how they may impact upon demand;

- changes in competition;

- the impact of changing technology on the types of products the industry produces;

- the likely growth in the market;

- the way in which market changes will occur in different areas or countries;

- market maturity and expected life;

- the market shares of competing firms in the industry.

Second, there are issues relating to the production technology of the industry. Forecasting here is a difficult process, but an awareness of changes occuring in other countries or other industries is helpful. Such changes will also have an impact on the supply of labour and the skills required of employees. It can even have profound implications for both suppliers and customers (for example, the use of just-in-time stock control in the motor industry has had a marked effect on component suppliers). In addition to these factors, there is the importance of regulatory changes and political awareness; an example is the effect of environmental legislation and concern on industry.

5.2.3 Company-specific factors

Necessary background information on the company includes the following:

- group structure and management;

- list of susidiary and associated companies in the group, including country of incorporation, date of acquisition, and proportion and class of capital held;

- names of senior managers and directors, together with profiles of experience where possible;

- full accounting information, including interim results, all published accounts for at least the last five years and results of subsidiaries and associates where possible;

- an outline of the accounting policies used, with particular reference to any changes in policies and any exceptional features of such policies;

- major limiting factors on output (e.g. demand, skilled labour, capital investment, supplies, etc.);

- unusual operating conditions (e.g. strikes, temporary shortage of supplies).

In can be helpful to perform what is sometimes referred to as a Strengths, Weaknesses, Opportunities and Threats ('SWOT') analysis. Properly carried out this can serve as a useful checklist when reviewing the realism of the assumptions made when preparing the forecast; furthermore, it also helps when applying scenario modelling (*see* below) to the forecast. When conducting such an analysis, company visits have a vital role to play, because this allows the possibility of making judgements about issues such as the quality of the management team and the nature of the workplace. It is important to note that this requires visits to the workface, not just the boardroom. If it is not possible to gain access to the firm itself, it may be possible to make use of any contacts with suppliers, customers or financiers and obtain their impressions of the valuation target.

Further to the SWOT analysis, it is also useful to perform an analysis of risk factors. One type of risk is what might be called economic risk exposure; this type of risk is what is being captured through beta which as explained in the previous chapter measures the relationship between returns on the company's equity and returns on the stock market as a whole. Since 'the market' is driven by economic prospects, this relative measure gives us an idea of how the company reacts to changes in these economic prospects. Although exposure to economic factors is already been picked up through beta, and hence is implicit in the discount rate used, it can still be useful to specify the effect of such factors on the SBU. For example, a highly leveraged buyout of a luxury car dealership can run into severe problems in the face of sustained high real levels of interest rates. Other risk factors might include:

- failure to renew major contracts for existing work;
- failure of new products to win anticipated market share;
- loss of key personnel;
- industrial relations problems;
- political risks;
- exchange rate risk.

In relation to the latter, apparently remote factors can affect company value; for example, any leisure activity which depends upon overseas tourists clearly is subject to some degree of exchange rate risk, as is any manufacturer which depends upon imported raw materials or components. Less obviously, a firm which manufactures entirely from domestically sourced material and sells in domestic markets might also be at risk in the longer term from currency movements, since a manufacturer in a country undergoing exchange rate appreciation will face an increasing threat from imports by foreign manufacturers who find that their competitive position has improved.

If the SBU is a foreign subsidiary, a range of other risk factors needs to be considered. Some of the major factors will be:

- political risk including:
  - regulatory controls
  - threat of nationalisation
  - cultural factors
  - government stability
  - human rights record
  - relationship with neighbouring countries;
- exchange rate risk;
- exchange controls;
- transfer pricing legislation;
- infrastructure development;
- availability of investment incentives and subsidies;
- labour availability.

The final consideration on risk should be to what extent such risks can be hedged, and at what cost. While a detailed discussion of hedging is beyond the scope of this book, we should note that it is by no means clear that a quoted company should hedge such risks. To start with, investors can diversify away many of these risk factors simply by holding a balanced portfolio; furthermore, they may actually want to take on currency and foreign economic risks as a way of limiting their exposure to the UK economy. Second, it is difficult to hedge long-run uncertain cash flows.[3] Third, we have the alternative of relying upon the type of long-run economic equilibria described above. Finally, it can be that the most effective method of limiting such risk is to finance expansion in foreign countries with local borrowing, although this will not always be possible.

The specific factors which need to be forecast concern the key variables or value drivers, depending on how the cash flow forecast is to be operationalised (*see* later in this chapter and Chapter 6). Looking first at the operational value drivers, we have the following factors which need to be considered as part of the forecasting process:

Sales revenue/sales growth

- Limiting factors on output
- Markets (share, positioning and strategy)
- Marketing (prices, demand, advertising and promotion, economic factors)
- Sales growth (historic, competitors, economic factors)
- Nature of sales (contract, non-contract, etc.)
- State of current order book
- Dependence on key customers
- Market research
- Distribution
- Seasonality

Cost of sales

- Technology and structure of processes
- Capacity
- Technological change
- Materials (price, supplies, stockholding requirements)
- Labour (skills, costs, availability, training, redundancy, pension and other employment costs)
- Other costs (administration, overheads, stock control, distribution, quality control)
- Cost drivers
- Cost structure (fixed, variable, etc.)
- Allocated costs vs stand-alone costs vs economies of scale
- Research and development costs (relationship with sales, lead times, current state of products/production technologies)

Margins

- Historical margins and trends
- Competitors' margins
- Product quality
- Product type
- Seasonality

Taxes

- Domestic and overseas tax rates
- Cash tax rate (as opposed to profit tax rate)[4]
- Asset purchasing patterns

Second, the relationship between operating cash flow and free cash flow is examined. The two key factors are working capital investment rates and fixed capital investment rates.

Working capital investment rates

- Stockholding requirements of raw materials, work-in-progress and finished goods stocks
- Seasonality
- Credit allowed/taken
- Relationship between sales growth and working capital requirements

Fixed capital investment

- Asset purchase pattern:
  - timing
  - inflation
  - relationship between asset formation and sales growth
- Existing plant and equipment:
  - age
  - replacement cycle

The final 'value driver', cost of capital, has been explained in the previous chapter.

5.3 FORECASTING FREE CASH FLOWS: THE FORECAST PERIOD AND HORIZON VALUES

A real problem is that specific FCF cannot reasonably be forecast more than a certain number of years ahead. To get around this problem, conventionally a simplifying assumption is made about the nature of the change in these cash flows. This allows the estimation of the *terminal* or *horizon value* of the business at the forecast horizon (that is, the end of the explicit forecast period). There are alternative methods of estimating this value which involve making the following assumptions:

- that the FCF grows at a constant rate;

- continuous replication;

- erosion of economic rents (this simply means that after a certain time the economic advantage of the business is diminished to the extent that only zero NPV projects are available to it);

- that the growth in FCF can be captured through the use of a prospective PE multiple.

Below we look at the merits of each of these in turn. Before doing so, the explicit forecast FCF period and the preparation of FCF forecasts are explained.

5.4 THE EXPLICIT FORECAST PERIOD

If the company did not have to invest in any fixed assets or increase its working capital investment, all of the operating cash flows after tax could be paid out as dividends; in such an event, there would be nothing else to be done with them. However, real businesses need to invest in order to maintain the existing asset base (because of inflation and the 'lumpy' nature of investment flows, this investment is not the same as accounting depreciation) and in order to expand. Sales, profit and cash flow growth can only come about through investment. In such a growth situation, if we simply took the expanding after-tax cash flows from operations and discounted them, we would overestimate the value of the firm because we would fail to take account of the sacrifice necessary in order to achieve the expansion. That sacrifice is measured by the cash flow retained in the firm and not paid out as dividends. As was noted in Chapter 3, in the case of a business financed entirely by equity, where investment was made directly (that is no cash is placed on deposit) and no new shares were issued, free cash flow and dividend would be identical. However, given that businesses can use cash deposits, borrow, receive and make interest payments and issue new equity, normally dividends and free cash flows differ.

In Chapter 3, free cash flow was defined. To explain how FCF estimates can be made from published accounting data, the British Vita accounts (as summarised from Appendix A) shown in Table 5.1 are used as an illustration.

Table 5.1   Summary of British Vita plc accounts

	Free cash flow	Item ref	1996	1997
s	Operating cash flow pre working capital investment (OCF)	47	70.4	81.4
t	Cash taxes (CT)	59	−14.1	−15.6
u	OCF post tax (CFAT)	s + t	56.3	65.8
v	Working capital investment (WCAP)	51	18.3	27.4
w	Fixed asset investment (INV)	66	−61.3	−52.3
x	Free cash flow (FCF)	u + v + w	13.3	6.1

It is this free cash flow which needs to be forecast for the chosen horizon. As a general rule, this should be a minimum of five years and should always be for the maximum number of years possible. The aim is to forecast as far into the future as is necessary in order to ensure that the 'steady-state' scenario, necessary to forecast the terminal or horizon value of the SBU, is a reasonable approximation of reality. 'Steady-state' means that the return on new investment (RONI), the proportion of earnings which are retained for reinvestment (RE) and hence the FCF growth rate (g) can be approximated as constant *to perpetuity*. (This set of assumptions is implicit whenever a PE multiple is applied to a forecast earnings figure.[5])

5.5 TRANSITION PERIOD FORECASTS

While ideally it should be possible to forecast explicit cash flows until a steady-state period can reasonably be assumed, sometimes the phenomenon occurs of a period of growth of above (or below) normal long-run rates for a certain period. One useful approach in such cases is to model a transitional period between the explicit forecast period and the horizon period using some form of change process; the easiest of these is the assumption of a linear rate of change.

In general, if there is some disparity between the growth rate of FCF in the final years of the explicit forecast period and the sustainable long-run rate of growth (*see* below), serious thought should be given to the inclusion of some transitional period to model the rate of change.

5.6 THE CALCULATION OF THE HORIZON (OR TERMINAL) VALUE

The horizon, or terminal, value of a business is its value at the end of the explicit forecast period; in practice, the estimation of such a figure is a necessary component of any valuation. In theory, any firm could be valued by taking the explicit forecast out far enough for the terminal value not to matter very much. Unfortunately, depending on growth and discount rates, this might involve forecasting cash flows anything from fifty to one hundred years ahead. The only practical alternative is the adoption of some form of terminal value calculation.

All such models are approximations, since we do not *literally* expect a steady state to occur. In particular, it is important to realise that the real expectation is that trade cycles will take place. As such, the 'steady-state' model implicit in any horizon value must reflect *average* expectations of costs and demand, in other words those that exist at the mid-point of the trade cycle. For this reason, the final year of the specific forecast period must be carefully chosen so that it reflects neither economic boom nor slump conditions.

A popular criticism of DCF valuations is that the majority of the value comes from the assumed terminal value of the company. Whether or not this is true depends upon the length of the specific forecast period, the growth rate of the SBU's free cash flows and the cost of capital. While one possibility is to recommend that the forecast horizon be extended until the terminal value is a relatively small percentage of total value, this would result in a fairly long specific forecast period for the 'average' business (average being defined as one which grows at the same rate as the economy). In fact all that is necessary is to forecast far enough ahead for a 'steady-state' assumption to be a reasonable approximation of forecast reality. The real point is that *any* forecasting method makes a similar assumption, the difference being that a DCF approach does so explicitly rather than implicitly. For example, applying a PE ratio to a forecast earnings estimate one year ahead actually assumes that 100% of the value is terminal value.

Turning to the various terminal valuation alternatives, the choice is between a simple constant growth model, a positive present value of growth opportunities model, a continuous replication model, a zero growth opportunities model and a PE valuation approach. These are examined in turn.

5.6.1 The constant growth model

This is simply the basic FCF growth model from Chapter 3, which adapted for the cost of capital calculation from Chapter 4 gives:

$$V_H = \frac{FCF_{H+1}}{WACC - g}$$

V_H is the horizon value of the firm at the end of the explicit forecast period (year H), so that we need to use the free cash flow for the next period (which by our steady-state assumption is $FCF_H \times (1 + g)$).

To find today's value of the company, this horizon value is discounted by the WACC and added to the present value of all the free cash flows for the specific forecast period.

An important issue when using this formula is to understand what constitutes a reasonable assumption for g, the long-run growth to perpetuity. A serious question is whether it is reasonable to assume that growth will be much different from the rate of growth in GDP in the long run. Taking the average industrial or retail firm operating in domestic markets[6] as an example, it is quite possible that for a time maintainable growth may exceed GDP growth. However, eventually market saturation is likely to occur; depending on the type of product, demand might then simply remain constant (in which case a working assumption is that FCF just grows in line with inflation) or increase in line with GDP growth. Which will in fact happen depends on the nature of the product or service.

The first point to note is that in the case of abnormally high or low growth companies there may be an argument for using some form of transition model.

The second point concerns the factors which determine the growth rate. From the analysis in Chapter 3 $g = RONI \times RE$, where RE represents that proportion of earnings which is retained by the firm. This means that as g declines, so must either RONI or RE or both. The special problems of defining and estimating RONI are discussed below, but if some form of reversion to the average is assumed for a high growth company, it is evident that both are likely to change since eventually the NPV of further investments will decrease to zero (so RONI = WACC), at which point the only need for earnings retentions would appear to be the replacement of existing assets. In the case where RONI declines to WACC but growth occurs at the same rate as any increase in GDP (which might be the case for companies in the leisure industry, for example), then RE needs to reflect the increase in capital necessary to maintain this rate of growth.

The conclusion on growth rate estimation is that it can be too easy to adopt unrealistically 'bullish' views of *long-term* growth prospects; in the medium term, it is quite feasible that abnormal growth can be achieved but there must be considerable doubt that many firms can grow at a much faster rate than GDP growth in perpetuity. There will be some genuine outperformers and some underperformers (where growth may be negative). However, there is evidence that:

- over/under performing companies revert to poorer/better performance on average in the longer run;[7]

- analysts overestimate long-run earnings growth for high growth companies, and underestimate it for low growth companies.[8]

5.6.2 The present value of growth opportunities model

An SBU or firm can be valued by calculating the perpetuity value of the sustainable current earnings after tax and adding to this the present value of the growth opportunities. It is possible to show that if the return on the new investment made in any period remains constant, the value of the growth opportunities can be described by the sum of the present values of each year's investment (net of any tax allowances) multiplied by the return on that new investment (RONI) less the cost of capital, divided by that cost of capital. Formally, with the cost of capital given as the weighted average cost of capital (WACC) for the SBU or firm, the horizon value is given by:

$$V_H = \frac{ENGS_H}{WACC} + \sum_{t=H+1}^{t=N} \frac{INV_t(RONI_t - WACC)}{WACC(1 + WACC)^t}$$

The derivation of this formula is somewhat complicated and is not given here (but for a formal derivation *see* Gregory (1992), appendix to chapter 8).

The point of this formula is that positive NPV investments come about because of some special advantage which the firm has; this may be attributable to brand names, patents, efficiency, location or some other factor. The essential feature of all these (except, perhaps, location) is that eventually such advantages can be competed away; the question is one of timescale. That is what the formula attempts to capture; for how many years does the investment advantage continue? In the above formula, this is assumed to be for N years. At the point when RONI falls to the WACC, the NPV of new investments has become zero, so the value of future growth is nil. This model therefore attempts to encapsulate this into the valuation. However, there is a difference in assumption between this and the perpetual growth model coupled with a transition period forecast. Where the perpetual growth model with a transition period is used, the assumption is that *all* project cash flows change at the same rate. With the model described in this section, the assumption is that return changes progressively on all *new* investments, while the return on investments once in place remains constant.

Which of these assumptions is likely to prove the most reasonable in practice? The answer is that in the case of growth prospects diminishing through market saturation and/or new competition arriving, all cash flows are likely to decline at some rate. However, in the case where the expansion is into more marginal investment areas and there are barriers to entry in existing markets, the assumptions of the growth opportunities model might be more defensible.

5.6.3 The continuous replication model

The assumption underlying this approach to terminal values is that the firm simply continues to invest in the same bundle of projects that it has at the end of the forecast horizon. This assumption amounts to saying that there will be no additional growth opportunities, and that the only investment necessary is that required to replace the existing asset base. Unlike the zero NPV model described below, the continuous replication model assumes that the NPV on the replacement investment is the same as that on the existing investment.

If these assumptions are appropriate (and cases where this might be so include utility companies or ventures such as Eurotunnel), the terminal value in year H is simply the annual equivalent cash flow divided by the cost of capital. This calculation was described in Chapter 3; further examples are given in the discussion of accounting rates of return and RONI below.

5.6.4 The zero NPV model

This method of arriving at the terminal value assumes that all of the business's economic advantage has been competed away by the end of the specific forecast period (economists call this the erosion of economic rents). If this is the case, then the value of the firm is simply that value arrived at by estimating the value of the existing operations at the specific forecast horizon. In effect, this is a special case of the growth opportunities model, where the growth opportunities sum to zero. This suggests that the horizon value should be:

$$V_H = \frac{ENGS_H}{WACC}$$

Since in such a case the shareholders would be strictly indifferent between further investment by the company or dividend payout, the value is also given by $FCF_H/WACC$.

5.6.5 The price-earnings multiple model

As was shown in Chapter 3, in a steady-state situation it is always possible to derive a prospective PE multiple to apply to the forecast earnings figure. The general formula, adapting that derived in Chapter 3 by recognising that the required return is the WACC, is:

$$PE = \frac{(1 - g / RONI)}{WACC - g}$$

In the case where g, RONI and WACC are all industry averages such a PE ratio will itself be the industry average PE. However, for the reasons discussed in Chapter 2, it does not follow that the current industry average PE ratio will be representative of the forecast PE at the end of the specific forecast horizon, since cost of capital, growth rates and RONI figures may all change, at least in part because of inflation changes and cyclical factors. In this respect, we need to note that the steady-state scenario reflects *average* trading conditions and not those experienced during booms or recessions. Provided such factors are properly taken account of (in particular, *see* the comments below on accounting), it may be possible to use some average historical industry PE multiple, suitably adjusted, as a proxy for the horizon prospective PE multiple.

5.7 AN EXPLANATION OF THE RELATIONSHIP BETWEEN ACCOUNTING PROFIT AND PRESENT VALUES

Given that several of the above models require inputs either of earnings or of RONI, it is important to appreciate the relationships between accounting profits and 'earnings' as used in the above models, and between the accounting rate of return and RONI.

Unfortunately, accounting profits and accounting rates of return may be of surprisingly little help in estimating economic worth. As Edwards, Kay and Mayer (1987) note: 'Much of the economics literature is ... very pessimistic about the applicability of accounting information to economic analysis.'

More recently, a series of papers by Ohlson has investigated the relationship between accounting earnings, book values and return. The Ohlson analysis is useful in that it shows that, over the life of the firm, accounting return equals economic return. The problem is that the Ohlson framework assumes 'clean surplus' accounting (which means that all changes in asset values flow through the P&L account, something which does not occur in UK accounting at present). Furthermore, there is nothing in the Ohlson analysis which shows that in any individual year economic return equates with accounting return.

A detailed explanation of the relationship between accounting rates of return, economic rates of return and firm value is beyond the scope of this briefing, but an excellent introduction to the topic can be found in O'Hanlon and Rees (1995). However, in this section, we look at this issue using some simple examples to illustrate the main points;[9] for simplicity we shall ignore the effect of taxation throughout but discuss the implications of taxation at the end of our analysis. In the next chapter, the examples below are used to illustrate the various metrics used in shareholder value based approaches to valuation.

5.7.1 The single investment case

The following information relates to Tamar plc, a single-product company. Initially, assume no inflation, no gearing and an equity cost of capital of 10% and that the product is made using a piece of machinery costing £400 000 which needs to be replaced every four years (assume that the machinery is worthless at the end of this period). Further assume that net cash inflows are £130 000 p.a. and will continue at that level for the foreseeable future. Tamar plc has just replaced the machinery in question.

The value of each of Tamar plc's investment decisions is simply:

$$\text{NPV (£000)} = \frac{130}{1.1} + \frac{130}{1.1^2} + \frac{130}{1.1^3} + \frac{130}{1.1^4} = +12.082$$

The firm can be valued by calculating the annual equivalent cash flow that this represents, given that the firm will reinvest in such equipment every four years. The annual equivalent (AE) can be found from:

$$\text{AE (£000)} = \frac{\text{NPV}}{\text{4yr, 10\% annuity factor [3.1699]}} = 3.812$$

As this is the annual equivalent each year to perpetuity, it follows that the NPV of the firm into perpetuity is 3.812/0.10 = £38.120. To find the value of the firm, add this to the capital just invested to replace the machine, giving a value (the gross present value) of £438.12(000).

The first question which arises is what is the return on this new investment? Clearly, if a conventional accounting definition of profit is used with straight line depreciation, the accounting rate of return will rise each year as the asset base falls. The average accounting rate of return (AARR) will be:

$$\text{AARR} = \frac{\text{Average profit (cash flow – depreciation)}}{\text{Mid-life book value of machinery}} = 15.0\%$$

This figure turns out to be of no real help in valuation, because AARR and any other accounting-based return measure ignores the time value of money. A more fruitful way of approaching the problem is to ask what return the shareholders expect and how this relates to the new investment. Given that the company has constant cash flows, no growth opportunities and needs only to retain sufficient cash to reinvest in asset replacement, surplus cash can be paid out as dividends in which case the value of the firm remains constant.

As shareholders require a 10% return, and since the firm is valued at £438 120, this implies a required dividend of £43 812 p.a. if the market value of the firm is to remain constant. This equates to a return on new investment of £43 812/£400 000 which is equivalent to 10.95%. This is not the AARR; neither is it the internal rate of return.[10] Note also that since the investment pattern is not constant, it is not possible to use the accounting earnings figure of £30 000 p.a. (calculated using straight line depreciation) in any meaningful sense in the valuation process.[11]

As a side issue, the dividend payment can also be calculated by working out how much cash needs to be reinvested each year in order to yield the £400 000 replacement cost of the equipment in year 4. This is found by dividing £400 000 by the future value of a four-year annuity at 10% p.a., or £400 000/4.641 = £86 188. The cash available for the dividend, net of this amount, is therefore £130 000 − £86 188 = £43 812 that the shareholders require to give a fair return.[12]

5.7.2 Multiple investment projects

In general, the multiple project case involving 'lumpy' investment flows can be solved by extending the above analysis. However, the aim here is to show when the accounting rate of return *might* be useful for the purposes of valuing a business. Essentially, the accounting rate of return is only of use where investment flows are not lumpy in nature, the cash flows from such projects are constant (at least in real terms) and where the returns on all projects are similar. In order to illustrate this, suppose that Tamar plc expands each year by adopting a similar project until the end of year 3, when the expansion programme is complete. The cash flows, in £000s, will now be:

		Yr 0	Yr 1	Yr 2	Yr 3	Yr 4	Yr ...
(1)	Investment	400	400	400	400	400	400
(2)	Inflows		130	260	390	520	520
(3)	FCF (2 − 1)	−400	−270	−140	−10	120	120
(4)	Depreciation		100	200	300	400	400
(5)	Profit (2 − 4)		30	60	90	120	120

The value of the firm can now be calculated in one of two ways. First, using the 'continuous replication' model described above, the perpetual value of each project, continually replicated, is £38 120 in year 0 terms. One of these is added each year until year 3, giving an NPV of:

$$\text{NPV of firm} = 38\,120 + \frac{38\,120}{1.1} + \frac{38\,120}{1.1^2} + \frac{38\,120}{1.1^3} = 132\,910$$

Adding this to the £400 000 year 0 cost gives us the gross PV of £532 908, which is the year 0 value of the firm. Alternatively, the same result can be obtained by discounting the FCF figures for each year to perpetuity. (This process is made easier by realising that the value of the firm in year 3 and – and beyond – will be £1.2 million, the present value of a perpetual £120 000 free cash flow from year 4 onwards.)

The *accounting* rate of return from year 4 onwards will be given by the profit figure of £120 000 divided by the opening net book value of the assets, £1 million (the assets purchased over the previous four years will have net book values of £400 000, £300 000, £200 000 and £100 000 in ascending order of age); this figure now remains constant at 12%. Unless there is any future growth, there is no role for such a rate of return anyway, since all earnings are paid out as dividends. However, there is a role for the accounting profits figure since we can use the 'zero NPV model' (or, more correctly in this case, a zero growth model). As we have seen, this type of analysis could be used to give a horizon value. Since a steady state exists from year 4 onwards, the year 3 horizon value is:

$$V_3 = \text{Earnings/WACC} = 120/0.1 = £1200 \; (£000)$$

This is the same as the present value of cash flows to perpetuity.

However, so far the important questions of growth and inflation have been ignored.

5.7.3 The multiple investment project firm with growth

Extend the above example further by assuming that from the end of year 5 onwards Tamar plc invests its £400 000 in new projects but expands this investment by 3.75% p.a. thereafter. The cash flows on these new investments are proportionate to those received on existing projects. All this produces the cash flows and profits shown in Table 5.2 (note that from year 9 onwards the firm has a steady rate of expansion).

Table 5.2 Tamar plc: cash flows and profits

End of year	Investment	6	7	8	9	10	11	12
Initial investment		*Cash inflows in year (£000)*						
2	400.00	130						
3	400.00	130	130.00					
4	400.00	130	130.00	130.00				
5	400.00	130	130.00	130.00	130.00			
6	415.00		134.88	134.88	134.88	134.88		
7	430.56			139.93	139.93	139.93	139.93	
8	446.71				145.18	145.18	145.18	145.18
9	463.46					150.62	150.62	150.62
10	480.84						156.27	156.27
11	498.87							162.13
12	517.58							
Total cash inflow		520	524.88	534.81	549.99	570.61	592.01	614.21
Total new investment		415	430.56	446.71	463.46	480.84	498.87	517.58
FCF		105	94.31	88.10	86.53	89.77	93.14	96.63
Growth in FCF			−10.18%	−6.59%	−1.78%	3.75%	3.75%	3.75%
Depreciation		400	403.75	411.39	423.07	438.93	455.39	472.47
Earnings		120	121.13	123.42	126.92	131.68	136.62	141.74
Growth in earnings			0.94%	1.89%	2.84%	3.75%	3.75%	3.75%

Notes

1. Depreciation is calculated on a straight line basis on the assets owned at the beginning of the year.
2. All asset purchases and operating cash flows are assumed to occur on the last day of the year.
3. All disposals of written-down assets occur on the last day of the year.

From this we can deduce several things. First, the firm is actually in a 'steady state' of growth from year 9 onwards. Second, using the FCF growth formula, we can value the company at, say, the end of year 10 as:

$$V_{10} = \frac{FCF_{11}}{WACC - g} = \frac{93.14}{0.10 - 0.0375} = 1490.23 \; (\pounds000)$$

The accounting book value of the new assets at the beginning of year 10 is found by calculating the net book value of each of the four assets, in £000s, as follows:

Gross BV of opening assets	1755.73
Accumulated dep'n on opening assets	638.21
NBV of opening assets	1117.52

The year 10 profit is £(000) 131.68 so that the accounting rate of return on the new investment is 131.68/1117.52 = 0.1178 or 11.78%. (Note that because of the year end cash flow assumption behind NPV, consistent accounting rates of return can only be found by using opening book values.)

It should also be possible to arrive at a year 10 value for the new investment projects by using the price-earnings multiple formula discussed in Chapter 3.

Inserting the relevant numbers gives:

$$PE = \frac{1 - 0.0375/0.1178}{0.10 - 0.0375} = 10.91$$

As this is a prospective PE ratio, it must be applied to the forecast year 11 earnings to give the year 10 valuation. Doing so gives:

$$V_{10} = 10.91 \times 136.62 = 1490.23 \ (\pounds 000)$$

Note, however, that this only works with constant rates of growth, cash flow and asset replacement. Finally, this horizon value can be discounted back to year 0 and added to the present value of the year 1 to 10 cash flows.

5.7.4 The growth case with inflation

Suppose that from the end of year 5, a consistent rate of inflation of 5% p.a. occurs; inflation continues at this level to perpetuity. A recalculation of the above numbers gives the accounting earnings, investments and cash flows shown in Table 5.3.

Table 5.3 Tamar plc: recalculation of cash flows and profits

End of year	Initial investment Investment	Cash inflows in year (£000) 6	7	8	9	10	11	12
2	400.00	136.50						
3	400.00	136.50	143.33					
4	400.00	136.50	143.33	150.49				
5	400.00	136.50	143.33	150.49	158.02			
6	435.75		148.70	156.13	163.94	172.14		
7	474.70			161.99	170.09	178.59	187.52	
8	517.12				176.47	185.29	194.56	204.28
9	563.34					192.24	201.85	211.94
10	613.69						209.42	219.89
11	668.54							228.14
12	728.29							
Total cash inflow		546	578.67	619.11	668.51	728.26	793.35	864.26
Total new inv.		435.75	474.70	517.12	563.34	613.69	668.54	728.29
FCF		110.25	103.98	101.99	105.18	114.58	124.82	135.97
Growth in FCF			−5.69%	−1.92%	3.13%	8.94%	8.94%	8.94%
Depreciation		400	408.94	427.61	456.89	497.73	542.21	590.67
Earnings		146	169.74	191.50	211.62	230.54	251.14	273.59
Growth in earnings			16.26%	12.82%	10.51%	8.94%	8.94%	8.94%

First, note that none of this poses any problems for the FCF growth model, provided a true steady state has been reached. This still occurs in year 9, since the replacement cost of the assets is automatically reflected in the FCF figure. Growth is now at the nominal rate of 8.94% p.a. (3.75% in real terms) and the nominal cost of capital is now 15.5% p.a.[13] This gives a horizon value of the company in year 10 of:

$$V_{10} = \frac{124.82}{0.155 - 0.0894} = 1901.95 \ (\pounds 000)$$

In year 5 price levels, this is equivalent to the value calculated above. However, if we now take our earnings figure and attempt to derive a PE ratio on the basis of year 9 or year 10 data, the result will be compatible with that obtained by the FCF model but *only* because the rate of inflation has been constant. In general, if the accounting book values and depreciation charges reflect a number of different rates of inflation, (for example 0% and 5%, as in year 7) it will not be possible to derive a PE ratio compatible with a FCF valuation. However, once the point is reached where a *constant* inflation rate has uniformly affected all asset and depreciation figures,[14] then a PE multiple can be successfully applied. Taking year 10 as a point where this is possible, the net book values of the assets are:

Gross BV of opening assets	1990.90
Accumulated dep'n on opening assets	693.44
NBV of opening assets	1297.46

This implies an accounting rate of return of 230.54/1297.46, which is equivalent to 17.77%. Applying this to the PE formula produces the following ratio:

$$PE = \frac{1 - 0.0894/0.1777}{0.155 - 0.0894} = 7.75$$

We can now value the company in year 10 by applying this PE multiple to the prospective (year 11) earnings:

$$V_{10} = 7.57 \times 251.54 = 1901.95 \ (\text{£}000)^{15}$$

It is also worth noting that inflation has the effect of increasing the retention rate since replacement cost is greater than that provided for with historic cost depreciation.

Finally, note the fact that the PE approach only works if a consistent inflation rate is experienced throughout the life of all the assets held *and* during the horizon value period. The alternative, if a PE methodology is to be used, is to restate all asset values and depreciation charges in horizon period price levels to give a real earnings figure, and then carry out the exercise using a real RONI, RE and *g* to give an appropriate multiple of real terms. This is generally the safer approach to apply, although there is a need to know the age structure of the assets in order to estimate the inflation-adjusted horizon depreciation and asset value figures.

5.7.5 Conclusions on the use of accounting numbers in the valuation process

In general, numbers derived from accounting data can only be used where the investment flows are constant. This has important implications for the 'shareholder value' models described in the next chapter. Constant rates of growth, inflation and returns on new investment are also necessary. The latter group of requirements constitute the standard assumptions of most of the horizon valuation methods (including, implicitly, the 'traditional' PE approach) and as such may not be unreasonable. However, the requirement that investment flows be constant may cause difficulties. While both the growth opportunities and continuous replication models can cope with the situation where growth is not constant, those which rely upon accounting data inputs cannot. In this respect, it is should also be noted that with the growth opportunities model some care is needed in defining RONI.

The good news is that it appears that the circumstances under which accounting numbers are of most use are those that are often assumed to apply beyond the explicit forecast horizon. The bad news is that such a situation will almost certainly *not* have applied to any historic periods which may have been under review when preparing the forecast. Empirical results on whether such historic numbers are of any use in predicting economic value are somewhat lacking, but a study by Kelly and Tippett (1991) suggests that the accounting rate of return 'is a potentially poor proxy for the future economic return'. The further bad news is that to make any sense of the accounting numbers it is necessary to know the age structure of the assets themselves. This is not a problem for a valuation being conducted with access to internal information, but it is so for an 'external' valuation. The best that can be done is to look back through past annual reports in order to try and establish past patterns of asset replacement and the likely age of the assets. This approach is described in detail in the next chapter.

5.8 TAXATION AND HORIZON VALUES

In those horizon models which assume growth, we need to consider the impact of taxation. The continuous replication model automatically does this provided that the cash flows considered are those that arise after tax. In the case of the FCF growth and the PE multiple models, the steady-state period must be set in such a way as to ensure that it is the after-tax cash flows which are expanding at a constant rate. Where writing-down allowances are less than 100% p.a. and assets are retained for a long period of time, this can necessitate the specific forecasting of cash flows for some time into the future.

5.9 VALUING THE SBU

So far in this chapter, the following have been estimated:

- a set of cash flows for the specific forecast period;
- a horizon valuation;
- depending on the methodology chosen, possibly a transition period forecast as well.

The next step is to discount these values at the WACC for the SBU and sum them.

Ideally, the model would be extended to produce the forecast profit and loss accounts and balance sheets at each year end. An important reason for producing such forecast accounting statements is to serve as consistency and logic checks on the process.

Finally, it is always useful to perform a sensitivity analysis or 'scenario modelling' exercise. All the key variables or value drivers should be analysed in this way. Where there is a mixture of growth opportunities and existing business (as in the case of Tamar plc), each has to be analysed separately in order to examine the effect of changes on value.

In the case of multi-line business entities interactions between business areas in particular the question of covariance must be considered when performing any sensitivity or scenario analysis at company level.

5.10 VALUING THE BUSINESS

Having valued the SBU and analysed the sensitivity of the value to changes in the key variables, it is a relatively simple step to value the firm as a whole.

First, the value of the firm is the sum of the present values of the individual component SBUs, or their disposable values (appropriately discounted and with full allowance for selling costs) if these are greater than such going concern values. Note that, as regards the correlation of cash flows between different SBUs, whilst this affects the probability distribution of values, the *expected* present value of the firm will simply be the sum of the present values of each SBU.

Second, we need to add in the value of any *financial* assets owned by the business. Discounted FCFs at the WACC properly values the operational aspects of the company but any items like trade investments, cash invested in government bonds and so on will not have been included. If capital markets are largely price efficient, the appropriate value for such financial assets will be their current market value.

Finally, it is often the case that the value of *equity* is needed rather than the value of the firm as a whole. The financing structure of the firm simply divides up the value of the firm between various claimants, so that the value of the equity is the total value of the firm less the value of the other claims, such as debt, convertibles and preference shares.

Contemporary methods for operationalising the FCF method

6.1 INTRODUCTION

Ideally, all valuations made should feature an explicit forecast of free cash flows for the longest period feasible, and certainly until a 'steady state' occurs, as described in the previous chapter. Once this steady state can be assumed to exist, the horizon valuation methods explained can be applied.

Unfortunately, the preparation of FCF forecasts is onerous and only really practicable with access to internal information. This has provided an incentive for consultancy firms to develop packages which adopt what are essentially short-cut methods to generate such forecasts. In principle, these methods make use of information available from either the published financial statements or internal financial records in the case of, say, an SBU analysis or a management buyout.

These packages can also be linked to 'shareholder value' or 'value based management' techniques through the use of value drivers. For example, the ALCAR package uses value drivers to build up cash flow forecasts, and Rappaport (one of the founders of ALCAR) links each of the value drivers to a cost leadership strategy.[1]

In broad terms, the packages on offer use one of two methods of estimating value. Either they use accounting data derived from the balance sheets and profit and loss account to calculate some concept of 'economic profit', or they use cash flow data in conjunction with asset values to infer a cash flow return.

The 'economic profit' type model essentially does the following:

- takes the accounting profit;
- deducts from this a capital charge (this is the required return (WACC) $\times$ the net operating assets);
- capitalises the surplus or deficit using the WACC;
- adds this capitalised surplus or deficit to the net operating assets to give the value of the enterprise's operations.

This basic concept has been around in the academic literature for years, and is known as 'residual income'. Academic authors such as Edwards and Bell, Peasnell and Ohlson have explained the rational link between 'economic profit' or 'residual income', book asset values and firm value. More recently, valuation packages based upon the residual income model have been marketed by Stern Stewart & Co. under the registered trade mark 'EVA®', or 'Economic Value Added'.

The alternative approach is to map cash flow data onto balance sheet information to calculate what is sometimes termed the 'cash flow return on investment' (CFROI), which is simply the IRR of the firm's investment set. This is then used in the valuation. Valuation packages using this metric have been marketed by the Boston Consulting Group and by Holt Value Associates®/Braxton Associates. The basics of this type of cash flow return (CFR) model are as follows:

- Take the cash from operations figure, before working capital investment.
- Take the gross book value of the fixed assets and net working capital required to generate these cash flows.
- Estimate the average life of the fixed assets.
- From the above, estimate the internal rate of return (called 'CFR').
- Calculate the difference between CFR and the WACC.
- Capitalise this difference at the WACC.
- Add this capitalised surplus or deficit to the net operating assets to give the value of the enterprise's operations.

Naively applied, both models suffer from the inherent weakness of assuming that current or past performance is a guide to future performance. However, in focusing upon value drivers, the models can help in identifying key areas where management can take action to add value to the company.

Both models are potentially affected by the weaknesses of historic cost accounting. Because of this, both require adjustments to the profit and loss and balance sheet items reported using conventional accounting techniques.

To illustrate the problems which potentially affect these models, the analysis below makes extensive use of the example of Tamar plc used in the previous chapter. Note that the models described are representative of the *general* types of approach and are *not* intended as detailed examples of any actual valuation models in current use. Having explained the models by way of this illustration, they are then applied to the case example of British Vita plc.

6.2 RESIDUAL INCOME OR EP MODELS AND CFR EXPLAINED

The basic case of the EP model simply charges operating profit with a capital charge equal to the WACC multiplied by the net operating assets. CFR works by inferring an asset life from the accounting data and calculating the IRR implied on the initial investment. To illustrate how this is done, and to show the weaknesses of the models if appropriate adjustments are not made, the following analyses are made using the example of Tamar plc (*see* Chapter 5):

- single investment project case;
- multiple investment (constant rate per annum);
- multiple investment with growth;
- multiple investment with growth and inflation.

6.2.1 The single investment project case

> **EXAMPLE**
>
> Tamar plc – initially, assume no inflation, no gearing and an equity cost of capital of 10%, and that the product is made using a piece of machinery costing £400 000 which needs to be replaced every four years (assume that the machinery is worthless at the end of this period). Net cash inflows are £130 000 p.a. and will continue at that level for the foreseeable future. Tamar plc has just replaced the machinery in question. From the analysis in the previous chapter, the rational value of the firm is £438 120.

The EP model

First, the EP model is illustrated (see Table 6.1). In the case of Tamar plc, the simplifying assumption of no working capital investment was made. In the more realistic case where there is working capital investment, net current operating assets would be added on to the fixed assets when calculating the capital charge.

Table 6.1 Application of the EP model – single asset case (all figures in £000s)

	Item	Year 1	Year 2	Year 3	Year 4
1	Operating cash flow	130	130	130	130
2	Depreciation	100	100	100	100
3	Operating income (1) − (2)	30	30	30	30
4	Opening net book value	400	300	200	100
5	Return on ONBV (3)/(4)	7.5%	10%	15%	30%
6	Capital charge on ONBV 10% 3 (4)	40	30	20	10
7	Economic profit or residual income (3) − (6)	−10	0	10	20
8	Capitalised residual income (7)/0.10	−100	0	100	200
9	Financial asset − Cash balances at year end	86.19	180.99	285.28	400
10	Implied value of firm CNBV[(4)−(2)] + (8) + (9)	286.19	380.99	485.28	600

Notes

1. As in Chapter 5, it is assumed that sufficient cash is retained each year, which, when invested at an assumed 10%, generates the £400 000 replacement cost of the asset in year 4.
2. The balance of the FCF, £43 812 p.a., is paid out as dividend.

141

The calculations are straightforward. Economic profit (EP) is calculated net of the capital charge. This EP is capitalised into perpetuity by dividing the EP by the WACC (in general, if surplus EP is expected to decline over time, the EP would simply be discounted for the appropriate number of years at the WACC). This capitalised value is added to the ONBV of the operating assets. If financial assets were owned, these would be added to this calculated operating market value to give the enterprise value.

As can be seen, EP suffers from a major problem, which is generalisable to any case where investment replacement patterns are uneven. EP rises over time, as assets age. This is because the capital charge is levied on the net book value (NBV) of the assets,[2] which under the conventional application of straight line accounting depreciation declines over the life of the asset (the problem is amplified if reducing balance depreciation is used). If no adjustment is made in such circumstances, we have the absurd result that in general the capitalised EP will be negative for the early years of the replacement cycle, and positive in the later years. As the EP model capitalises the EP at the WACC and adds this to the NBV of the operating assets, the EP model miscalculates the fair value of the firm, which given a constant dividend payout policy and constant replication of the investment cycle, must logically remain constant at £438 120 (*see* Chapter 5 for an explanation).

In fact, this problem is well known in accounting theory and in the management accounting literature, where the residual income (RI) model was developed. The problem can be difficult to solve, depending on the complexity of the investment cycle and the cycle cash flows, but various different solutions have been suggested to ensure that RI/EP can give the correct signals about project value and management incentives.[3] In the simple case of a single investment project with constant annual cash flows, the problem is easily solved – an alternative depreciation method known as *annuity depreciation* can be used.

Annuity depreciation is easily calculated by taking the annual equivalent cost of the asset and deducting from that an implied capital charge on the ONBV of the asset:

$$\text{Annual equivalent cost} \quad = \quad \frac{\text{Asset cost} - \text{PV of scrap value}}{\text{Annuity factor (life of asset, } r\%)}$$

$$\text{Annuity depreciation} = \text{Annual equivalent cost} - r\% \times \text{ONBV of asset}$$

In the case of Tamar plc, the annuity factor is for four years at 10% (3.1699), and the annual equivalent cost is therefore £400 000/3.1699 = £126 188.

Applying annuity depreciation to the example yields the following result shown in Table 6.2.

Table 6.2 Application of the EP model with the annuity depreciation (all figures in £s)

	Item	Year 1	Year 2	Year 3	Year 4
1	Operating cash flow	130 000	130 000	130 000	130 000
2	Annuity depreciation	86 188	94 807	104 288	114 717
3	Operating income (1) − (2)	43 812	35 193	25 712	15 283
4	Opening net book value	400 000	313 812	219 005	114 717
5	Return on ONBV (3)/(4)	10.95%	11.21%	11.74%	13.32%
6	Capital charge on ONBV 10% × (4)	40 000	31 381	21 900	11 472
7	Economic profit or residual income (3) − (6)	3 812	3 812	3 812	3 812
8	Capitalised residual income (7)/0.10	38 120	38 120	38 120	38 120
9	Financial asset − Cash balances at year end	86 188	180 995	285 283	400 000
10	Implied value of firm CNBV[(4) − (2)] + (8) + (9)	438 120	438 120	438 120	438 120

Notes

1. As in Chapter 5, it is assumed that sufficient cash is retained each year, which, when invested at an assumed 10%, generates the £400 000 replacement cost of the asset in year 4.
2. The balance of the FCF, £43 812 p.a., is paid out as dividend.

The major result from this is that the EP model is capable of giving the theoretically correct value of the firm *but only if an unusual (although acceptable under GAAP) depreciation method is used.* Firms in general do not use this method – nor is it possible to recalculate the depreciation charge on an annuity basis without detailed knowledge of asset lives and scrap values. This requires access to the internal records of the company. Furthermore, annuity depreciation does not yield the desirable result above unless investment cash flows are constant, at least in real terms.

The CFR model

Unlike the EP model, the CFR model is cash flow rather than accounting profits based. It does not therefore suffer in quite the same way if (as is quite likely) straight line depreciation is used in preparing the financial statements. Paradoxically, the use of straight line depreciation is of some advantage in the CFR model as it allows a rough estimate of the asset life to be arrived at by simply dividing the gross book value (GBV) of the assets by the annual depreciation charge. While this will be totally accurate in the case of Tamar plc, in general it will be an approximation because of problems caused by non-constant rates of asset replacement, inflation and the fact that companies in practice may retain fully written-down assets.

The first step in the calculation is the estimation of this asset life. Taking GBV divided by the annual depreciation charge for any individual year yields 400/100 = 4 years as the life estimate. Next, the assumption is made that on a four-year cycle basis the GBV is invested to yield the annual operating cash flow. In this case, the implication is that the cash flows are −£400 000 initially, followed by inflows of £130 000 p.a. The CFR model works by computing the IRR on this investment (i.e. finding the rate of return which equates the NPV on this investment to zero). The IRR is 11.39%, which the model terms 'cash flow return on investment' or CFR. Note that if working capital investment is required, it is treated as an outflow at the beginning of the investment cycle, with subsequent recovery at the end.

The next step is the calculation of the 'spread', or the difference between the CFR and the WACC; this is simply 11.39% − 10%, or 1.39%. In the CFR model this is the surplus earned on the assets over and above that required by the shareholders.

This 'spread' is now multiplied by the GBV of the assets and capitalised. As in the case of the EP model, this spread is assumed to last into perpetuity in the case of Tamar plc, but in general can be assumed to last for a limited number of years and discounted appropriately. This gives a capitalised value of:

$$\frac{(11.39\% - 10\%) \times 400\,000}{0.10} = £55\,600$$

The final step is to add this capitalised value to the CNBV of the assets. This gives a value of:

$$(£400\,000 - £100\,000 \text{ dep'n}) + £55\,600 + £86\,188^* = £441\,788 \text{ for year 1}$$
$$^* \text{ Financial assets calculated as above}$$

This value is above the theoretically correct value of the firm in year 1. Why is this the case?

The answer is that, like any IRR-based calculation, the implicit assumption is that surplus cash flows can be reinvested at the IRR. In the previous chapter, we assumed that surplus cash was in fact invested at the WACC of 10%; furthermore, we explicitly assumed no expansion, and constant replication, the implication being that it will be quite impossible to earn the IRR on surplus cash.

How important this problem is in practice will depend upon the actual bundle of projects the company has available and the CFR spread. Since economic theory predicts diminishing marginal returns on projects, it might reasonably be expected that reinvestment will be at lower rates of return than implied by the IRR or CFR.

Following the calculation for years 2–4 inclusive yields a CFR value for the firm of:

Year 2:

(£300 000 − £100 000 dep'n) + £55 600 + £180 995* = £436 995

*Financial assets calculated as above

Year 3:

(£200 000 − £100 000 dep'n) + £55 600 + £285 283* = £440 883

* Financial assets calculated as above

Year 4:

(£100 000 − £100 000 dep'n) + £55 600 + £400 000* = £455 600

* Financial assets calculated as above

Thus CFR valuations are affected to a limited (though not serious, compared to the EP method) extent by the use of straight line depreciation. Using annuity depreciation, the value is constant each year. For example, the first year valuation is:

Year 1:

(£400 000 − £86 188 dep'n) + £55 600 + £86 188* = £455 600

* Financial assets calculated as above

Finally, note that the implicit assumption of the way CFR has been calculated is that cash flows are constant throughout the life of the investment. If this is not the case, the estimated CFR is likely to be a biased estimate of the true IRR the firm owns on its fixed asset investment. In practice, both CFR and EP models would try and mitigate the effects of non-constant cash flows by looking at trends in CFR/EP over time. Even so, misleading conclusions might be drawn if the pattern of flows over the investment and trade cycles was not clearly understood.

6.2.2 The multiple investment case

As was seen in the previous chapter, the multiple investment case with constant rate of investments is the situation in which accounting-based measures of return are likely to yield the most promising results. As such, we might expect both EP and CFR models to perform well in such circumstances. These are essentially the very least challenging conditions for either of these models. Given this, because they work well, it does *not* imply that they are likely to be successful in all circumstances.

Again, as in the previous section, the two models are compared by using the second example of Tamar plc.

EXAMPLE

Tamar plc now expands each year by adopting a similar project until the end of year 3, when the expansion programme is complete. The value of the firm from year 3 onwards is now £1.2 million, as explained in Chapter 5

Given that the firm only reaches a steady state at the end of year 3, the firm will be valued using year 4 data in all cases.

The EP model

The EP model is illustrated in Table 6.3.

Table 6.3 Application of the EP model – multiple asset case (all figures in £000s)

	Item	Year 4
1	Operating cash flow	520
2	Depreciation	400
3	Operating income (1) − (2)	120
4	Opening net book value	1000
5	Return on ONBV (3)/(4)	12%
6	Capital charge on ONBV 10% × (4)	100
7	Economic profit or residual income (3) − (6)	20
8	Capitalised residual income (7)/0.10	200
9	Implied value of firm £1000 + (8)	1200

Note: In the case of constant replacement, the depreciation each year exactly covers the purchase of the next asset. Financial assets at each year end are therefore zero, and all FCF (which is equal to EP) is distributed as dividend.

In this case the EP model has valued the firm at its theoretical value of £1.2 m. Note also that even if annuity depreciation had been used, the result would have been identical. This is because with constant rates of asset replacement, the effects of differing depreciation policies cancel each other out.

The CFR model

As above, the asset life is calculated as GBV/Annual depreciation = 1600/400 = 4 years.

The investment pattern is still calculated by reference to the GBV of the assets and the operating cash flows. Thus the cash flow patterns are assumed to be the investment of £1.6 m at the start of the four-year cycle, with cash generation of £520 000 p.a. for four years. As before, this yields an IRR (CFR) of 11.39%.

Capitalising this 'spread' multiplied by the GBV of the assets (£1.6 m) yields:

$$\text{Capitalised 'spread'} \quad = \quad \frac{(11.39\% - 10\%) \times £1.6\text{ m}}{10\%} \quad = \quad £222\,400$$

Adding this to the value of the CNBV of the firm yields an estimated value of £1.224 m, which marginally overestimates the true value of the firm. Again, this is because of the implicit reinvestment assumption made in the IRR calculation. The CFR model assumes all the future receipts from the project are reinvested at the firm's IRR. In fact, only the retained cash flows (£400 000 p.a.) are actually reinvested at this rate. The balance, £120 000, is paid out to the shareholders as a dividend. The implied opportunity cost of capital on this element is therefore 10% p.a.

6.2.3 The multiple investment project firm with growth

In the previous chapter, we explained the impact of growth on the valuation by extending the Tamar example further by assuming that from the end of year 5 onwards Tamar plc invested its £400 000 in new projects but expanded this investment by 3.75% p.a. thereafter. The cash flows on these new investments were assumed to be proportionate to those received on existing projects. This produced a valuation of £1 490 230 at the end of year 10.

As year 10 was chosen as the point where the firm was in a 'steady state', both EP and CFR calculations are made as at the end of that year. In order to provide some background to the calculations which follow, the GBV and NBV of the assets is first calculated for years 10 and 11 (see previous chapter for detailed figures) as shown in Table 6.4.

Table 6.4 Calculation of GBV and NBV (all figures in £000s)

	Item	Year 10	Year 11
1	Gross BV of opening assets	1755.73	1821.57
2	Accumulated dep'n on opening assets	638.21	662.14
3	NBV of opening assets	1117.52	1159.43
4	Depreciation provided	438.93	455.39
5	Estimated life (1)/(4)	4	4
6	Accumulated dep'n on closing assets	662.14	686.97
7	Estimated average age (6)/(4)	1.5	1.5

The EP model

In the 'with growth' case, the EP has to be capitalised in a way which allows for growth in this variable over time. As in earlier chapters, the basic formula for valuing a cash flow with constant growth into perpetuity is:

$$\text{Value at time } t = \frac{\text{Cash flow (in this case, EP) at time } t+1}{\text{WACC} - \text{Growth}}$$

In the case example of Tamar, growth in cash flows and assets was 3.75% p.a. If the valuation is being carried out at the end of year 10, the EP for year 11 therefore needs to be estimated in the capitalisation calculation (*see* Table 6.5).

Table 6.5 The EP model with growth (all figures in £000s)

Economic profit valuation	Year 10	Year 11
Capital charge on ONBV @ 10%	111.7523	115.943
Economic profit	19.93	20.67
Growth in EP		3.75%
Capitalised EP (Year 11 EP / (0.10 − 0.0375)	330.7975	
CNBV of assets	1159.43	
Value = CNBV + Capitalised EP	1490.23	

Thus the EP model gives the correct valuation in the case of a company with constant investment rates and constant growth.

The CFR model

As in the case of the EP model, the spread needs to be capitalised including a growth term. The capitalisation calculation uses the same formula given above for the EP capitalisation (*see* Table 6.6).

Table 6.6	CFR valuation model with growth		
		Year 10	*Year 11*
IRR		11.39%	11.39%
Spread		1.39%	1.39%
Spread × OGBV assets		25.28	26.23
Growth in spread			3.75%
Growth in gross assets		3.75%	3.75%
Capitalised spread		404.51	
Value (Capitalised spread + Net assets)		1563.94	

As before in the constant investment case, the CFR model overestimates the true value of the firm. Again, this is because of the implicit reinvestment assumption made in the IRR calculation. In general, the CFR model will always overestimate the value of firms where the IRR > WACC, and underestimate those where the IRR < WACC.

The overvaluation will be more serious when:

- growth is particularly high, relative to the WACC;

- IRR is high relative to the WACC;

- the assumed period for which positive NPVs can be earned on new investments is long.[4]

6.2.4 The multiple investment project firm with growth and inflation

Unless appropriate adjustments are made to asset values, both EP and CFR models will perform badly in the presence of inflation. In descriptions of the CFROI model, Madden (1996) describes how gross and net assets are adjusted for inflation. There is less public information on how EVA® handles inflation, although a recent article in *CFO Europe* claims that both models involve 'arbitrary adjustments' to the reported accounts and notes that

> Stern Stewart [the owners of the EVA® trademark] recommends anything up to 164 modifications – such as adding spending on R&D and marketing back to the balance sheet on the ground that this creates value and so should be treated as an asset.

In fact, it turns out that provided the rate of inflation is constant throughout the life of the assets (something that in practice seems a highly unrealistic assumption) the EP model does not need adjusting for inflation. The CFR model does, but unless the *actual* asset purchase pattern is known, the real CFR will be estimated with error. This is important as some analysts apparently estimate the inflation adjustment using an assumed average age of the assets (*see* below).

The 'with growth and inflation' case is the final version of the Tamar plc example. The relevant figures are given on p. 133 of Chapter 5. These were the data assumed in section 6.2.3 above (i.e. with real growth of 3.75% p.a. and a real WACC of 10%), but inflation is now assumed to occur at the rate of 5% p.a. from year 5 onwards.

Summary data for the analysis, assuming this inflation level, are given in Table 6.7.

Table 6.7 Summary data for analysis of EP and CFR with growth and inflation

	Item	Year 10	Year 11
1	Gross BV of opening assets	1990.90	2168.84
2	Accumulated dep'n on opening assets	693.44	755.42
3	NBV of opening assets	1297.46	1413.43
4	Depreciation provided	497.73	542.21
5	Estimated life (1)/(4)	4	4
6	Accumulated dep'n on closing assets	755.42	822.93
7	Estimated average age (6)/(4)	1.52	1.52

The estimate of average age is not necessary unless adjustment for inflation is being considered. However, note that the impact of growth and inflation has a distorting effect on the age estimate. Given the assumption of year end asset replacement, the true ages of the four assets are respectively 0, 1, 2 and 3 years; this is an average of 1.5 years. The approximation used above results in an estimate of 1.52 years. The consequences of this are discussed below.

The EP model

The EP model is set out in nominal terms. That is, the actual historic cost balance sheet and profit and loss figures are used, but the WACC is now calculated in nominal terms. From the explanation in Chapter 4, we have the following relationship:

$$(1 + WACC_{nominal}) = (1 + WACC_{real}) \times (1 + Inflation)$$

Thus Tamar's WACC in nominal terms is:

$$(1.1 \times 1.05) - 1 = 0.155 \text{ or } 15.5\%$$

Applying this to the Tamar plc data gives Table 6.8.

Table 6.8 Economic profit valuation with growth and inflation

	Year 10	Year 11
Capital charge on ONBV @ 15.5%	201.11	219.0809
Economic profit	29.43	32.06
Growth in EP		8.94%
Capitalised EP (Year 11 EP/(0.155 − 0.0894))	488.5243	
CNBV of assets	1413.43	
Value = CNBV + Capitalised EP	1901.95	

Thus the EP valuation in year 10 agrees with the theoretical correct value worked out for Tamar plc of £1 901 950 in Chapter 5. However, if the rate of inflation or asset growth is not constant over time, the EP method will not produce such a congruent result.

The CFR model

The CFR model attempts to get around the problem of inflation by re-estimating the book values of the assets using an estimate of asset age and inflation. Note that in the UK, non-depreciating assets (freehold land and possibly buildings) are generally valued at current market values. Depreciable assets generally are not – it is therefore this second group that needs to be adjusted in value. This can be done in one of two ways. In the first instance, an approximation can be used based upon the average age of the assets and an average rate of inflation.

Applying this approach to the Tamar example yields a restated opening gross book value of assets of:

Original OGBV	×	$(1 + \text{Average inflation})^{\text{Average asset age}}$	
1990.9	×	$(1.05)^{1.52}$	= 2143.93 (£000s)

This is the *opening* value, i.e. it is at year 9 price levels. As we have assumed throughout that cash flows occur at the year end, the year 10 cash flows will be stated at end year 10 price levels. Thus the 2143.93 needs to be uplifted by a further 5% to state the value in comparative price levels, which is £2251.12.

The NBV is then easily estimated by multiplying the GBV by the ratio of the historic cost (GBV) of the assets to the historic cost (NBV) of the assets (the 'net : gross ratio'). This is equivalent to uplifting the accumulated depreciation by the same inflation factor that was applied to the historic cost of the assets

This approach yields the inflation adjusted gross and net asset values shown in Table 6.9.

Table 6.9 Inflation adjustments in the CFR valuation model

	Year 10	Year 11
Inflation adjusted OGBV (to end year 10 price levels)	2251.12	2335.54
Net : Gross ratio (HC GBV : HC NBV)	0.6517	0.6517
Inflation adjusted ONBV (Net : gross ratio × Inflation adjusted OGBV)	1467.05	1522.06

The next step is to calculate the estimated real IRR. The annual cash inflows for the four-year life of the asset at year 10 price levels are £728.26 p.a. (from Chapter 5). Solving for the IRR (CFR) yields an estimated IRR of 11.17%. This is a real estimate as all asset values and cash flows have been stated in real terms.

Unfortunately, it is incorrect as it *should* be identical to the 11.39% estimate we derived above – all that has happened to the earlier analysis is that we have added in inflation at a constant 5%. This error in the IRR/CFR estimate is caused by the approximation of the inflation-adjusted asset values. However, as this is an approximation commonly used by some consultants and analysts a valuation using this approach is shown in Table 6.10.

Table 6.10 CFR valuation with growth and inflation (all figures in £000s)

	Year 10
IRR estimate (real)	11.17%
Spread	1.17%
Spread × OGBV assets	27.37
Growth in gross assets	3.75%
Capitalised spread	437.94
'Net/Gross' factor	0.6517
CNBV (Yr 11 OGBV × Net : Gross factor)	1522.06
Value (Capitalised spread + Adjusted net assets)	1960.00

Several points arise concerning this valuation:

- the 'reinvestment assumption' problems of IRR explained above affect this valuation;
- the inflated gross asset values are estimated with error (overstated), and hence the IRR is an underestimate;
- this causes the value of the capitalised value of the spread to be understated;
- this is partly offset by the fact that the understated spread is added to the overstated net asset value.

In other words, in the approximation used to adjust asset values, there will always be opposite and to some degree offsetting errors.

6.3 THE APPLICATION OF EP AND CFR MODELS IN PRACTICE

The above examples overstate the ease with which either model can be applied. In practice, several issues arise:

- Real difficulties can arise because of accounting practices for example:
  - not all costs and revenues flow through the P&L account (e.g. asset revaluations);
  - some real assets may not be capitalised (e.g. goodwill, development expenditure);
  - some short-term avoidable costs are essential for the long-term survival of the business (e.g. R&D spending, marketing expenditure).
- Asset replacement and new asset expenditures are usually non-constant.
- Inflation and real growth rates tend to vary through time.
- Events such as takeovers and mergers make comparative analysis of the business over time very difficult – in particular, it makes estimation of asset ages and lives problematic.

Given that both models are intended to facilitate the forecasting of *specific forecast* period cash flows, the above represent real difficulties. Clearly, both models perform reasonably well under conditions where growth and investment patterns are constant. Yet these are the conditions typically associated with horizon period forecasts rather than specific forecast periods.

One further input to the EP and CFR models has not been analysed so far, and that is the period over which abnormal performance is likely to persist. In the examples above, it was assumed that the firm could continue to invest in positive NPV projects into perpetuity. In practice, this is unlikely to occur, as competitive advantages are competed away. When all competitive advantage has disappeared, the firm will be investing in 'marginal' projects, i.e. those where the NPV is just zero. Under such circumstances the value of the firm is simply the replacement cost of its assets.

Both CFR and EP models face this difficulty. In the case of the CFR model, the issue is the number of years that the spread is maintained, or the rate of decline in the spread. For the EP model, the equivalent problem is the rate of decline in the EP itself. In both cases the spread or EP is capitalised by discounting the declining pattern of cash flows over the appropriate number of years. The rate and period of decline can either be estimated by:

- specific forecasting of competitive advantage period; or
- cross-sectional analysis based upon large samples of historical data.

An example of the latter can be found in Madden (1996), where changes in CFROI (or 'fade' as Madden describes it) are analysed by growth rate, initial CFROI and variability (standard deviation) of CFROI. Essentially this shows that firms with high initial CFROI, with high variability and high growth are most likely to decline in relative CFROI rankings over time. Those with low CFROI are likely to improve. The growth measure used is based upon accounting earnings. The finding of mean reversion in CFROI and earnings growth is compatible with findings elsewhere in the academic literature.[5]

6.3.1 EP and CFR compared

The relative performance of both models depends entirely upon the conditions assumed to apply in terms of:

- asset replacement patterns;
- relationship between sales growth, margin growth and asset growth;
- changes in the rate of inflation through time;
- changes in asset growth through time.

For both models, it is essential that a reasonable number of years' data are used in the analysis to avoid any distortions caused by any one year being unrepresentative of general trends.

In general, the EP model performs well if there are reasonably constant rates of asset replacement and when either the accounting system is 'clean surplus' or appropriate adjustments can be made. This is not surprising, given that with assumptions of constant relationships between the key 'value drivers' referred to above, the link between accounting and market values has been well established in the academic literature by authors such as Edwards and Bell, Peasnell and Ohlson.

However, the relationships break down where asset replacement patterns are 'lumpy' in nature, unless accounting depreciation methods are adjusted. While annuity depreciation is an improvement, it is difficult to estimate from published data, and in any event breaks down when cash flows from assets are not contant.[6] To the extent that the CFR model uses asset GBVs, it is not dependent on the accounting depreciation method chosen in the same way that EP is.[7]

Against this, the CFR model suffers from the weakness inherent in the use of IRR. This is the assumption that cash flows can always be reinvested at the IRR or CFR. By contrast, the EP model makes the more reasonable assumption that surplus cash flows are reinvested at the firm's WACC. This is the standard textbook advantage claimed for NPV over IRR.

6.3.2 Estimating the EP and CFR models from published UK accounting data

Using CFR and EP models without access to information more detailed than that presented in the annual report and accounts is fraught with difficulty. To start with, a reasonable run of data is desirable to work out average asset ages and lives, as the CFR calculation can be highly sensitive to such estimates. Second, in reality it is clearly unrealistic to assume year end cash flow timing. One approach to get around this problem is to use average (i.e. assumed mid-year) asset values.

In the case of the CFR model, when the business changes over the year through, say, acquisitions and disposal of discontinued businesses, one alternative approach is to estimate the opening gross assets on continuing operations by estimating the opening gross assets as the closing gross assets less acquisitions during the year (*see* Madden, 1996, for an example).

To illustrate these approaches, the case example of British Vita is used. Note that the figures given below are approximations based on just one year's data for the purposes of illustration only. They are not meant to be representative of the actual value of British Vita in any way.

6.3.3 Case example – British Vita plc

The first step is the estimation of a real and nominal WACC for British Vita. British Vita plc has a comparatively simple capital structure with no listed debt. From the 1997 Annual Report and Accounts, all the debt is in the form of bank loans and finance leases. If these are assumed to carry variable interest rates, so that book value of debt is approximately equal to market value, the firm has a current portion of short-term debt of £7.8 m plus medium and long-term debt of £30.1 m, giving a total of £37.9 m. However, it also has term deposits of £42.5 m, so that for our purposes we may assume the firm has virtually zero gearing.

British Vita's equity has a beta of 1.13. Taking the approximation of a risk-free real rate of interest of 2% and a market risk premium of 3% (*see* Chapter 4), an approximation of British Vita's real equity cost of capital can be found using the CAPM:[8]

$$r_{\text{British Vita}} = 2 + (3 \times 1.13) = 5.4\%$$

As British Vita has been assumed to have no long-run gearing, this is also the real WACC. The nominal WACC can be found by adjusting for inflation. Assuming an inflation rate of approximately 2.5% we have:

$$WACC_{nominal} = (1.054 \times 1.025) - 1 = 0.804 \text{ or approximately } 8\%$$

These costs of capital can now be applied to the CFR and EP models respectively.

The EP model applied to British Vita

The EP model is far simpler to apply in practice than the CFR model. Following the accounting adjustments known to be made in the EVA® model, the following adjustments are made:

- R&D spending is added back to profit and capitalised.

- Cumulative goodwill written off is added back to the asset values.

- To arrive at net operating profit after taxes (NOPAT) a tax rate of 31% is assumed for illustrative purposes.

This gives the estimate of EP value shown in Table 6.11 (all number references are to the British Vita data given in the Appendix).

Table 6.11 Economic profit valuation for British Vita plc

			1997
a	Operating profit	6	55.5
	Add back:		
b	R&D expenditure	N1	2.4
c	Restated operating profit	(a) + (b)	57.9
d	Assumed taxes	(c) × 31%	17.95
e	NOPAT	(c) − (d)	39.95
	Adjusted invested capital		
f	Net fixed assets	20	225.8
g	Net working capital	32	95.7
h	Term dep. and borrowing in (5)	N6 − 29	20.6
I	Def. tax and other liabilities	35	18.7
j	Cum. goodwill w/o	N5	68.1
k	Restated invested capital	(f) + (g) − (h) − (i) + (j)	350.3
l	Capital charge @ 8%	8% × (k)	28.02
m	Economic profit	(e) − (k)	11.93
n	Capitalised EP into perpetuity	(l)/0.08	149.09
o	Value of operating assets	(m) + (j)	499.39
p	Enterprise value	(n) + 22	591.69
q	Equity value	o + N6 − 34 − 29	577.89

Note that a key point in establishing the theoretical relationship between accounting profits and net asset values and market value is the requirement that accounting is 'clean surplus' in nature. This simply means that all changes in asset values flow through the profit and loss account. This is not currently the case for UK accounting, although US GAAP mean that US profits are closer to this concept. As UK accounting is not 'clean surplus' in nature, adjustments are necessary. These were not needed in the simplified setting of Tamar plc in the previous sections but is important in reality. In the example above, this is why the cumulative goodwill written off (to reserves) in the past has been added back to the balance sheet value.

Finally, the whole question of 'fade' or decline in competitive advantage has been ignored. For simplicity, the analysis assumed that the EP would continue to be earned in perpetuity. Alternatives are the estimation of growth and subsequent decay in EP over time. This is a simple exercise on a spreadsheet and is left for the reader to attempt. For the record, the market capitalisation of British Vita at the end of December 1998 was £474 m. Various plausible patterns of EP change can be found which are broadly compatible with such a valuation.

The CFR model applied to British Vita

Applying the CFR model is considerably more complex than the EP model. In the Tamar example above, no adjustments were necessary to opening assets because the business was unchanged from one year to the next. Unfortunately, in the case of British Vita this does not apply, as some operations have been added by acquisition.

In the calculation that follows, this has been ignored. Ideally, the cash flows would be analysed separately for continuing and new operations, but this would overcomplicate the example given and could only be done by making assumptions about the relationship between profits, assets and cash flows. An alternative would be to use average assets and assume mid-year cash flows. For simplicity, the example has been simplified to use just the closing book values of the assets. This probably has the effect of overstating the asset investment required to generate the cash flows shown, and hence underestimates the CFR.

The calculation of the CFR valuation model is shown in Table 6.12 (again, all references are to the British Vita accounting data given in Appendix A at the end of the briefing).

The first point that needs explanation is the calculation of the IRR/CFR. Following the calculation to item (f), we have an estimated life of 12.86 years. This is rounded up to 13 years for the IRR calculation. To earn this, the company needs the following 'assets invested':

- investment (gross, inflation adjusted) in depreciable assets – this calculation is given in item (j);

- investment in land and buildings (stated in the accounts at approximately current values);

- investment in working capital, net of short-term investments and current portion of long-term financing – this calculation is given in items (l)–(m).

Table 6.12 CFR valuation for British Vita plc

				1997
a	Operating cash flow		47	81.40
b	Cash taxes	Assumed 31% × (a)		25.23
c	OCF after tax	(a) − (b)		56.17
d	Opening gross plant assets		18	311.20
e	Depreciation provided	N2a		24.20
f	Estimated life of assets	(d)/(e)		12.86
g	Net : Gross ratio (plant)	20/18		0.36
h	Estimated age of assets	19/42		8.29
i	Inflation adjustment	(h) @ 3% est. p.a.		1.28
j	Curr. gross cost of opening plant	(i) × (d)		397.65
k	Land and buildings		20	115.30
l	Net working capital		32	95.70
m	Term dep. and borrowing in (5)	N6 − 29		20.60
n	Assets invested	(j) + (k) + (l) − (m)		588.05
o	Assets recovered at end	(k) + (l) − (m)		190.40
p	CFR	IRR of cash flows (13 yrs)		5.96%
q	Spread	(p) − 5.4%		0.56%
r	Capitalised spread into perpetuity	((q) × (n))/0.054		61.08
s	Closing gross plant		18	311.20
t	Closing L&B		20	115.30
u	Closing net infl. adj. plant	18 × (g) × (l)		141.20
v	Infl. adj. net assets	(t) + (u) + (l) − (m)		331.60
w	Value of operating assets	(v) + (r)		392.68
x	Non-operating assets and inv.	22 + N6		48.60
y	Enterprise value	(w) + (x)		441.28
z	Equity value	(y) − 34 − 29		384.98

While the depreciable assets have a finite life, the land and buildings, along with the working capital, are assumed recoverable at the end of the investment cycle.[9]

All this gives the components of the IRR calculation:

- Year 0: invest the 'assets invested' figure of £588.05 m.

- Year 1–13: earn the real cash flow, net of tax, £56.17 m.

- Year 13: recover the 'recoverable assets' (assets invested less the inflation-adjusted depreciable assets) of £190.4 m.

This yields the real IRR (CFR) of 5.96%, or 0.46% above the WACC.

Note that there is an argument for including some element of goodwill in the assets invested. However, given that the goodwill has been recorded based upon historic cost of the assets, and that historic cost has been increased to some degree by the inflation adjustment, the inclusion of an element of goodwill is debatable.

It turns out that the IRR/CFR is quite sensitive to changes in assumption concerning assets invested. This is partly because such changes influence the calculated length, and hence number of years cash inflow, in the IRR calculation.

Against this disadvantage of the CFR model is the probability that it deals with the impact of inflation more appropriately than the EP model. At the time of writing, inflation rates in the UK have declined from levels found over the length of the investment cycle being assumed. As current rates are below historical rates, the EP model is applying a WACC based upon current inflation rates to a P&L and balance sheet which is a function of past inflation rates. In relative terms, this means that the WACC is understated relative to the depreciation charge and net asset values used in the calculation of EP.

6.4 SUMMARY AND CONCLUSIONS

Both the EP and CFR models can be viewed as attempts to ease the burden of making specific FCF forecasts for firms. Branded EP-type models are simply the application of the well-known capitalised residual income valuation approach described in the academic literature. The CFR model adopts a different approach by relating cash flow data to the inflation-adjusted balance sheet values and calculating an implied IRR.

Which performs better in practice is an empirical question. Performance of the models depends upon:

- the pattern of cash flows over the investment cycle;
- whether or not the investment in new assets takes place at a constant rate or is 'lumpy' in nature;
- whether the rate of inflation is constant or not.

Both models can be error-prone under certain circumstances. Both can be expected to work well in conditions where cash flows, investment, inflation and growth take place at roughly constant rates. That said, these are undemanding conditions where any simplifying model can be expected to work. For example, in Chapter 3 it was shown that the PE model is compatible with DCF when growth, return on new investment and payout rates were constant into perpetuity.

Finally, it should be borne in mind that a naive application of both models could give highly misleading answers. Taken to an extreme, if only the current year's data is used in valuing a firm or SBU, both rest upon the assumption that the current year's profit, cash flow and asset values are representative of the long-run position. This suggests that, as a minimum, a long-run analysis should be made of the relationships between asset values and EP, and between inflation-adjusted asset values and the CFR, depending on which model is used. This is particularly important given the central role such models currently have in evaluating major strategic decisions such as takeovers or divestment of SBUs.

7

Additional factors in valuation for takeovers

7.1 INTRODUCTION

In this chapter we consider the special case of the additional value created by takeovers and mergers (which for simplicity we refer to throughout this chapter as 'mergers').

In the case of mergers involving listed companies, successful acquirers normally pay a figure in excess of the current market price, which can be viewed as a control premium paid to purchase certain special benefits; the value of these benefits is discussed below. In an efficient equity market, the market value of listed companies should reflect the going concern value of firms following existing and currently planned strategies.

7.2 THE VALUE OF MERGER BENEFITS

There is considerable evidence to suggest that many acquiring firms pay premia which may be too high; estimates of these premia vary considerably, but 30% plus for a typical premium seems compatible with the evidence. For example, a UK study by Limmack (1991) reports an average premium as high as 37.1% which is similar to Firth's (1980) finding of 38%. In the US Jensen and Ruback (1983) find an average premium of 30%. For France, Eckbo and Langohr (1986) report 53% on cash offers and 20% for those in exchange for securities.

Some examples of firms paying too much for their targets include Marks and Spencer's acquisition of Brooks Brothers,[1] Boots' acquisition of Ward White (*FT*, 14 November 1991) and Ford's acquisition of Jaguar.

The scale of the premia described above are extremely demanding in terms of the merger benefits required, and this begs the question of whether or not firms are over-optimistic in their estimation of these benefits. Accordingly, we shall attempt to investigate the sources of such benefits. The first of these is synergy, which basically assumes that the profitability of a business combination is greater than the profitability of the two component companies added together because some efficiency gain will result from the merger.

7.2.1 Synergy

Synergy might reasonably be expected to occur because of economies of scale. Such benefits can also relate to production through:

- the more intensive use of plant and equipment (the implication here may well be the rationalisation of some of the post-combination assets of the firm);
- increased throughput moving the labour force further down the so-called 'experience' or learning curve (for example, the Boston Consulting Group

believe that this is an important factor in the claimed association of market share and profitability[2]);

■ increased purchasing power in raw materials markets.

Other cost benefits relate to administration costs and marketing and distribution costs. Gains may also be experienced in the area of research and development. The common feature of all these benefits is that they are likely to be associated with horizontal integration, that is a merger between firms in the same industry. The cash flow saving resulting from these benefits can normally be estimated without too much difficulty, although over-optimism needs to be carefully guarded against. In particular, acquiring company management should be able to quantify such savings, and should also be capable of specifying when and how such savings will be achieved. Since such business combinations will be in common lines of business, the existing cost of capital can normally be used as the discount rate, but due allowance must be made for changes in gearing (*see* Chapter 5).

Some synergystic benefits might be expected to occur in vertical integrations. A vertical integration is one where companies at different stages of the manufacturing process combine; examples include clothing retailers taking over their suppliers and computer manufacturers buying software houses. Benefits here might include the elimination of selling costs and obtaining security of sourcing or outlets; besides the gain in terms of risk elimination, a direct result might be the need for lower stock levels.[3] When valuing these benefits, the general comments on value made above are relevant. However, the discount rate chosen now needs to reflect the systematic or market risk of the SBU where the savings arise.

There may also be benefits in terms of financial synergy. Financial synergy comes about when either direct borrowing costs or transactions costs are reduced. It is worth examining why such savings may come about in a little more detail. The evidence clearly suggests that size is an important factor in the determination of corporate cost of capital, for several reasons:

■ the transaction costs of any capital issue tend to vary in inverse proportion to the amount being raised;

■ access to certain markets can only be obtained by companies of a minimum size, e.g.

 – the ability to list shares on foreign stock exchanges;

 – issuing bonds on the Euromarkets;

■ the shares of larger companies will be more marketable (in a liquidity sense), resulting in:

 – a lower bid–ask spread;

 – a reduction in any liquidity premium required by shareholders.

It is also possible that both equity and borrowing costs are reduced for larger firms because of the wider availability of information on such companies. Large firms are very much in the public eye; they are studied by a significant number of analysts, by the financial press and may also be rated by credit rating agencies such as Dun & Bradstreet. All this means that for either an equity investor in, or a potential lender to, a large firm, the costs of acquiring information are considerably reduced compared to the cost for smaller firms. Even if these smaller firms are listed, they may be studied by comparatively few analysts and it may be unlikely that there will be much publicly available information on such companies, except for the published accounts. Furthermore, in this situation there is a greater risk of 'informed' investors being able to deal at the expense of the 'naive' or 'uninformed'; this should lead to an increase in the bid–ask spread for such firms, again implying an increased cost of capital.[4] Note that financial synergies of the type discussed here will be size driven, and as such it does not matter whether the merger takes the form of a vertical, horizontal or conglomerate integration.

Another reason why borrowing costs tend to be lower for large companies is because of risk reduction. This might, in part, be due to the enhanced visibility of the company, but it is more likely to be associated with benefits from diversification. To the extent that a diversified company is less prone to a costly liquidation risk, it may be able to borrow more and if it is the case that this gives rise to increased valuable tax shields, a gain in the value of the combined equity may result. Furthermore, a similar benefit may result without any increased gearing if the combined firm is more likely to benefit from debt tax shields because of lower profit volatility.

However, the argument that lower borrowing costs are achieved for reasons other than the avoidance of liquidation costs or the gain of realised tax shields is suspect. This is because the reduction of risk achieved by debt holders is simply offset by a loss in the value of limited liability achieved by shareholders. It should be noted that this argument applies to the positions of *existing* debt holders; if two firms merge, the value of the outstanding debt will tend to increase because each firm now effectively guarantees the other's debt position. Since, in the absence of other synergies, the value of the two firms remains the same in total, if the value of the debt rises, the value of the equity should fall.[5]

In the case of *new* debt issued by the combined firm, both debt and equity holders will merely receive a fair return for the systematic risk they are taking on. It must always be borne in mind that rational investors will hold diversified portfolios; a pure conglomerate merger does not help them because they can replicate the investment portfolio that the combined firm represents themselves for a minor payment in transaction costs. However, as we have noted above, the tax shield issue and the ability to avoid costly liquidations changes this result, although it does not seem credible to believe that the effect could be large enough to justify anything other than a marginal bid premium.

7.2.2 Strategic value from mergers

In addition to the desire to benefit from synergy, there are several strategic motives for mergers, some of which are rational and some of which are irrational. In this sense, 'rational' means value adding; that is, the acquirer must gain a positive net present value from the business combination. Strategic reasons can be dichotomised into those which are defensive and those which are aggressive. Defensive reasons can include:

- protection from cyclical exposure or exposure to one industry;
- protection of markets or supplies;
- buying needed expertise;
- capacity reduction;
- the need to achieve a certain minimum size;
- moving away from a concentration in a declining industry.

Some of these have been discussed under 'synergy' above, and some can be immediately dismissed as irrational motives from the investors' perspective, although they may well be rational from a managerial one. If we take the general case of diversification, management are merely performing a task that shareholders can do for themselves. There are clear and powerful incentives for management to diversify, since they receive added protection from cyclical and industrial exposure,[6] although unless subsequent performance is satisfactory, there is always the danger of the market 'disciplining' an under-achieving acquiring firm. The question here is under what circumstances it might make sense for managers to do this rather than the shareholders.

Liquidation costs

First, as liquidations are costly affairs, business combinations that diversify away some risk do offer something to the shareholders. However, they gain only the present value of the reduction in *expected* liquidation costs. These are hard to estimate, but there have been academic attempts to do so, for example in two US studies:

- Warner (1977) estimates that the average bankruptcy costs for a sample of 11 US railroad companies was in the order of 1.4% of their market value five years before bankruptcy.
- Altman (1984) gives a much higher figure of 11 to 17% of the market value three years prior to bankruptcy.

To predict the expected bankruptcy cost for other US companies from this data, we would need to multiply this percentage by the probability of the company becoming bankrupt and discount this figure back to the present, which is likely to produce a small figure. Without extrapolating too much from small-sample US studies, it seems highly unlikely that the avoidance of expected liquidation costs is a significant justification for the observed level of bid premia.

Taxation

Diversification may allow some tax shield benefits on increased borrowing to be realised; this point was discussed above. However, related to this argument, there may be other taxation benefits. To some extent, corporation tax has option-like properties in that taxation authorities receive a positive payment when the firm makes a profit, but do not make a payout themselves when the firm makes a loss;[7] it is true, of course, that carry-forward provisions and the like exist, but these still represent a timing disadvantage. If two firms with less than perfectly correlated profit flows merge, the value of the taxation authority's 'option' is reduced, since to some extent the losses of one part of the firm can be used to offset the profits of the other; since the value of the taxing authority's position is reduced, it follows that that of the shareholders must be improved.

However, it must be concluded that while there are undoubtedly some benefits to diversification that can be achieved only through merger, they are unlikely to be particularly large. Recent empirical studies by Morck et al. (1990) and Gregory (1997) find that acquisitions driven by diversification are associated with poor post-merger performance, which is precisely what we would expect if acquirers paid a high premium to acquire marginal benefits. It may also be the case that these benefits are lost in the additional problems generated by managing a business outside the realms of existing experience.

Threat elimination

Clearly, the combination of firms to eliminate threats (be these to outlets, supplies or market share) might yield some benefits to the shareholders of combining companies. For example, it has long been recognised in the economics literature that collusion in price setting leads to the increased profitability of the co-operating parties.[8] One way of achieving such an effect is through merger; the resulting shareholder gain is, of course, achieved at the expense of society in general, which is why many countries have legislation in place to prevent the abuse of oligopolistic and monopolistic positions. However, many of the actions available to government (such as the referral of a bid to a monopolies and mergers commision) are discretionary, and to some extent this means that companies may be able to realise such benefits by judicious use of lobbying etc.

The position of declining industries

The desire of the management of firms in stagnant or declining industries to diversify into other activities is understandable, but rarely reflects the interests of the shareholders. Unless management have a competitive advantage in the area they wish to move into (and in general this is unlikely to be the case), they may well do better to concentrate on extracting the best results possible from the industry they are currently in and pay out surplus cash to the shareholders as dividends.

There are two possible exceptions to this; first, there is the perversity of legislation in many countries (including the UK) which only allows dividends to be paid out of past or current profits. This can prevent loss-making companies in declining industries from rationalising assets and distributing the proceeds to shareholders, which would be the economically efficient solution; however, in some countries (including the UK) this difficulty can be avoided by various routes, including an application to the courts to allow a capital restructuring. The second problem, which will affect companies with a large percentage of higher rate taxpayers among the shareholders, can be the tax implication of such a payout or of share buy-back programmes.

Aggressive reasons

Turning to the aggressive strategic reasons for acquisitions, we again find market share to be one such reason, along with an ability to employ price increases; this general class of gains is sometimes referred to as the 'product-market-power argument' (Krinsky, Rotenberg and Thornton, 1988). In addition, we have considerations such as:

- the extension of existing markets (including overseas expansion);
- joint ventures;
- the purchase of growth opportunities;
- acquiring assets at a discount;
- the purchase of valuable brands;
- the acquisition of technological advantage;
- the purchase of valuable options.

In general, a great deal of care is needed in the evaluation and appraisal of these areas; the closer the expansion activity is to the firm's existing business, the more likely it is that management will understand the processes involved and be able to value them. Note that with several of these reasons, expansion can take place though direct investment (sometimes called *organic growth*) or through acquisition. If market values are less than replacement costs of the physical assets, then acquiring assets through takeover may be attractive; this relationship is measured through the q-ratio. If this is less than 1.0, it may be cheaper to adopt the acquisition route rather than the direct purchase one.

Given that the observed US ratio has sometimes been less than 0.6, some commentators have suggested that the q-ratio phenomenon may partially explain the size of observed bid premia. A US study by Bartley and Boardman (1984), using a sample of 33 matched pairs, reports that the average q-ratio for target companies, at an average of 0.57, was significantly less than that observed for non-targets (0.75); a further US study by Chappell and Cheng (1984) supports this view that q-ratios are important factors in mergers. The theoretical issues relating to q-ratios have already been discussed, but it is worth emphasising that both the achievable returns (measured by NPV) and the true replication costs of the business (including the non-physical assets) need to be considered.

Brand values

Such values are implicit in the going concern price of the business, and if capital markets are operating efficiently their values should be reflected in the existing market capitalisation of the acquisition target. The key question which needs to be addressed is why the brands may be worth more to the acquirer than they are in the hands of the extant management. To some extent, the answer might lie in the efficiency of the brands' current managers (efficiency considerations are discussed below) and to a degree increased value may result from a more intense use or marketing of the brand. Nonetheless, problems can arise for acquirers here; first, brand values can easily be overestimated (for example, many commentators feel that Ford paid too much for Jaguar's brand name), and a more intensive development of a brand can, in some cases, devalue it through the loss of 'exclusivity'.

Cross-border synergies

An area where particular strategic issues may be important is in cross-border acquisitions. It has been suggested that cross-border acquisitions allow multinational enterprises (MNEs) to capitalise on monopoly rents particularly in respect of research and development activity as R&D creates barriers to entry and monopoly power through the development of patents.[9] Markets can be inefficient in allowing technology transfer because licensing arrangements and the like can be abused. In addition, the need to recover extensive R&D costs requires larger markets.

Other reasons for MNE cross-border acquisitions might include differential tax advantages, different accounting treatments between domestic and foreign reporting (in theory this should not motivate takeovers but in practice it may), and differential currency strength (although this implies that capital markets are either pricing cost of capital inefficiently or that the currencies themselves are mispriced). A US study by Harris and Ravenscraft (1991) found the following:

- that foreign buyers consistently pay substantially higher premiums for US firms than do US buyers (39.8% against 26.3%);

- that cross-border takeovers tend to be more concentrated in R&D intensive industries than domestic takeovers;

- that three-quarters of their sample of cross-border takeovers occur between companies in related industries;

- that currency strength also is an explanatory factor – when the buyer's currency is strong relative to the dollar, the bid premium is higher.

Valuing potential benefits

It is apparent from the above list of aggressive strategic motivations that identifying the cash flows associated with the claimed benefits is likely to be difficult. In many cases, what is being acquired is effectively an *option*. In the finance literature, this type of option has been termed a *real option* (as opposed to a *financial option*). For example, buying growth opportunities, research expertise and products under development, and all manner of other potential benefits, can all be viewed as the purchase of a right (but not an obligation) to enter a possibly profitable market in the future. Unfortunately, a DCF methodology is not particularly useful at dealing with this type of problem and a PE approach is wholly inadequate.

Where possible, such cases can be thought about in terms of option pricing; the application of such techniques is given in the next chapter. However, given the unknowns involved and the sheer complexity of the necessary calculations, in many cases the valuation of such options will be highly subjective.

7.2.3 Efficiency improvement gains

The type of benefit of concern here is not efficiency gain from synergy or strategic benefit, but from the acquiring company's management realising greater value from the business than the incumbent management. Such gains can come from cost reduction, revenue increases, greater asset utilisation or more effective capital investment. Takeovers may also be a way of allowing swifter adjustment to changing market conditions,[10] or an effective means of bringing about a cultural change in the organisation which in some way improves productivity or efficiency.

It is important to separate differential efficiency from the issue of general managerial inefficiency. With the former, we have a position where a management team can be managing well, but a rival team may be better at managing those particular resources; this would perhaps be an explanatory factor in horizontal mergers. The point here is that differential efficiency suggests that one particular management team may have an exclusive, or near exclusive, ability to produce efficiency gains. If target firm management are simply incompetent, a number of rival management teams may be able to generate improvements. Ironically, this can lead to a competitive bid situation with a higher premium being paid for the target.

Roll (1986) in his famous 'hubris hypothesis' suggests that managers are generally over-optimistic when evaluating takeover benefits; as such, they tend to overbid so that most (or even more than 100%) of the gains end up being received by the acquired company's shareholders.

7.2.4 Evaluating the benefits in efficient markets

One way of valuing the benefits of a merger is to value the acquired company in its current state, add on the value of the improvements and finally add on the present value of any synergistic benefits which might arise in the acquiring company. The considerations involved in evaluating these components has been discussed above. However, if stock market prices are efficient and a listed company is being valued, there would be no need to perform the first part of this task, since the current market value would represent the consensus view of the fair value of the company.

This perhaps suggests that most attention should be paid to the *additional* value that a merger is expected to lead to. Several points emerge here:

- If the company is viewed by the market as a likely takeover prospect, the market price will already reflect the expected value of any future bid premium.
- The price will also be affected by:
  - the number of interested bidders and the specificity of the benefits to be realised (important, since the benefits of past tax losses, replacing generally incompetent management, etc. can be realised by several acquirers);
  - in an efficient and well informed market the values of the options we discussed above will already be impounded in the share price.
- The value of brands etc. should also be present in the share price.

7.3 SPECIAL CONSIDERATIONS RELATING TO THE VALUATION OF OVERSEAS OPERATIONS

In Chapter 4, it was argued that the cost of capital should reflect the systematic risk of the investment, but should not take account of other risk factors which are really types of specific risk. If the discount rate is not adjusted for country-specific risk factors, analysis of this risk can be conducted in terms of the cash flows. Sensitivity analysis and scenario modelling approaches will be of particular value here.

In general, the rule is to forecast the cash flows for the foreign SBU on an expected value basis; we can then *either*:

- discount using an appropriate local cost of capital, giving today's value in the foreign currency which can be translated at current spot rates; *or*:
- translate all the cash flows at predicted future spot rates into the domestic currency, which must then be discounted at a rate which allows for domestic inflation (since the inflation differential is implicit in exchange rate movements).

Provided there are no exchange controls, and no foreseeable risks of such controls being introduced, the former approach will be less prone to errors. However, it should be noted that it is rarely possible to avoid forecasting exchange rates because of cross-border transactions made by the foreign SBU and because of transfer prices charged for goods and services between the foreign SBU and the rest of the group. Issues relating to exchange rate forecasting were discussed in Chapter 5; given the long-run nature of the valuation problem, it will generally be useful to make use of the economic relationships explained between interest rates, inflation rates and exchange rates.

7.3.1 Forecasting local currency cash flows

Whichever method that we use to value the foreign SBU, the starting point is always to forecast cash flows (or earnings flows) in the local currency; this includes translating any non-local transactions into that currency. (For example, if valuing a Dutch subsidiary supplying goods to other European countries (including the UK), all revenues must first be translated back into guilders.) It is at this stage that any political and other specific risks should be reflected through the use of probabilistic analysis; in general, the forecasting of political risk requires specialist advice.[11] Considerations involve not only the type and probability of such risks (which can range from asset expropriation to tax changes or regulatory changes), but also the degree to which such risks can be managed.

7.3.2 Estimating the cost of capital

The second stage of the process is the estimation of the cost of capital for the foreign SBU. The general considerations involved in setting the discount rate were discussed in Chapter 4.

If capital markets are integrated, then in theory it makes no difference whether the beta of the investment from a domestic viewpoint is used in conjunction with a domestic risk premium, or whether the local beta is used in conjunction with a local risk premium. Alternatively, a global CAPM with a global risk premium can be used. A full analysis of when the use of a global or local CAPM makes a difference to the cost of equity estimate is beyond the scope of this briefing, but a useful analysis with a case example applied to Nestlé can be found in Stulz (1995).

The appropriate capital structure to use in any weighted average cost of capital calculation is the long-run target gearing achievable by a stand-alone subsidiary in its own country of operation. Note that the weights used should reflect market capitalisations of debt and equity (in the usual manner) and that therefore local 'cultural' factors on the debt–equity mix are taken into account. Any special considerations, such as the availability of subsidised loans or government regulations specifying the required level of equity financing, are best reflected through the use of an adjusted present value framework

It is also necessary to remember that the relevant tax rate to be used in the computation of the value of debt tax shields and WACC must reflect local corporation tax.

7.3.3 Translating value into parent's currency

A DCF calculation can be carried out in the normal way, looking at cash flows for the specific forecast period and adding in the terminal value of the firm. As, by definition, the present value is the value today, this resultant valuation can be translated to the parent's domestic currency at the current spot rate. The final step is to consider the present value of any special benefits which accrue to the parent that would not occur if the subsidiary was truly a stand-alone enterprise. For example, multinational enterprises (MNEs) will attempt to gain some tax advantages by the judicious use of transfer pricing; the best approach when valuing any overseas operation is to ignore such gains initially, value the subsidiary on a genuine arm's length basis, and then include the value of these gains at the final stage of the process.

This method of valuing the SBU in a 'local' context is perfectly reasonable provided there are no exchange regulations in force. However, if it is expected that there will be restrictions on capital flows the approach has to be modified to take account of the cash flows which can actually be remitted to the group by one means or another. (For example, if dividend payments are restricted, transfer prices can sometimes be used to move cash flows around.) In such situations, the value to the parent can only be calculated by forecasting the cash flows remitted in the parent's currency, discounted at a rate which reflects the inflation rate of the parent's currency and the systematic rate of the foreign SBU.

7.4 THE EMPIRICAL EVIDENCE ON MERGERS

The overwhelming weight of the evidence from extensive empirical studies in the US, UK and other countries is that acquiring company shareholders do not, on average, gain from mergers. In fact, a considerable amount of evidence exists which suggests that acquiring company shareholders actually lose significantly from mergers in the long term.

For example, in the US Agrawal et al. (1992) show that for the merger sample as a whole, the underperformance of acquirers is −4.94% after 24 months, −7.38% after 36 months and increasing to −10.26% after 60 months. For the UK, Gregory (1997) shows that underperformance exists no matter what benchmark is used – all that varies is the scale of the underperformance, with estimates varying between −11.82% and −18.01% after 24 months. Results from a later paper[12] show that this underperformance continues at a similar rate for at least 36 months post merger. This research study also shows that acquirers are, on average, strong outperformers in the 36 months before the merger.

Those studies that investigate the impact of factors on long-run post-bid returns seem unanimous in finding that equity financing acquirers perform significantly worse than acquirers who use cash or mixed consideration.[13] Hostile bidders appear to perform better than non-hostile bidders although the differences are not statistically significant in the UK.[14] The evidence on conglomerate bidders is mixed, and appears to be specific to given time periods. In the US, Agrawal et al. (1992) report superior performance by conglomerate acquirers compared to non-conglomerates, whereas in the UK Gregory (1997) finds non-conglomerate acquirers have less poor performance, especially in the 1989–92 period.

In all, the evidence is compatible with a systematic overestimation of the value of merger benefits by acquirers. That is not to say that *all* acquisitions are wealth-reducing events. For example, the recent UK evidence shows that roughly 50% of cash deals and around one-third of equity financed deals are value-creating for the acquirer.[15] However, the fact that the majority of deals fail to be value-enhancing suggests that acquirers should exercise a certain scepticism in reviewing financial forecasts that suggest large potential benefits justifying substantial bid premia.

8

Value added through flexibility

8.1 INTRODUCTION

In this chapter, a brief review is given of how management choices concerning the investment decision can be valued. In principle, flexibility arises in a least three ways:

- discretion over the expansion of investments;
- discretion over the abandonment of operations;
- discretion over the timing of investments.

Other types of option can include the flexibility to alter the scale of the investment, the ability to shut down processes temporarily, and so on. Two general themes emerge:

- flexibility always adds value to any capital investment;
- 'keeping one's options open' is generally desirable.

The latter point explains one interesting phenomenon. In an investment situation where output cash flows are highly uncertain, firms which do not have production capacity will often be ill-advised to invest. This is because the option to *possibly* invest at some point in the future (a call option) is best kept alive but unexercised (i.e. there is more value in holding on to the option than exercising it). However, for the same reason, firms that already have production capacity will be better off retaining that capacity and not exercising their option (a put option) to abandon it. Thus the desirability of having a production capability is a function of whether or not it is already owned.

In principle, all types of flexibility can be valued using option pricing techniques. Three basic techniques are needed:

- a model for pricing call options;
- a model for pricing put options;
- a model for pricing options on dividend paying stocks.

Examples of the application of all three are given below. However, before going through the analysis, three important caveats should be noted:

- In an efficient market, the valuing of any existing options owned by a company should already be reflected in its share price.
- Option valuations relating to timing ignore issues such as 'first mover advantage'.
- Option valuations assume that exercise prices are known with certainty.

The first caveat also means that if 'analogue' companies possessing similar options are used in any analysis, option values will be implicit in any beta or PE estimates used. The second caveat is important. There is a tendency in recent finance literature to justify high discount rates as a rational response to the presence of timing options. While this may be justified in some cases, in others an appeal to the value of timing options can fail to take account of the real value a firm can achieve by being the first entrant to a particular product market. The third caveat can also mean that option values are overstated. With a financial option, exercise prices are known with certainty. With real options, this may not be the case. For example, if a project is abandoned because of poor demand conditions for a product, it might reasonably be expected that the disposable value of the manufacturing plant might be affected by this.

8.2 BASIC TYPES OF OPTION IN COMPANY EVALUATION

Real options can be either call options or put options. In Chapter 4 when warrants and convertibles were being valued (these are financial options), valuation techniques for call options were described. Call options are those where there is a right, but not an obligation, to acquire an asset at some fixed price (the exercise price) at some future date. Where the option is exercisable on one date only (the expiry date), it is described as a *European* option. If exercise can take place on any date up to expiry, it is described as an *American* option.

Examples of call options are:

- the option to develop a building site at some future date (an American call);
- the option to expand production facilities (an American call).

Put options are those where there is a right, but not an obligation, to sell an asset at a fixed price at some future date. Again, put options can be American or European options.

Examples of put options include:

- the option to abandon a mine (an American put);
- the option to contract production facilities (an American put).

In Chapter 4, it was noted that the Black-Scholes (BS) option pricing model could not be simply applied to the problem of valuing an option on a dividend-paying share. The BS model actually values a European call option. It can be shown that provided a share does not pay dividends, the early exercise of an American call option is never worthwhile. As such, the BS model can be used to value an American call on a non-dividend paying stock.

The BS model can also be used in valuing a European put option. There is a well-known relationship between the values of call and put options that arises because the payoff at expiry from owning a call option on a share is similar to the payoff from owning a share together with a put option with an identical exercise price to the call. Both allow an investor to avoid the downside of a fall in share price, and both allow the investor to profit by the difference between the share price and the exercise price if the value of the share goes up. The difference is that the former requires less investment – the exercise price does not have to be paid until expiry of the option. Thus the difference in value between the two alternatives is simply the present value of the exercise price. Thus we have:

> Value of call + PV exercise price = Value of put + Value of share

Rearranging terms to solve for the value of a put we have:

> Value of put = Value of call − Value of share + PV of exercise price

This is sometimes called the 'put–call parity' relationship. While it is useful in finding the value of a European put (using either the BS or binomial models), it only gives an approximation of the value of an American put. This is because under some circumstances it can be worth exercising such an option early if it is an 'in the money' option.[1] In fact, the value of an American put is at least as great as the value of a European put.

As was noted in Chapter 4, the BS model fails in the valuation of an American option on a dividend-paying share because early exercise can be desirable on an 'in the money' option if the dividend payment is large enough. Under such circumstances the binomial model can be used, though, provided the dividend payments are known. For many capital investment projects, the types of real option that arise are analogous to an American option on a dividend paying stock because:

- exercise can take place at different points in time;
- projects produce interim cash flows (analogous to dividend payments).

An example is the option to delay an investment, which is described in more detail below.

8.3 VALUING REAL OPTIONS

The valuation of real options is explained using three case examples:

- development of a building site (i.e. expansion);
- abandonment of an investment;
- the option to delay investment in a project.

179

In all cases, the general principle is that flexibility adds value to the project. The relationship is simple, although the valuation of the option element can be complex. The value of an investment with an option attached is:

Value of investment with flexibility = Value of investment with no flexibility + Value of the attaching option

---

The first component on the right-hand side of the above expression (Value of investment with no flexibility) is calculated using normal DCF principles. The second component is estimated using the option pricing models described below.

8.3.1 The option to expand

Suppose Supertours plc has a portfolio of international operations in hotels and tourism. It is considering the purchase of the Far Eastern Hotel Group, which is a private company. The group has been valued on a DCF basis using the FCF model at $95 million. Unfortunately, the current owners of the group require a price of $100 million. Part of the problem is that the markets in which the group operate face a very uncertain future. If the conditions are favourable the Far Eastern Hotel Group owns some potentially valuable sites which could be exploited. The necessary development would be made five years from now with a cost of development amounting to around $120 million; on the basis of *expected* cash flows, the present value of the inflows (discounted back to end year 5 values) would only be $100 million, which suggests that the investment is not going to be worthwhile (and hence none of the associated cash flows have been included in the appraisal of current value). However, because of the uncertainty in the market, the standard deviation of the value of these projected cash flows is large, around 60% per annum.[2] It is possible, therefore, that buying the Far Eastern Hotel Group might end up giving access to a growth market. The problem, of course, is how to value the option that the purchase of the group represents.

The additional information needed is the cost of capital of the venture itself (suppose that this is 23% p.a.) and the risk-free rate of interest – suppose that on a continuously compounded basis this is 10% p.a. As the example assumes any decision to go ahead will not be made until five years from now, the option being valued is a European call. In terms of the option input variables:

- the exercise price of the option is $120 million;
- *today's* value of the asset on which we have the option is $100 million discounted for five years at 23% giving a present value of $35.52 million.[3]

From Chapter 4 the value of a call option is given by the BS model as:

$$C = S.N(d_1) - X.e^{-R_f.t}N(d_2)$$

In the original model, S is the current share price, X the exercise price and $e^{-R_f.t}$ is a continuously compounded discount factor for t years at a risk-free rate, where t is the number of years to expiry of the option. The appendix to Chapter 4 gives the spreadsheet formulae necessary to compute the value of the option. In this case, all the terms have the same meaning except that S becomes the present value of the asset being acquired. The values of d_1 and d_2 are given by:

$$d_1 = \frac{\ln(S/X) + R_f.t}{\sigma.\sqrt{t}} + (0.5.\sigma.\sqrt{t})$$

and:

$$d_2 = d_1 - \sigma.\sqrt{t}$$

In this case $\ln(S/X)$ is the natural logarithm of the ratio of the present value of the asset to the exercise price and σ is the standard deviation of the asset's present value.

The first step in arriving at the value of the option is the calculation of the values for d_1 and d_2:

$$d_1 = \frac{\ln(35.52/120) + (0.10 \times 5)}{0.6 \times \sqrt{5}} + (0.5 \times 0.6 \times \sqrt{5}) = 0.1361$$

$$d_2 = 0.1361 - (0.6 \times \sqrt{5}) = -1.2055$$

Either from normal area tables or from the spreadsheet model given at the end of Chapter 4, the value for $N(d_1) = 0.5541$; for $N(d_2)$ the value $= 0.1140$. Using these in the option pricing formula yields:

$$C = (35.52 \times 0.5541) - (120 \times 0.6065 \times 0.1140) = \$11.39 \text{ million}$$

Thus we find that by going ahead with the purchase, Supertours plc would be acquiring an option with an approximate value of $11.39 million; adding this to the present value of cash flows from existing businesses produces a value for the Far Eastern Hotel Group of $106.21 million. On this basis, an acquisition for $100 million looks like a better deal.

Of course, in reality there are additional complications; for example, the adoption of the expansion project might in turn produce options on further expansion (for example, the extension of the new hotels).

8.3.2 The option to abandon investments

Returning to the example of the Far Eastern Hotel Group above, extend the facts by assuming that the company has as part of its assets a nearly completed hotel in Thailand. Given the current state of the Thai economy and the level of the Thai baht, there is some uncertainty about the value of this hotel and its long-run viability. The estimated present value of the hotel's expected cash flows is $5 m, but the family selling the group have offered to guarantee to buy the hotel back at $4 m in a year's time if the new owners of the group wish. Supertours plc estimates that the standard deviation of the hotel's NPV over the next year is 30%. The risk-free rate is again assumed to be 10% p.a.

This amounts to the new acquirers having a put option on an asset with a current value of $5 m and an exercise price of $4 m. As there is a 'one-off' exercise opportunity, the option is a European put and can be valued using the BS model and the put–call parity relationship described above. The steps are:

- value a call option with the same exercise price and date as the put;
- calculate the present value of the exercise price;
- calculate the value as: Call value − Share value + PV exercise price.

Calculating the value of the call is similar to the steps described above. Using the Chapter 4 spreadsheet model yields a call value of $1.472 m.

The present value of the exercise price (using continuous compounding) is:

$$\$4\text{ m} \div e^{0.10} = \$4\text{ m} / 1.1052 = \$3.619$$

Using the put–call parity relationship gives a put option value of:

$$\$1.472 + \$3.619 - \$5 = \$0.091\text{ m}$$

This is the value of the abandonment option on the Thai hotel and can be added to the calculated value of the Far Eastern Group.

One problem with abandonment values is that option valuation models assume the exercise price is known with certainty. In the above example it was, but more realistically the abandonment value of an asset is likely to depend on market conditions prevailing at the time of disposal.

8.3.3 The option to delay investment

Suppose that a firm has a project under consideration that costs £4 m and that the eventual outcome depends upon year 1 demand for the product. This demand for the product manufactured is highly unpredictable at present, as this depends on whether a rival product (which depends on the success of an untried technology) can be produced. However, all of this uncertainty will be resolved by the end of year 1. If year 1 demand is high, it will be £600 000 (in real terms) and the demand from year 2 to infinity is also expected to be £600 000 p.a. (again in real terms). Further assume that the relevant real discount rate is 10% p.a., so that the value of this stream of cash flows in perpetuity is £6 m. If year 1 demand is low (£300 000), low demand is likely in perpetuity, giving a PV in perpetuity of £3m. Thus at the end of year 1, the payoffs are either:

- high demand: £600 000 + £6 m = £6.6 m; or
- low demand: £300 000 + £3 m = £3.3 m.

Suppose that the probabilities of these two occurrences are each 0.5, and that the uncertainty over demand (which we assumed to depend on technological developments) is entirely unsystematic in nature. It follows that the required discount rate is still 10% p.a. and that the present value of the project at year 0 is $[(0.5 \times 6.6 \text{ m}) + (0.5 \times 3.3 \text{ m})] \div 1.1 = £4.5$ m. Using a conventional NPV approach gives an NPV of £4.5 m − £4 m = £0.5 m. This would normally suggest going ahead with the project.

However, if we wait until the end of year 1 before making the investment decision, we keep our 'call' option on doing the project alive. This call option is worth either:

- £6 m − £4 m = £2 m if demand is high; or
- £0 (at the limit)   if demand is low.

The underlying asset (the project) is worth either £6.6 m or £3.3 m at year 1 (including the project cash flow, equivalent to the dividend on a share), depending on demand. Applying the binomial option pricing model, the delta is:

$$2/(6.6 - 3.3) = 0.6061$$

Suppose the risk-free rate is 5% p.a. A hedged portfolio would result from 'writing' $1/0.6061 = 1.65$ 'calls' on the project. Since the payoff is then a certain £3.3 m, it follows that the value of the call, C, can be found from:

$$(4.5 \text{ m} - 1.65C) \times 1.05 = 3.3 \text{ m}$$

Solving for X gives the value of the call at £0.8225 m. Thus the option is worth £0.8225 m if kept 'alive', or only £0.5 m (the NPV) if exercised today. In other words, more value results from delaying investment than from going ahead today. thus the value of the firm as a whole is increaed by (£0.8225 m − £0.5 m) or £0.3225 m as a result of having the option to delay investment.

This option could also have been valued using the 'risk-neutral' method described in Chapter 4. The synthetic probability of a rise in value is 0.4318 (as opposed to the real probability of 0.5). This synthetic probability would have been used to compute the expected payoff on the option, and this payoff would have been discounted at the risk-free rate to give the same option value of £0.8225 m.

In conclusion, on the value of abandonment options, note that a critical assumption is that the value of either potential cash flow streams is assumed to be unaffected by a delay in exploitation of the project. In some cases, this is likely to be a valid assumption. For example, mines and oil wells are reasonable examples of where such option pricing techniques can be employed. Given the volatility of underlying commodity prices, there may be some advantage in delaying investment in such cases.

By contrast, firms that develop a technologically based design advantage are unlikely to have the luxury of being able to delay investment – if they do so, rival firms may well catch up with them quickly. As such, any attempt to value options to delay should take into account the loss in competitive advantage that may result from not going ahead with the investment immediately.

Appendices

British Vita plc – data adapted from the 1997 Annual Report and Accounts

RESTATED P&L

Item no.	Item	1997 Cont.	1997 Aqns	1997 Total	1996 Cont.	1996 Disc	1996 Total
1	Sales	800.4	8.0	808.4	873.5	22.3	895.8
2	COS	605.6	6.5	612.1	676.9	20.2	697.1
3	Gross prof.	194.8	1.5	196.3	196.6	2.1	198.7
4	Dist. costs	51.9	0.2	52.1	54.2	1.4	55.6
5	Admin.	88.1	0.6	88.7	92.5	1.6	94.1
6	Operating prof.	54.8	0.7	55.5	49.9	−0.9	49.0
7	Share of ass. pr.	9.6		9.6	8.3		8.3
8	Net op. inc.	64.4	0.7	65.1	58.2	−0.9	57.3
9	Restr. costs				0.0	7.6	7.6
10	Less 95 prov'n				0.0	7.5	7.5
11	Profit on ord. BIT	64.4	0.7	65.1	58.2	−1.0	57.2
12	Net int. rec.	1.2	−0.1	1.1	0.0	0.0	0.0
13	Prof on ord. pre-tax	65.6	0.6	66.2	58.2	−1.0	57.2
14	Tax on ord. act.	22.0	0.2	22.2	20.3	−0.3	20.0
15	Profit on ord.	43.6	0.4	44.0	37.9	−0.7	37.2
16	Min. Int.	0.2		0.2	0.3		0.3
17	EAT	43.4	0.4	43.8	37.6	−0.7	36.9
	Dividends			19.4			18.2
	Per share (p)			8.75			8.25

Notes				
N1	R&D expend.	2.4		2.4
N2	Depreciation	27.3		31.1
N2a	P&M dep'n	24.2		
N3	Tax on assoc.	3.4		3.0
N4	G'will w/o to res.	23.1		?

RESTATED BALANCE SHEET

Item no	Item	1997 Land & bldg.	1997 Plant	1997 Total	1996 Land & bldg.	1996 Plant	1996 Total
18	At cost or valn.	118.5	311.2	429.7	117.6	316.0	433.6
19	Accm. depn.	3.2	200.7	203.9	0.0	203.8	203.8
20	Net book value FA	115.3	110.5	225.8	117.6	112.2	229.8
		Listed	UL + other	Total	Listed	UL + other	Total
21	Investments NBV	9.6	9.2	18.8	13.0	9.4	22.4
22	Investments, valn.	81.8	10.5	92.3	81.8	10.5	92.3
23	Fixed assets			244.6			252.2
24	Stocks			75.1			76.4
25	Debtors, <1yr			159.5			159.7
26	Debtors, >1yr			2.0			2.0
27	Cash and STI			60.0			55.1
28	Current assets			296.6			293.2
29	Borrowings, <1yr			21.9			19.8
30	Other creditors			179.0			182.7
31	Current liabilities			200.9			202.5
32	Net current assets			95.7			90.7
33	Total assets less CL			340.3			342.9
34	LT liabilities			34.4			21.7
35	Def. tax + other liabs			18.7			22.2
36	Net assets			287.2			299.0
37	Shareholders' funds			286.1			298.0
38	Minority interests			1.1			1.0
39	Total equity			287.2			299.0

Notes

N5	Cum. g'wil w/o			68.1			45.0
N6	Term deposits			42.5			35.7
N7	P&M additions			31.3			
N8	L&B additions			12.2			

RESTATED CASH FLOW STATEMENT

		1997			1996	
40	Operating profit		55.5			49.0
41	Add back non-cash items					
42	Depreciation		27.3			31.1
43	Gov't grants	−0.2			−0.3	
44	Profit on sales of assets	−0.5			−1.0	
45	Decrease in provision	−0.7			−8.4	
46	Total other adjs		−1.4			−9.7
47	Op. CF pre w. cap inv. (ent. cash engs)		81.4			70.4
48	(Inc.) Dec. in stock	−1.6			13.0	
49	(Inc.) Dec. in dtrs	−4.4			−0.1	
50	(Dec.) Inc. in creds.	−1.4			5.4	
51	Working capital investment		−7.4			18.3
51	Operating cash flow		74.0			88.7
52	Investment and servicing of finance					
53	Interest received	3.4			2.5	
54	Interest paid	−1.7			−2.7	
55	Int. paid on leases	−0.2			−0.3	
56	Divs from associates	1.5			1.2	
57	Minority interests	−0.1			−0.1	
58	Cash inflow from inv.-servicing		2.9			0.6
59	Taxation paid		−15.6			−14.1
60	Capital expenditure					
61	Purchase of fixed assets	−38.6			−38.0	
62	Sale of fixed assets	5.6			4.3	
63	Grants received	0.1			0.1	
64	Purchase of subs.	−19.4			−34.9	
65	Sales of subs.				7.2	
66	Total Capex		−52.3			−61.3
67	Changes in inv. and assocs		−0.5			10.5
68	Equity dividends paid		−18.8			−17.6
69	Increase in deposits, etc.		−9.8			−4.4
70	Issue of equity	1.2			2.3	
71	Net increase in loans	16.3			0.3	
72	Net decrease in leases	−0.2			−0.3	
73	Inflow from financing		17.3			2.3
74	(Dec.) Inc. in cash		−2.8			4.7
75	Year-end shares in issue		221.7			220.9
76	Weighted average		221.2			220.2
77	EPS FRS3		19.8			16.8
78	EPS co. stated		19.8			17.2
79	EPS IIMR		20.0			17.5

Discount tables

Interest rate Years	1%	2%	3%	4%	5%	6%	7%	8%	9%	10%	11%	12%	13%	14%	15%	16%	17%	18%	19%	20%	25%	30%	35%	40%
1	0.9901	0.9804	0.9709	0.9615	0.9524	0.9434	0.9346	0.9259	0.9174	0.9091	0.9009	0.8929	0.8850	0.8772	0.8696	0.8621	0.8547	0.8475	0.8403	0.8333	0.8000	0.7692	0.7407	0.7143
2	0.9803	0.9612	0.9426	0.9246	0.9070	0.8900	0.8734	0.8573	0.8417	0.8264	0.8116	0.7972	0.7831	0.7695	0.7561	0.7432	0.7305	0.7182	0.7062	0.6944	0.6400	0.5917	0.5487	0.5102
3	0.9706	0.9423	0.9151	0.8890	0.8638	0.8396	0.8163	0.7938	0.7722	0.7513	0.7312	0.7118	0.6931	0.6750	0.6575	0.6407	0.6244	0.6086	0.5934	0.5787	0.5120	0.4552	0.4064	0.3644
4	0.9610	0.9238	0.8885	0.8548	0.8227	0.7921	0.7629	0.7350	0.7084	0.6830	0.6587	0.6355	0.6133	0.5921	0.5718	0.5523	0.5337	0.5158	0.4987	0.4823	0.4096	0.3501	0.3011	0.2603
5	0.9515	0.9057	0.8626	0.8219	0.7835	0.7473	0.7130	0.6806	0.6499	0.6209	0.5935	0.5674	0.5428	0.5194	0.4972	0.4761	0.4561	0.4371	0.4190	0.4019	0.3277	0.2693	0.2230	0.1859
6	0.9420	0.8880	0.8375	0.7903	0.7462	0.7050	0.6663	0.6302	0.5963	0.5645	0.5346	0.5066	0.4803	0.4556	0.4323	0.4104	0.3898	0.3704	0.3521	0.3349	0.2621	0.2072	0.1652	0.1328
7	0.9327	0.8706	0.8131	0.7599	0.7107	0.6651	0.6227	0.5835	0.5470	0.5132	0.4817	0.4523	0.4251	0.3996	0.3759	0.3538	0.3332	0.3139	0.2959	0.2791	0.2097	0.1594	0.1224	0.0949
8	0.9235	0.8535	0.7894	0.7307	0.6768	0.6274	0.5820	0.5403	0.5019	0.4665	0.4339	0.4039	0.3762	0.3506	0.3269	0.3050	0.2848	0.2660	0.2487	0.2326	0.1678	0.1226	0.0906	0.0678
9	0.9143	0.8368	0.7664	0.7026	0.6446	0.5919	0.5439	0.5002	0.4604	0.4241	0.3909	0.3606	0.3329	0.3075	0.2843	0.2630	0.2434	0.2255	0.2090	0.1938	0.1342	0.0943	0.0671	0.0484
10	0.9053	0.8203	0.7441	0.6756	0.6139	0.5584	0.5083	0.4632	0.4224	0.3855	0.3522	0.3220	0.2946	0.2697	0.2472	0.2267	0.2080	0.1911	0.1756	0.1615	0.1074	0.0725	0.0497	0.0346
11	0.8963	0.8043	0.7224	0.6496	0.5847	0.5268	0.4751	0.4289	0.3875	0.3505	0.3173	0.2875	0.2607	0.2366	0.2149	0.1954	0.1778	0.1619	0.1476	0.1346	0.0859	0.0558	0.0368	0.0247
12	0.8874	0.7885	0.7014	0.6246	0.5568	0.4970	0.4440	0.3971	0.3555	0.3186	0.2858	0.2567	0.2307	0.2076	0.1869	0.1685	0.1520	0.1372	0.1240	0.1122	0.0687	0.0429	0.0273	0.0176
13	0.8787	0.7730	0.6810	0.6006	0.5303	0.4688	0.4150	0.3677	0.3262	0.2897	0.2575	0.2292	0.2042	0.1821	0.1625	0.1452	0.1299	0.1163	0.1042	0.0935	0.0550	0.0330	0.0202	0.0126
14	0.8700	0.7579	0.6611	0.5775	0.5051	0.4423	0.3878	0.3405	0.2992	0.2633	0.2320	0.2046	0.1807	0.1597	0.1413	0.1252	0.1110	0.0985	0.0876	0.0779	0.0440	0.0254	0.0150	0.0090
15	0.8613	0.7430	0.6419	0.5553	0.4810	0.4173	0.3624	0.3152	0.2745	0.2394	0.2090	0.1827	0.1599	0.1401	0.1229	0.1079	0.0949	0.0835	0.0736	0.0649	0.0352	0.0195	0.0111	0.0064
16	0.8528	0.7284	0.6232	0.5339	0.4581	0.3936	0.3387	0.2919	0.2519	0.2176	0.1883	0.1631	0.1415	0.1229	0.1069	0.0930	0.0811	0.0708	0.0618	0.0541	0.0281	0.0150	0.0082	0.0046
17	0.8444	0.7142	0.6050	0.5134	0.4363	0.3714	0.3166	0.2703	0.2311	0.1978	0.1696	0.1456	0.1252	0.1078	0.0929	0.0802	0.0693	0.0600	0.0520	0.0451	0.0225	0.0116	0.0061	0.0033
18	0.8360	0.7002	0.5874	0.4936	0.4155	0.3503	0.2959	0.2502	0.2120	0.1799	0.1528	0.1300	0.1108	0.0946	0.0808	0.0691	0.0592	0.0508	0.0437	0.0376	0.0180	0.0089	0.0045	0.0023
19	0.8277	0.6864	0.5703	0.4746	0.3957	0.3305	0.2765	0.2317	0.1945	0.1635	0.1377	0.1161	0.0981	0.0829	0.0703	0.0596	0.0506	0.0431	0.0367	0.0313	0.0144	0.0068	0.0033	0.0017
20	0.8195	0.6730	0.5537	0.4564	0.3769	0.3118	0.2584	0.2145	0.1784	0.1486	0.1240	0.1037	0.0868	0.0728	0.0611	0.0514	0.0433	0.0365	0.0308	0.0261	0.0115	0.0053	0.0025	0.0012
21	0.8114	0.6598	0.5375	0.4388	0.3589	0.2942	0.2415	0.1987	0.1637	0.1351	0.1117	0.0926	0.0768	0.0638	0.0531	0.0443	0.0370	0.0309	0.0259	0.0217	0.0092	0.0040	0.0018	0.0009
22	0.8034	0.6468	0.5219	0.4220	0.3418	0.2775	0.2257	0.1839	0.1502	0.1228	0.1007	0.0826	0.0680	0.0560	0.0462	0.0382	0.0316	0.0262	0.0218	0.0181	0.0074	0.0031	0.0014	0.0006
23	0.7954	0.6342	0.5067	0.4057	0.3256	0.2618	0.2109	0.1703	0.1378	0.1117	0.0907	0.0738	0.0601	0.0491	0.0402	0.0329	0.0270	0.0222	0.0183	0.0151	0.0059	0.0024	0.0010	0.0004
24	0.7876	0.6217	0.4919	0.3901	0.3101	0.2470	0.1971	0.1577	0.1264	0.1015	0.0817	0.0659	0.0532	0.0431	0.0349	0.0284	0.0231	0.0188	0.0154	0.0126	0.0047	0.0018	0.0007	0.0003
25	0.7798	0.6095	0.4776	0.3751	0.2953	0.2330	0.1842	0.1460	0.1160	0.0923	0.0736	0.0588	0.0471	0.0378	0.0304	0.0245	0.0197	0.0160	0.0129	0.0105	0.0038	0.0014	0.0006	0.0002
30	0.7419	0.5521	0.4120	0.3083	0.2314	0.1741	0.1314	0.0994	0.0754	0.0573	0.0437	0.0334	0.0256	0.0196	0.0151	0.0116	0.0090	0.0070	0.0054	0.0042	0.0012	0.0004	0.0001	0.0000
35	0.7059	0.5000	0.3554	0.2534	0.1813	0.1301	0.0937	0.0676	0.0490	0.0356	0.0259	0.0189	0.0139	0.0102	0.0075	0.0055	0.0041	0.0030	0.0023	0.0017	0.0004	0.0001	0.0000	0.0000
40	0.6717	0.4529	0.3066	0.2083	0.1420	0.0972	0.0668	0.0460	0.0318	0.0221	0.0154	0.0107	0.0075	0.0053	0.0037	0.0026	0.0019	0.0013	0.0010	0.0007	0.0001	0.0000	0.0000	0.0000
50	0.6080	0.3715	0.2281	0.1407	0.0872	0.0543	0.0339	0.0213	0.0134	0.0085	0.0054	0.0035	0.0022	0.0014	0.0009	0.0006	0.0004	0.0003	0.0002	0.0001	0.0000	0.0000	0.0000	0.0000
100	0.3697	0.1380	0.0520	0.0198	0.0076	0.0029	0.0012	0.0005	0.0002	0.0001	0.0000	0.0000	0.0000	0.0000	0.0000	0.0000	0.0000	0.0000	0.0000	0.0000	0.0000	0.0000	0.0000	0.0000

Annuity tables

Interest rate / Years	1%	2%	3%	4%	5%	6%	7%	8%	9%	10%	11%	12%	13%	14%	15%	16%	17%	18%	19%	20%	25%	30%	35%	40%
1	0.9901	0.9804	0.9709	0.9615	0.9524	0.9434	0.9346	0.9259	0.9174	0.9091	0.9009	0.8929	0.8850	0.8772	0.8696	0.8621	0.8547	0.8475	0.8403	0.8333	0.8000	0.7692	0.7407	0.7143
2	1.9704	1.9416	1.9135	1.8861	1.8594	1.8334	1.8080	1.7833	1.7591	1.7355	1.7125	1.6901	1.6681	1.6467	1.6257	1.6052	1.5852	1.5656	1.5465	1.5278	1.4400	1.3609	1.2894	1.2245
3	2.9410	2.8839	2.8286	2.7751	2.7232	2.6730	2.6243	2.5771	2.5313	2.4869	2.4437	2.4018	2.3612	2.3216	2.2832	2.2459	2.2096	2.1743	2.1399	2.1065	1.9520	1.8161	1.6959	1.5889
4	3.9020	3.8077	3.7171	3.6299	3.5460	3.4651	3.3872	3.3121	3.2397	3.1699	3.1024	3.0373	2.9745	2.9137	2.8550	2.7982	2.7432	2.6901	2.6386	2.5887	2.3616	2.1662	1.9969	1.8492
5	4.8534	4.7135	4.5797	4.4518	4.3295	4.2124	4.1002	3.9927	3.8897	3.7908	3.6959	3.6048	3.5172	3.4331	3.3522	3.2743	3.1993	3.1272	3.0576	2.9906	2.6893	2.4356	2.2200	2.0352
6	5.7955	5.6014	5.4172	5.2421	5.0757	4.9173	4.7665	4.6229	4.4859	4.3553	4.2305	4.1114	3.9975	3.8887	3.7845	3.6847	3.5892	3.4976	3.4098	3.3255	2.9514	2.6427	2.3852	2.1680
7	6.7282	6.4720	6.2303	6.0021	5.7864	5.5824	5.3893	5.2064	5.0330	4.8684	4.7122	4.5638	4.4226	4.2883	4.1604	4.0386	3.9224	3.8115	3.7057	3.6046	3.1611	2.8021	2.5075	2.2628
8	7.6517	7.3255	7.0197	6.7327	6.4632	6.2098	5.9713	5.7466	5.5348	5.3349	5.1461	4.9676	4.7988	4.6389	4.4873	4.3436	4.2072	4.0776	3.9544	3.8372	3.3289	2.9247	2.5982	2.3306
9	8.5660	8.1622	7.7861	7.4353	7.1078	6.8017	6.5152	6.2469	5.9952	5.7590	5.5370	5.3282	5.1317	4.9464	4.7716	4.6065	4.4506	4.3030	4.1633	4.0310	3.4631	3.0190	2.6653	2.3790
10	9.4713	8.9826	8.5302	8.1109	7.7217	7.3601	7.0236	6.7101	6.4177	6.1446	5.8892	5.6502	5.4262	5.2161	5.0188	4.8332	4.6586	4.4941	4.3389	4.1925	3.5705	3.0915	2.7150	2.4136
11	10.3676	9.7868	9.2526	8.7605	8.3064	7.8869	7.4987	7.1390	6.8052	6.4951	6.2065	5.9377	5.6869	5.4527	5.2337	5.0286	4.8364	4.6560	4.4865	4.3271	3.6564	3.1473	2.7519	2.4383
12	11.2551	10.5753	9.9540	9.3851	8.8633	8.3838	7.9427	7.5361	7.1607	6.8137	6.4924	6.1944	5.9176	5.6603	5.4206	5.1971	4.9884	4.7932	4.6105	4.4392	3.7251	3.1903	2.7792	2.4559
13	12.1337	11.3484	10.6350	9.9856	9.3936	8.8527	8.3577	7.9038	7.4869	7.1034	6.7499	6.4235	6.1218	5.8424	5.5831	5.3423	5.1183	4.9095	4.7147	4.5327	3.7801	3.2233	2.7994	2.4685
14	13.0037	12.1062	11.2961	10.5631	9.8986	9.2950	8.7455	8.2442	7.7862	7.3667	6.9819	6.6282	6.3025	6.0021	5.7245	5.4675	5.2293	5.0081	4.8023	4.6106	3.8241	3.2487	2.8144	2.4775
15	13.8651	12.8493	11.9379	11.1184	10.3797	9.7122	9.1079	8.5595	8.0607	7.6061	7.1909	6.8109	6.4624	6.1422	5.8474	5.5755	5.3242	5.0916	4.8759	4.6755	3.8593	3.2682	2.8255	2.4839
16	14.7179	13.5777	12.5611	11.6523	10.8378	10.1059	9.4466	8.8514	8.3126	7.8237	7.3792	6.9740	6.6039	6.2651	5.9542	5.6685	5.4053	5.1624	4.9377	4.7296	3.8874	3.2832	2.8337	2.4885
17	15.5623	14.2919	13.1661	12.1657	11.2741	10.4773	9.7632	9.1216	8.5436	8.0216	7.5488	7.1196	6.7291	6.3729	6.0472	5.7487	5.4746	5.2223	4.9897	4.7746	3.9099	3.2948	2.8398	2.4918
18	16.3983	14.9920	13.7535	12.6593	11.6896	10.8276	10.0591	9.3719	8.7556	8.2014	7.7016	7.2497	6.8399	6.4674	6.1280	5.8178	5.5339	5.2732	5.0333	4.8122	3.9279	3.3037	2.8443	2.4941
19	17.2260	15.6785	14.3238	13.1339	12.0853	11.1581	10.3356	9.6036	8.9501	8.3649	7.8393	7.3658	6.9380	6.5504	6.1982	5.8775	5.5845	5.3162	5.0700	4.8435	3.9424	3.3105	2.8476	2.4958
20	18.0456	16.3514	14.8775	13.5903	12.4622	11.4699	10.5940	9.8181	9.1285	8.5136	7.9633	7.4694	7.0248	6.6231	6.2593	5.9288	5.6278	5.3527	5.1009	4.8696	3.9539	3.3158	2.8501	2.4970
21	18.8570	17.0112	15.4150	14.0292	12.8212	11.7641	10.8355	10.0168	9.2922	8.6487	8.0751	7.5620	7.1016	6.6870	6.3125	5.9731	5.6648	5.3837	5.1268	4.8913	3.9631	3.3198	2.8519	2.4979
22	19.6604	17.6580	15.9369	14.4511	13.1630	12.0416	11.0612	10.2007	9.4424	8.7715	8.1757	7.6446	7.1695	6.7429	6.3587	6.0113	5.6964	5.4099	5.1486	4.9094	3.9705	3.3230	2.8533	2.4985
23	20.4558	18.2922	16.4436	14.8568	13.4886	12.3034	11.2722	10.3711	9.5802	8.8832	8.2664	7.7184	7.2297	6.7921	6.3988	6.0442	5.7234	5.4321	5.1668	4.9245	3.9764	3.3254	2.8543	2.4989
24	21.2434	18.9139	16.9355	15.2470	13.7986	12.5504	11.4693	10.5288	9.7066	8.9847	8.3481	7.7843	7.2829	6.8351	6.4338	6.0726	5.7465	5.4509	5.1822	4.9371	3.9811	3.3272	2.8550	2.4992
25	22.0232	19.5235	17.4131	15.6221	14.0939	12.7834	11.6536	10.6748	9.8226	9.0770	8.4217	7.8431	7.3300	6.8729	6.4641	6.0971	5.7662	5.4669	5.1951	4.9476	3.9849	3.3286	2.8556	2.4994
30	25.8077	22.3965	19.6004	17.2920	15.3725	13.7648	12.4090	11.2578	10.2737	9.4269	8.6938	8.0552	7.4957	7.0027	6.5660	6.1772	5.8294	5.5168	5.2347	4.9789	3.9950	3.3321	2.8568	2.4999
35	29.4086	24.9986	21.4872	18.6646	16.3742	14.4982	12.9477	11.6546	10.5668	9.6442	8.8552	8.1755	7.5856	7.0700	6.6166	6.2153	5.8582	5.5386	5.2512	4.9915	3.9984	3.3330	2.8571	2.5000
40	32.8347	27.3555	23.1148	19.7928	17.1591	15.0463	13.3317	11.9246	10.7574	9.7791	8.9511	8.2438	7.6344	7.1050	6.6418	6.2335	5.8713	5.5482	5.2582	4.9966	3.9995	3.3332	2.8571	2.5000
50	39.1961	31.4236	25.7298	21.4822	18.2559	15.7619	13.8007	12.2335	10.9617	9.9148	9.0417	8.3045	7.6752	7.1327	6.6605	6.2463	5.8801	5.5541	5.2623	4.9995	3.9999	3.3333	2.8571	2.5000
100	63.0289	43.0984	31.5989	24.5050	19.8479	16.6175	14.2693	12.4943	11.1091	9.9993	9.0906	8.3332	7.6923	7.1428	6.6667	6.2500	5.8824	5.5556	5.2632	5.0000	4.0000	3.3333	2.8571	2.5000

Notes

CHAPTER 1 INTRODUCTION

1. *See*, for example, Glover (1987) and Gregory and Hicks (1995).

2. An intriguing argument put forward by two well-known economists, Grossman and Stiglitz (1981), is that in a world where vast sums are spent on the search for misvalued securities, absolute market efficiency is logically impossible. This is because in a rational world, the marginal expenditure on such search activity must, in equilibrium, be equal to its marginal benefit – which implies at least some degree of inefficiency.

3. Note that in the case of large target companies, this may be unlikely, particularly when one considers the international nature of acquisitions. Perhaps more typical is the case where a particular company has a special strategic value to a few potential bidders, as in the case of some recent large takeovers and mergers. Examples include the Daimler-Chrysler merger and the proposed but failed merger between Glaxo and SmithKline Beecham.

4. Finance theory usually assumes that the objective is to maximise shareholder wealth. However, the basic approach encapsulated in the DCF valuation model is useful even if one assumes a less 'purist' objective such as producing a satisfactory rate of return for shareholders.

5. A spin-off is where the shares in a subsidiary are distributed directly to the shareholders of the parent, the spun-off subsidiary then having its own stock market quotation, as in the case of Argos from BAT. Divestment covers the actual sale of a subsidiary, either to its existing management (*a management buyout*) or to another buyer.

6. See Keane (1992) and Collier et al. (1999).

7. For a review of comparative international accounting, see Nobes and Parker (1991).

8. The research looked at five-year forecast and actual growth by US analysts using the I/B/E/S data tape.

9. There is little evidence of the long-run performance of continental European acquirers.

10. Quoted in full in Rappaport (1998).

CHAPTER 2 REVIEW OF TRADITIONAL VALUATION MODELS AND THEIR CONTEMPORARY OPERATIONALISATION

1. For example, Arnold and Moizer (1984) and Day (1986) surveyed investment analysts, and Keane (1992) and Collier et al. (1999) surveyed chartered accountants. Pike et al. (1993) compared the approaches used by German and UK analysts, and reports that the earnings multiple approach is the dominant method in both countries, although net assets per share is also regarded as an important indicator.

2. In some respects, residual income based methods of valuation (*see* Chapter 6) are not dissimilar.

3. For an explanation of the relationship between inflation and required rates of return, *see* Chapter 3, pp. 46–8.

4. In general, one plus the difference is equal to one plus the inflation rate to the power of the number of years over which the difference accumulates; in this case $(1.05)^5$.

5. All this assumes that the market sees the reality which lies behind the historic cost accounting numbers.

6. *See* Collier et al. (1999).

7. There is now considerable evidence from many markets (the bulk of it relating to the US and UK stock markets) which show that returns are inversely related to firm size. In rational markets, this implies that large firms have a lower cost of capital than small firms.

8. For a full definition *see*: *The Definition of IIMR Headline Earnings* (Institute of Investment Management and Research, 1993), plus supplementary note on FRS 10, January 1998.

9. Price to cash earnings figures are quoted on services such as Datastream but care needs to be exercised with definitions of these items as there is no universally accepted description of 'cash earnings per share'.

10. It should be noted that the assumptions necessary to use market-based earnings multiples are, in their way, just as onerous as those needed to use the market-based discount rates discussed in the next chapter; it might be just that in the former case the assumptions are 'in the closet' and therefore not discussed perhaps as often as they should be.

11. A discussion of this issue is beyond the scope of this text, but it should be noted that it is *unlikely* that an optimal management accounting solution is to price goods and services at 'market price'; *see*, for example, Emmanuel, Otley and Merchant (1991) for a discussion.

12. The estimation of profits on long-term contracts is subjective and has real implications for the reliability of reported profit numbers.

CHAPTER 3 FUNDAMENTAL DCF MODELS

1. In this example, we assumed risk-free and certain cash flows so that the opportunity cost is simply the interest rate. In a risky environment, higher returns will be demanded – *see* Chapter 4 for an explanation of cost of capital in DCF models.

2. The general formula for an annuity factor is given by:

$$[1 - (1 + r)^{-n}]/r$$

3. For an informal derivation of this, take the annuity formula in note 2 above and see what happens when n becomes very large. The answer is that $(1 + r)^{-n}$ becomes very small, so the annuity factor reduces to $1/r$. Multiplying this by the cash flow gives the perpetuity formula.

4. This is discussed in detail in Chapter 4.

5. A more precise solution would allow for changing expectations of real rates of return and the actual (semi-annual) timing of the coupon payments. For a full explanation of spot rate calculation and gilt valuation *see* Rutterford.

6. A review of the evidence on this hypothesis is beyond the scope of this briefing, but in general it is probably safer to use domestic expectations of inflation where possible.

7. For an introduction to the issues involved, *see* Brealey and Myers (1996).

8. An example of the 'dividend irrelevance' proposition of Modigliani and Miller referred to earlier.

9. While the exact relationship is explored in Chapter 4, increasing gearing leads to an increase in the cost of equity capital, thus *ceteris paribus* increasing the payout ratio means increasing the discount rate. To a degree, the same type of logical error can beset the FCF method, since via the same argument if gearing changes then so *might* the weighted average cost of capital.

CHAPTER 4 THE COST OF CAPITAL IN DCF MODELS

1. Because equity is enterprise value less the value of non-equity claims.

2. That is, a dividend of £2.75 is received per £100 invested in the index – hence the use of 100 in the calculation which follows.

3. Black and Scholes (1974), Fama and MacBeth (1973, 1974) and Stambaugh (1982).

4. The fact that over the long run small companies earn higher returns than large companies is well documented, both in the US and the UK. This may be because of additional risks imposed by the lack of liquidity in small stocks or by different exposures to macroeconomic risk factors, or it may reflect the higher transaction costs of dealing in the shares of smaller firms. Alternatively, it could (at least in part) be an example of a stock market 'anomaly'.

5. Fama and French (1992, 1996).

6. For a full explanation *see*, for example, Rutterford (1995).

7. Mehra and Prescott (1985); Burnside and McCurdy (1992).

8. But *see* section 4.4 for an explanation of the shortcomings of this approach.

9. This is, of course, similar to the use of analogues in the earnings multiple approach described in Chapter 2.

10. This data is from the January–March 1999 issue.

11. Note that market risk and specific risk cannot be simply added to give the total risk (variability) of British Vita's shares. In fact, the formula is:

$$\text{Variability}_{\text{British Vita}} = (\text{Beta}_{\text{British Vita}}^2 \times \text{Variability}_{\text{Market}}^2) + (\text{Specific risk}^2)$$

12. Fama and French (1996).

13. Because there are well over 2000 firms listed in most years on the LBS data tape from which these portfolios were formed, even the largest decile includes more than 100 firms from outside the FT100 – hence the small positive gamma coefficient for the *average* firm in this group.

14. *See* Schnabel (1983) and Buckley (1981) for a detailed derivation.

15. As noted above, in general the acquirer's WACC should be used only when the risk of the investment is the same as the risk of the firm as a whole.

16. Miles and Ezzell (1980).

17. Gregory and Rutterford (1999).

18. Actually, it turns out that even companies with straight debt have option-like properties due to the concept of limited liability.

19. This approach gives an identical answer to the 'portfolio' approach above, and while not as intuitive as that method has the advantage for any mathematical solution to the option pricing problem that expected asset prices calculated using these synthetic probabilities are *martingales* (essentially a random walk) when discounted at the risk-free rate. A full explanation can be found in Chapter 3 of Neftci (1996).

20. This is an oversimplification – for a thorough but intuitive explanation of the mathematics involved, *see* Neftci (1996).

21. So called because writing $1/N(d_1)$ call options for every share owned results in a risk-free investment position, subject to the assumptions of the model. The hedge ratio needs to be revised continuously.

22. Including that the firm does not pay dividends.

23. See Copeland and Weston (1988), chapter 8.

24. Strictly speaking, the standard deviation of the log price relative should be used – *see* Blake (1990) for a detailed explanation.

25. A more accurate analysis can be found in Ingersoll (1977).

26. Note that this implies (a) that new debt is issued when conversion takes place and (b) that debt is issued throughout the life of the company so that target levels of gearing are maintained.

27. For a formal proof of the concept, *see* Strong and Appleyard (1992).

28. Gregory and Rutterford (1999).

CHAPTER 5 FORECASTING FREE CASH FLOWS AND CALCULATING HORIZON VALUES

1. In fact, this is precisely how market participants set the forward premium or discount; if they did not take these interest rate differences into account it would be possible for arbitrageurs to make risk-free gains.

2. Empirical research suggests that forward rates are unbiased predictors of future spot rates but not very accurate ones.

3. By contrast, short-run certain streams (such as receipts from contract payments) can be hedged through the forward market for virtually no cost.

4. Note that the P&L account of UK companies shows corporation tax provided rather than paid. The use of deferred tax accounting in the UK (a different form of deferred tax accounting is used in the US) means that the rate of taxation provided in the P&L account may be a poor guide to the cash tax rate.

5. *See* Chapter 3 (appendix) for an explanation.

6. Overseas SBUs should be valued separately; issues relating to cost of capital for such operations are discussed in Chapter 4, while those relating to cash flow estimation are covered above.

7. *See*, for example, Lakonishok et al. (1994); DeBondt and Thaler (1985, 1987).

8. Bulkley and Harris (1997).

9. For a detailed discussion of the area, together with an investigation of how accounting can be made to generate economically useful information, Edwards, Kay and Mayer (1987) offer an excellent analysis.

10. The internal rate of return (IRR) is the discount rate which gives an NPV of zero; in general the IRR should not be used for investment decisions. The reason that RONI ≠ IRR is that the latter assumes that retained cash can be reinvested at the IRR (in this case 11.4%), whereas the assumption made in the valuation is that in the interim surplus cash is reinvested at the company's opportunity cost of capital (this can either be achieved by the company or by the shareholders if all FCF is paid as dividends and a new capital issue is made at the time of asset replacement). For this reason, RONI is in fact a function of the opportunity cost of capital used.

11. It is always possible to find an implied PE ratio (in this case 14.6) but only once we already know the theoretical value of the firm. In other words, we cannot rationally determine *ex ante* what the PE multiple should be.

12. However, Modigliani and Miller's 'dividend irrelevance' proposition means that in the absence of transaction costs it makes no difference to the value of the firm if all the free cash flow is paid out in dividends each year with a new issue of shares being made to finance the replacement purchase.

13. Using the formula $(1 + \text{Real rate}) \times (1 + \text{Inflation rate}) = (1 + \text{Nominal rate})$.

14. Note that this requirement is particularly onerous in the case of long-life assets. In this example, if the asset life had been ten years cash flows and earnings would need to be projected to year 17 before a PE ratio dependent upon a steady state could have been used.

15. Corrected for minor rounding errors.

CHAPTER 6 CONTEMPORARY METHODS FOR OPERATIONALISING THE FCF METHOD

1. Rappaport (1998).

2. As noted in the previous chapter, the conventional 'year end' cash flow assumption of DCF means that the interest change should be applied to the *opening* NBV of the assets.

3. For example, *see* Gregory (1987).

4. In this example, this was assumed to be in perpetuity.

5. Lakonishok et al. (1994); Bulkey and Harris (1997).

6. At least in real terms. An inflation-adjusted annuity depreciation figure is easily calculated.

7. Although with inflation the average age estimate needed is influenced by the depreciation method chosen.

8. Whether or not this should be adjusted for 'size effects' is ignored here. *See* Chapter 4 for a discussion of this point. British Vita is one the companies in the FT Mid 250 index.

9. Note that British Vita depreciates its buildings. The net figure has been taken here, the assumption being that in real terms the value will not change over the investment cycle.

CHAPTER 7 ADDITIONAL FACTORS IN VALUATION FOR TAKEOVERS AND MERGERS

1. The *Independent on Sunday* (10 November 1991) quoted Rick Greenbury, the M&S chairman, as admitting to shareholders; 'The stores hadn't had a lick of paint for 30 years' and 'You were right, we paid too much.'

2. *See* Cooke (1986) for a detailed description.

3. It is possible in principle to obtain similar benefits by co-operative trade agreements; mergers might actually be an expensive and inefficient way of realising such benefits.

4. *See*, for example, Glosten and Milgrom (1985).

5. It is possible to prove this using option pricing models; *see* Galai and Masulis (1976) for an explanation.

6. Note that this will not benefit most of the employees, since they remain exposed to the economics of the sector in which they work. In fact, given the performance record of many conglomerates, one might argue that they lose out as a result of such mergers.

7. Ball and Bowers (1986).

8. For a discussion of this literature, *see* Dorward (1987).

9. Harris and Ravenscraft (1991).

10. Pound, Lehn and Jarrell (1986).

11. For a useful exploration of the topic, readers are referred to Eitman and Stonehill (1989) and Shapiro (1989).

12. Gregory (1998).

13. Aggrawal et al. (1992); Gregory (1997); Loughran and Vijh (1997).

14. Loughran and Vijh (1997); Kennedy and Limmack (1996); Gregory (1997).

15. Gregory (1997).

CHAPTER 8 VALUE ADDED THROUGH FLEXIBILITY

1. To see this, take the extreme example of a firm which goes bankrupt. As the share price cannot fall below zero, there is no value in waiting for expiry of the option to exercise it.

2. Note that this standard deviation is that of the present value of the project over the next five years.

3. Note that when an option on a share is valued, the market price has already discounted the company's estimated cash flow at the required rate of return, so that the price already is a present value.

References

Agrawal, A., Jaffe, J.F. and Mandelker, G.N. (1992) 'The post-merger performance of acquiring firms; a re-examination of an anomaly', *Journal of Finance*, 47 pp 1605–22.

Altman, E. (1984) 'A further empirical investigation of the bankruptcy cost question', *Journal of Finance*, September, pp. 1067–89.

Arnold, J. and Moizer, P. (1984) 'A survey of the methods used by UK investment analysts to appraise investments in ordinary shares', *Accounting and Business Research*, summer.

Ashton, D.J. (1989a) 'Textbook formulae and UK taxation: Modigliani and Miller revisited', *Accounting and Business Research*, summer, pp. 207–12.

Ashton, D.J. (1989b) 'The cost of capital and the UK imputation tax system', *Journal of Business Finance and Accounting*, vol. 16, no. 1.

Asquith, P. (1983) 'Merger bids, uncertainty and stockholder returns', *Journal of Financial Economics*, no. 11, pp. 51–83.

Asquith, P., Brunner, R.F. and Mullins, D.W. Jr (1983) 'The gains to bidding firms from merger', *Journal of Financial Economics*, no. 11, pp. 121–39.

Auerbach, A.J. and Reishus, D. (1987) *The effects of taxation on the merger decision*, National Bureau of Economic Research, Working Paper No. 2192.

Ball, R. and Bowers, J. (1986) *Distortions Created by Taxes which Are Options on Value Creation – The Case of Windfall Profits Taxes*, BAA Conference Paper, March.

Barclays Capital (1998) *Equity-Gilt Study – January 1997*, Barclays Capital. January.

Bartley, J.W. and C.M. Boardman, *The replacement cost adjusted valuation ratio as a discriminator among target and nontarget firms*, University of Utah, Working Paper.

Black, F. and Scholes, M. (1974) 'The effects of dividend yield and dividend policy on common stock prices and returns', *Journal of Financial Ecomonics*, vol. 1, pp 1–22.

Blake, D. (1990) *Financial Market Analysis*. McGraw-Hill.

Bookstaber, R.M. (1981) *Option Pricing and Strategies in Investing*. Addison-Wesley.

Brealey, R.A. and Myers, S.C. (1996) *Principles of Corporate Finance.* McGraw-Hill.

Brown, L.D., Griffin, P.A., Hagerman, R.A. and Zimijewski, M.E. (1987) 'Security analyst superiority relative to univariate time-series models in forecasting quarterly earnings', *Journal of Accounting and Economics*, vol. 9, pp. 61–87.

Buckley, A. (1981) 'Beta geared and ungeared', *Accounting and Business Research*, spring.

Buckley, G. and Harris, R. (1997) 'Irrational analysts' expectations as a cause of excess volatility in stock prices', *Economic Journal*, March.

Burmeister, E. and McElroy, M. (1987) *APT and Multifactor Asset Pricing Models with Measured and Unobserved Factors: Theoretical and Econometric Issues*, Discussion Paper, University of West Virginia.

Burmeister, E. and McElroy, M.B. (1988) 'Joint estimation of factor sensitivities and risk prremia for the arbitrage pricing theory', *Journal of Finance*, pp. 721–35.

Burnside, C. and McCurdy, T. (1992) 'The equity premium puzzle', in *The New Palgrave Dictionary of Money and Finance*.

Capstaff, J., Paudyal, K. and Rees, W. (1995) 'The accuracy and rationality of earnings forecasts by UK analysts', *Journal of Business Finance and Accounting*, January, pp. 67–86.

CFO Europe (1997) 'The metrics war', April.

Chappell, H.W. and Cheng, D.C. (1984) 'Firms' acquisition decisions and Tobin's q ratio', *Journal of Economics and Business*, pp. 29–42.

Chen, K.C., Roll, R. and Ross, S.A. (1986) 'Economic forces and the stockmarket', *Journal of Business*, vol. 58, pp. 383–403.

Clare, A.D. and Thomas, S.H. (1994) 'Macroeconomic factors, the APT and the UK stockmarket', *Journal of Business Finance and Accounting*, April, pp. 309–30.

Clark, J.J. (1995) *Business Merger and Acquisition Strategies.* Prentice-Hall.

Collier, P. A., Gregory, A. and Jeanes, E.L. (1999) *Accounting Firm Reputation and Company Valuation Practices: The UK Evidence*, University of Exeter Working Paper.

Conn, R.L. and Nielsen, J.F. (1997) 'An empirical test of the Larson-Gonedes exchange ratio determination model', *Journal of Finance*, vol. 32, no. 3.

Cooke, T.E. (1986) *Mergers and Acquisitions.* Blackwell.

Cooke, T.E. (1998) *International Mergers and Acquisitions.* Blackwell.

Cooke, T.E., Gregory, A. and Pearson, B. (1994) 'A UK empirical test of the Larson-Gonedes exchange ratio model', *Accounting and Business Research*, spring, pp. 133–47.

Copeland, T.E. and Weston, J.F. (1988) *Financial Theory and Corporate Policy*. Addison-Wesley.

Day, J.F.S. (1986) 'The use of annual reports by UK investment analysts', *Accounting and Business Research*, autumn, pp. 295–307.

DeBondt, W. and Thaler, R. (1985) 'Does the stock market overreact?', *Journal of Finance*, vol. 40, 793–805.

DeBondt, W. and Thaler, R. (1987) 'Further evidence on investor overreaction and stock market seasonality', *Journal of Finance*, vol. 42, 557–81.

DeBondt, W. and Thaler, R. (1990) 'Do security analysts overreact?', *American Economic Review, Papers and Proceedings*, vol. 80, 52–57.

Dempsey, M.J. (1991) 'Modigliani and Miller again revisited: the cost of capital under the assumption of unequal borrowing and lending rates', *Accounting and Business Research*, summer, pp. 221–6.

Dimson, E. and Marsh, P. (1989) 'The smaller companies puzzle', *Investment Analyst*, January.

Dimson, E. and Marsh, P. (1991) *The Hoare Govett Smaller Companies Index 1991*. Hoare Govett Investment Research Ltd.

Dorward, N. (1987) *The Pricing Decision*. Harper & Row.

Eckbo, E. and Langohr, H. (1986) *Disclosure Regulations and Determinants of Takeover Premiums*, University of California Working Paper.

Eckbo, B.E., Giammarino, R.M. and Heinkel, R.L. (1990) 'Asymmetric information and the medium of exchange in takeovers: theory and tests', *Review of Financial Studies*, vol. 3, pp. 651–75.

Edwards, J., Kay, J. and Mayer, C. (1987) *The Economic Analysis of Accounting Profitability*. Clarendon Press.

Eitman, D.K. and Stonehill, A.I. (1989) *Multinational Buisiness Finance*. Addison-Wesley.

Elton, E.J. and Gruber, M.J. (1991) *Modern Portfolio Theory and Investment Analysis*. John Wiley.

Emmanuel, C., Otley, D. and Merchant, K. (1991) *Accounting for Organizational Control*. Chapman & Hall.

Fama, E. (1998) 'Market efficiency, long-term returns and behavioural finance', *Journal of Finance*, vol. 49, 283–306.

Fama, E.F. and French, K.R. (1992) 'The cross-section of expected stock returns', *Journal of Finance*, vol. 47, no. 2, pp. 427–66.

Fama, E.F. and French, K.R. (1996) 'Multifactor explanations of asset pricing anomalies', *Journal of Finance*, vol. 50, pp. 131–55.

Fama, E.F. and MacBeth, J. (1973) 'Risk, return and equilibrium: empirical tests', *Journal of Political Economy*, May/June, pp. 607–36.

Fama, E.F. and MacBeth, J. (1974) 'Tests of the multi-period two-parameter model', *Journal of Financial Economics*, vol. 1, May, pp. 43–66.

Firth, M. (1980) 'Takeovers, shareholders' return and the theory of the firm', *Quarterly Journal of Economics*, March, pp. 235–60.

Franks, J.R. and Harris, R.S. (1989) 'Shareholders' wealth effects of corporate takeovers; the UK experience 1955–1985', *Journal of Financial Economics*, vol. 23, pp. 225–49.

Franks, J.R., Harris, R.S. and Mayer, C. (1988) 'Means of payment in takeovers: results for the United Kingdom and the United States', in A.J. Auerbach (ed.) *Corporate Takeovers: Causes and Consequences*. University of Chicago Press.

Galai, D. and Masulis, R.W. (1976) 'The option pricing model and the risk factor of stock', *Journal of Financial Economics*, Jan.–Mar., pp. 53–82.

Glosten, L.L. and Milgrom, P.R. (1985) 'Bid, ask and transactions prices in a specialist market with heterogenously informed traders', *Journal of Financial Economics*, vol. 14, pp. 71–100.

Glover, C. (1987) 'Valuation of unquoted shares', *Accountants Digest*, ICAEW, London.

Gregory, A. (1987) 'Divisional performance measurement with divisions as lessees of head office assets', *Accounting and Business Research*, summer, pp. 241–6.

Gregory, A. (1997) 'An examination of the long run performance of UK acquiring firms', *Journal of Business Finance and Accounting*, vol. 24, nos 7 and 8, pp. 971–1002.

Gregory, A. (1998) *The Long Run Performance of UK Acquirers: Motives Underlying the Method of Payment and Their Influence Upon Subsequent Performance*, University of Exeter Discussion Paper in Business and Management No. 98/01.

Gregory, A. and A. Hicks, (1995) 'Valuation of shares: a legal and accounting conundrum', *Journal of Business Law*, January.

Gregory, A. and Rutterford, J. (1999) *The Cost of Capital in the UK*. CIMA Research Monograph, forthcoming.

Grossman, S.J. and Stiglitz, J. (1980) 'The impossibility of informationally efficient markets', *American Economic Review*, June, pp. 393–408.

Harris, R.S. and Ravenscraft, D. (1991) 'The role of acquisitions in foreign direct investment: evidence from the US stockmarket', *Journal of Finance*, July, pp. 825–44.

Ingersoll, J. E. (1977) 'A contingent claims valuation of convertible securities', *Journal of Financial Economics*, vol. 4, May, pp. 289–322.

Jaganathan, R. and Wang, Z. (1996) 'The conditional CAPM and the cross-section of expected returns', *Journal of Finance*, vol. 51, no. 1, pp. 3–54.

Jensen, M.C. and Ruback, R.S. (1983) 'The market for corporate control: the scientific evidence', *Journal of Financial Economics*, vol. 11, April, pp. 5–50.

Keane, S. M. (1992) *A Survey of the Valuation Practices of Professional Accounting Firms*. ICAS.

Kelly, G. and Tippett, M. (1991) 'Economic and accounting rates of return: a statistical model', *Accounting and Business Research*, vol. 21, no. 84, pp. 321–30.

Kennedy, V.A. and Limmack, R.J. (1996) 'Take-over activity, CEO turnover and the market for corporate control', *Journal of Business Finance and Accounting*, March.

Kim, D. (1995) 'The errors in the variables problem in the cross-section of expected stock returns', *Journal of Finance*, vol. 50, no. 5, pp. 1605–34.

Kothari, S.P., Shanken, J. and Sloan, R.G. (1995) 'Another look at the cross-section of expected returns', *Journal of Finance*, March, pp. 185–224.

Krinsky, I., Rotenberg, W.D. and Thornton, D.B. (1988) 'Takeovers – a synthesis', *Journal of Accounting Literature*, vol. 7, pp. 243–79.

Lakonishok, J., Shleifer, A. and Vishny, R.W. (1994) 'Contrarian investment, extrapolation and risk', *Journal of Finance*, December, pp. 1541–78.

Larson, K.D. and Gonedes, N.J. (1969) 'Business combination: an exchange ratio determination model', *The Accounting Review*, October, pp. 720–8.

Lee, T.A. and Tweedie D.P. (1981) *The Insitutional Investor and Financial Information*. ICAEW.

Limmack, R.J. (1991) 'Corporate mergers and shareholder wealth effects: 1977–1986', *Accounting and Business Research*, summer, pp. 239–52.

Litzenberger, R.H. and Ramaswamy, K. (1979) 'The effect of personal taxes on capital asset prices: theory and empirical evidence', *Journal of Financial Economics*, vol. 7, pp. 163–96.

Loughran, T. and Vijh, A.M. (1997) 'Do long-term shareholders benefit from corporate acquisitions?', *Journal of Finance*, vol. LII, no. 5, December, pp. 1765–90.

Madden, B.J. (1996) 'The CFROI life cycle', *Journal of Investing*, summer.

Mehra, R. and Prescott, E.C. (1985) 'The equity premium: a puzzle', *Journal of Monetary Economics*, vol. 15, pp. 145–61.

Miles, J.A. and Ezzell J.R. (1980) 'The weighted average cost of capital, perfect capital markets and project life: a clarification', *Journal of Finance and Quantitative Analysis*, September, pp. 719–30.

Miles, J.A. and Ezzell, J.R. (1983) 'Capital project analysis and the debt transaction plan', *Journal of Finance Research*, spring, pp. 25–31.

Miller, M. (1977) 'Debt and taxes', *Journal of Finance*, May.

Modigliani, F. and Miller, M.H. (1963) 'Corporate income taxes and the cost of capital: a correction', *American Economic Review*, June.

Morck, R., Shleifer, A. and Vishny, R.W. (1990) 'Do managerial objectives drive bad acquisitions', *Journal of Finance*, July, pp. 31–48.

Neftci, S.N. (1996) *An Introduction to the Mathematics of Financial Derivatives*. Academic Press.

Nobes, C, and Parker, R.H. (1991) *Comparative International Accounting*, 3rd edn. Prentice Hall International (UK) Ltd.

O'Hanlon, J. and Rees, B. (1995) 'Links between accounting numbers and economic fundamentals', in B. Rees, *Financial Analysis*. Prentice-Hall.

Ohlson, J.A. (1991) 'A synthesis of security valuation theory and the role of dividends, cash flows, and earnings', *Contemporary Accounting Research*, spring, pp. 648–76.

Ohlson, J.A. (1991) 'The theory of value and earnings, and an introduction to the Ball-Brown analysis', *Contemporary Accounting Research*, vol. 8, no.1, pp. 1–19.

Ohlson, J. A. (1991) *Earnings, Book Value and Dividends in Security Valuation*, Working Paper, Columbia University, January.

Peasnell, K.V. (1982) 'Some formal connections between economic values and yields and accounting numbers', *Journal of Business Finance and Accounting*, autumn, pp. 261–381.

Pike, R., Meerjanssen, J. and Chadwick, L. (1993) 'The appraisal of ordinary shares by investment analysts in the UK and Germany', *Accounting and Business Research*, vol. 23, autumn, 489–499.

Pound, J.K., Lehn, K. and Jarrell, G. (1986) 'Are takeovers hostile to economic performance?', *Regulation*, September/October, pp. 25–56.

Rappaport, A. (1998) *Creating Shareholder Value*. Free Press.

Reinganum, M.R. (1992) 'A revival of the small-firm effect', *Journal of Portfolio Management*, spring, pp. 55–62.

Roll, R. (1977) 'A critique of the asset ricing theory's tests', *Journal of Financial Economics*, vol. 4, pp. 129–76.

Roll, R. (1986) 'The hubris hypothesis of corporate takeovers', *Journal of Business*, vol. 59, no. 2, pp. 197–216.

Rutterford, J. (1993) *Introduction to Stock Exchange Investment*, 2nd edn. Macmillan.

Schnabel, J.A. (1983) 'Beta geared and ungeared: an extension', *Accounting and Business Research*, spring, pp. 128–30.

Scholes, M. and Wolfson, M. (1990) 'The effects of changes in tax laws on corporate reorganisation activity', *Journal of Business*, no. 63, pp. S141–S164.

Shapiro, A.C. (1989) *Multinational Financial Managment*. Allyn & Bacon.

Smith, T. (1992) *Accounting for Growth*. Century.

Stark, A.W. (1990) 'Irreversibilty and the capital budgeting process', *Management Accounting Research*, vol. 1, no. 3, pp. 167–80.

Stern, J., Stewart, B. and Chew, D. (1998) 'The EVA financial management system', in Stern, J.M. and Chew, D.H., *The Revolution in Corporate Finance*, 3rd edn, Blackwell.

Strong, N.C. and Appleyard, T.R. (1992) 'Investment appraisal, taxes and the security market line', *Journal of Business Finance and Accounting*, vol. 19, no. 1, pp. 1–24.

Strong, N.C. and Xu, X.G. (1997) 'Explaining the cross-section of UK expected returns', *British Accounting Review*, March, pp. 1–23.

Stultz, R. (1995a) 'The cost of capital in internationally integrated markets: the case of Nestlé', *European Financial Management*, vol. 1, no. 1, pp. 11–22.

Stamburgh, R.F. (1982) 'On the exclusion of assets from tests of the two parameter model: a sensitivity analysis', *Journal of Financial Economics*, vol. 10, November, pp. 237–68.

Warner, J.B. (1977) 'Bankruptcy costs: some evidence', *Journal of Finance*, vol. 26, pp. 337–48.